FREEDOM FROM S.I.N.

Satan's Intended Notion

FREEDOM FROM S.I.N.

SATAN'S INTENDED NOTION

BY
LAWRENCE P. LUBY

www.hispubg.com
A division of HISpecialists, llc

Copyright © 2008 by Lawrence P. Luby. All rights reserved.

Permission to reproduce or transmit in any form or by any means, electronic or mechanical, including photocopying and recording, or by any information storage and retrieval system, must be obtained in writing from the author. Contact publisher at info@hispubg.com

Published by HIS Publishing Group, Dallas, Texas 75225
Division of Human Improvement Specialists, llc
For Information: visit: www.hispublishinggroup.com
Or Contact: info@hispubg.com

Cover design by Ty Walsworth at Culture Red
Visit the website: culture-red.com
Edited by Cindy Walsworth.

All scripture quoted in this book is from the New King James Version unless specified otherwise. "Scripture taken from the New King James Version. Copyright © 1982 by Thomas Nelson, Inc. Used by permission. All rights reserved."

Library of Congress Control Number: 2009936979
ISBN-13: 978-0-615-31708-3

Printed in the United States of America
10 9 8 7 6 5 4 3 2

Table of Contents

Acknowledgements.................................. 7

Dedications.. 9

Introduction....................................... 11

Chapter One
The Trinity.. 17

Chapter Two
Satan's Intended Notion............................ 37

Chapter Three
The Set-Up... 63

Chapter Four
Societal Addiction................................. 87

Chapter Five
Playing Life....................................... 107

Chapter Six
Climactic Deliverance.............................. 137

Chapter Seven
Stairway to Heaven................................. 169

Chapter Eight
Practice Rounds.................................... 203

Chapter Nine
God's Picture Puzzle............................... 233

Conclusion... 247

Free Gift.. 251

Appendix... 253

Acknowledgements

My Savior - Without Jesus Christ, I would be destined for a life separated from God.

The Word of God - Without the Word, my life would be meaningless, and there would be no foundation on which to present the material in this writing.

Dedications

Mother - She has been an unchanging, steady rock in our family. Many of her loved ones have come to her for care before they died. The Lord has blessed her with a strong and steadfast spirit. She has been a blessing to many in their last precious moments here on this side of eternity.

Sons - The love of a Father is straight from God, and I love my sons as He loves us. They have brought me great joy and taught me to love unconditionally.

Tisher - Satan thought he could kill her through the disease of Multiple Sclerosis, but in his ignorance, he resurrected her to eternal life.

> The righteous perishes, And no man takes it to heart; Merciful men are taken away, While no one considers That the righteous is taken away from evil. He shall enter into peace; They shall rest in their beds, Each one walking in his uprightness. (Isaiah 57:1-2)

Friends - They have a way of bringing the truth in love that I need. We all need the help of our loved ones to push us beyond our limits and to be there if we fall. They have not been mere cushions in my life, they have been my trampoline.

Introduction

In the title *S.I.N. is an acronym for Satan's Intended Notion*. It has been Satan's intention since the beginning of man to inflict as much pain on God's elect and to take as many as possible with him into an eternity separated from God. He has attempted to alter our society over time by physically infiltrating every aspect of our cultural environment. He has done so by corrupting our spiritual values and, in so doing, shaped and controled our lives. For this reason, one could argue that *S.I.N.* is also *Societal In Nature*.

We are all born into sin and are subject to its vices, so it makes sense that we need guidelines in order to break free from the bondage of sin. For this reason, I will be using the Bible as my ultimate resource and support for the theories and ideas contained herein. Of course, some reading this book might be asking, "How do we know the Bible is accurate?" Many of you acknowledge the Bible exists (kind of hard to deny), but many doubt the Bible's accuracy. So to satisfy those who have doubts, I offer the following history. For those of you who believe in the inspired word of God, it is my hope you would find the history interesting reading.

The factual reality is this: the Bible was divinely inspired by God to 40 writers and written over a period of 1,600 years. It is the most accurately verifiable piece of literature and history known to man.

> The Bible is a collection of writings from about forty contributors, thirty in the Old Testament and ten in the New

Testament. It is truly amazing that all forty of these authors, spread out over 1600 years, have such a unified message in spite of their great diversity in language, culture and time. There is a reason for that! The reason is that these forty or so writers are all secondary authors. There is actually only one primary author, the one who inspired all the human authors, the eternal God. (1)

The first recorded instance of God's Word being delivered to Moses at the top of Mount Sinai sometime between 1,400 BC and 1,500 BC.

The earliest scripture is the "Pentateuch", the first five books from Moses: Genesis, Exodus, Leviticus, Numbers, & Deuteronomy. The Old Testament scriptures were written in ancient Hebrew, a language substantially different than the Hebrew of today. These writings were passed down from generation to generation for thousands of years on scrolls made of animal skin, usually sheep, but sometimes deer or cow. When the entire Pentateuch is present on a scroll, it is called a "Torah". An entire Torah Scroll, if completely unraveled, is over 150 feet long! The Jewish scribes who painstakingly produced each scroll were perfectionists. If they made even the slightest mistake in copying, such as allowing two letters of a word to touch, they destroyed that entire panel (the last three or four columns of text), and the panel before it, because it had touched the panel with a mistake! This demonstrates the level of faithfulness to accuracy applied to the preservation of God's Word throughout the first couple of thousand years of Biblical transmission.

By approximately 500 BC, the 39 Books that make up the Old Testament were completed, and continued to be preserved in Hebrew on scrolls. As we approach the last few centuries before Christ, the Jewish historical books known as the "Apocrypha" were completed, yet they were recorded in Greek rather than Hebrew. By the end of the *First Century AD*, the New Testament had been completed. The oldest copies of the New Testament known to exist today are: The Codex Alexandrius and the Codex Sinaiticus in the British Museum Library in London, and the Codex Vaticanus in the

Vatican. They date back to approximately the *300's AD*. By *500 AD* the Bible had been translated into over 500 languages.

Just one century later, by *600 AD*, it has been restricted to only one language: the Latin Vulgate. The only organized and recognized church at that time in history was the Catholic Church of Rome, and they refused to allow the scripture to be available in any language other than Latin.

On the Scottish Island of Iona, in *563 AD*, a man named Columba started a Bible College. For the next 700 years, this was the source of much of the non-Catholic, evangelical Bible teaching through those centuries of the Dark and Middle Ages. The students of this college were called "Culdees", which means "certain stranger". The Culdees were a secret society, and the remnant of the true Christian faith was kept alive by these men during the many centuries that led up to the Protestant Reformation. In fact, the first man to be called a "Culdee" was Joseph of Aremethia. In the late 1300's, the secret society of Culdees chose John Wycliffe to lead the world out of the Dark Ages. Wycliffe has been called the "Morning Star of the Reformation". That Protestant Reformation was about one thing: getting the Word of God back into the hands of the masses in their own native language, so that the corrupt church would be exposed and the message of salvation in Christ alone, by scripture alone, through faith alone would be proclaimed again. (2)

Further evidence came to light in 1947 when Bedouin shepherds found the first of what we now know as the *Dead Sea Scrolls*. The scrolls are ancient texts that have been authenticated by numerous scholars and archeologists. The first scrolls discovered were believed to be the Isaiah Scroll, the Habakkuk Commentary and the Manual of Discipline.

Specific methods were employed to authenticate the scrolls. Archeology being the first, Paleography second and then Carbon 14 dating, which was later refined by a technique called *Accelerator Mass Spectrometry Testing*. All methods employed concurred that the scrolls were written during the first through the fourth centuries. (3)

I offer this history of the Bible to make this point: it would be ignorant to assume that the Bible is a hoax made up by one person or a group of people in order to deceive mankind. The people who penned the content of the Bible lived in different time periods and had no way of collaborating with one another.

Now for those of you who still have doubts about the authenticity of the Bible or are not open to acknowledge it in any way, please stop reading. Go explore other publications (they are too numerous to name) that will challenge you in the debate of whether the Bible is the true source of God's Word. It is not my intention in this book to engage in such an argument or in any way try to defend what the God of the Universe has divinely imparted to man.

Therefore, I will continue on. Why not allow God's Word to penetrate deep within your soul. After all, it "is living and powerful and sharper than any two-edged sword."

> For the word of God *is living and powerful, and sharper than any two-edged sword*, piercing even to the division of soul and spirit, and of joints and marrow, and is a discerner of the thoughts and intents of the heart. (Hebrews 4:12)

In the first chapter we will establish a foundation of truth. For us to understand God's divine nature, His purpose for earth and humankind, it is best to start with a definition of "The Trinity." The three distinct yet integrated personalities of the Godhead.

In the second chapter, we will expose Satan's business: his intent to destroy our society, through a gradual erosion of our societal values. Thus, showing that S.I.N. has become "Societal in Nature."

In the third chapter, we will proceed to expose Satan's "Set-Up." A methodology that Satan has used since the beginning of time with one goal and one goal only—drag as many to an eternity separated from God with him as will let him. We will go back to the beginning when Adam and Eve took up residence in the garden. We will see how Satan hatched his plan through original sin, so whenever a baby is conceived, Satan's seed is implanted in the heart of man.

In the fourth chapter, we explore the process of addiction and the eroding affect it has had on our society. Christ shows us how we have naively become addicted to our material possessions. Many have bought into a counterfeit system of determining worth and value. Those possessions have become our false indicators of success. Our hearts have become hardened like stone, and out of ignorance, we fail to embrace the vision of paradise, which is eternal life.

In the fifth chapter, "Playing Life," Christ shows us that we robotically move through life in hope that one day we will look back and see that our life had purpose and meaning. We follow the culturally defined leaders and media, to the edge of eternity only to realize that what we had been chasing was a dream, a mirage. We come to find that what we thought was real was really a lie.

In the sixth chapter, Christ offers the opportunity for us to be "Climactically Delivered" for all eternity. Not in the way the world would teach us—where one doesn't have to work toward or acknowledge the refining process necessary to unleash the power of the Holy Spirit. Instead, Christ wants to climactically deliver us in such a way that we desire to humble ourselves and are willing to take responsibility for the change that He wants to enact in our hearts.

Then it is on to chapter seven, where we take a ride on God's "Stairway to Heaven." This stairway, like an escalator, is always moving, but, unlike an escalator, never breaks down. Once we make the heartfelt-decision to put our trust in Him, no matter which direction we are walking on His stairway, we are always being led upward toward His eternal kingdom.

Christ tees it up with us in the eighth chapter through the "Practice Rounds" of life. He coaches, refines, and purifies us into His image. He allows us free will and even though we make the wrong choices, He continues playing with us, revealing His nature and love. As we reflect back over life's struggles, we develop testimonies that we can use to empower others on their journey through life.

In closing, we learn that we are all important pieces in God's eternal puzzle. We learn how our piece fits into the overall eternal scheme. We see how the enemy has attacked through the inadvertent dysfunction of the church to keep us from knowing our purpose in life. We will learn how to place the Trinity over our life in order to complete the spiritual covering God so desires to provide.

We all are born into this addictive world, which is one of pain and suffering. However, there is another world that is free of pain and suffering, a world that is unseen, but more real than the physical world we now live in. Through this book let me take you on a journey of regeneration, a journey that leads to eternal life. A life that is spiritually real. But before we begin, I would like to challenge you to answer one question.

If you were to die tonight, and found yourself standing face to face with the Almighty God of the Universe and He asked you, "Why should I let you in to Heaven? What would be your answer?

I am sure many of you know what to say. Some of you may have a pretty good idea. But many of you will be quietly wondering, not really knowing, about the answer God reveals in scripture. Thus, it is my goal through this writing that you will come to embrace God's love and the shutters over the eyes of your understanding will be opened or further enlightened.

Chapter One

The Trinity

Most of us, at one time or another, have cried out to God or to an unknown Creator. Think of the man sitting in a foxhole during WWII, almost out of ammunition, the enemy close to attacking. What goes through his mind? Think of a Father, sitting at the bedside of his daughter, watching as she suffers through the night because of an illness. What goes through his mind? Think of a Mother tossing and turning in her sleep fretting over sending her son off to war. What goes through her mind?

Yes, at some point in life we will cry out, looking skyward with both the understanding and assurance that God is there or in hopes that something, anything, is out there.

For many, God is an unknown Creator. Others might refer to God as their higher power or a spiritual force in nature. Some refuse to believe that God exists at all. There have been many discussions and disagreements with respect to whether God exists, who God is, and what is meant by the Trinity or God in three persons.

For those of you who already believe in God and understand the Trinity I challenge you to go deeper in your understanding. For those of you who don't understand God, the Trinity, or refuse to acknowledge God at all, I challenge you to open your hearts while reading this book. Open to the possibility that there is a Creator and that He wants to reveal Himself to you through a spiritual revelation of His divine nature.

I assuredly offer these challenges, because I believe He does exist, and He is who He says He is. I know that if you honestly ask Him to reveal Himself, He will not disappoint you.

> Trinity – The union of three persons (the Father, the Son, and the Holy Ghost) in one Godhead, so that all the three are one God as to substance, but three persons as to individuality. (4)

As we turn to the first chapter of John, one of the original 12 Disciples of Christ, we gain a deep insight into the Trinity. John sets up his writing by reminding us:

> *In the beginning was the Word, and the Word was with God, and the Word was God.* He was in the beginning with God. All things were made through Him, and without Him nothing was made that was made. *In Him was life, and the life was the light of men.* And the light shines in the darkness, and the darkness did not comprehend it. (John 1:1-5)

It is important to pause and meditate on this verse before continuing on with our reading in John. The "Word" is referred to as "Him." We have the word today in the form of the Bible. "Him" is Jesus Christ. Jesus is alive and the word comes alive in our hearts through the "Light" which is "Life." In the Greek, "Word" is "Logos" and "Light" is "Phos."

> Logos – In John, denotes the essential Word of God, Jesus Christ, the personal wisdom and power in union with God, his minister in creation and government of the universe, the cause of all the world's life both physical and ethical, which for the procurement of man's salvation put on human nature in the person of Jesus the Messiah, the second person in the Godhead, and shone forth conspicuously from His words and deeds. (5)

> Phos – a heavenly light such as surrounds angels when they appear on earth; a lamp or torch; God is light because light has the extremely delicate, subtle, pure, brilliant quality; the power of understanding esp. moral and spiritual truth. (5)

> Separate Note: A Greek philosopher named Heraclitus first used the term Logos around 600 B.C. to designate the divine reason or plan which coordinates a changing universe. (5)

John provides us with instruction so that we can come to a clear revelation of Jesus Christ and His connection to God and God's desire to guide us in life. Furthermore, John does not ask us to accept this information based entirely on his own observation and experience. But relates an eyewitness account, clearly understanding the need of supporting evidence in order to dispel the enemy's attempts to distort our thinking. He introduces us to John the Baptist (JTB), who was sent by God to bear witness to the Light.

> There was a man sent from God, whose name was John. *This man came for a witness, to bear witness of the Light that all through him might believe.* He was not that Light, but was sent to bear witness of that Light. (John 1:6-8)

JTB is bearing witness to the three parts of the Trinity: God the Father, God the Son and God the Holy Spirit. Word, light and life. Jesus and God are one in the word. Jesus was the word made flesh. Jesus became a human vessel by which God's light, the Holy Spirit, could come to life and shine on all His creation. Thus, bringing revelation of the truth: we all have "the right to become children of God."

> That was the true Light which gives light to every man coming into the world. He was in the world, and the world was made through Him, and the world did not know Him. He came to His own, and His own did not receive Him. *But as many as received Him, to them He gave the right to become children of God,* to those who believe in His name: who were born, not of blood, nor of the will of the flesh, nor of the will of man, but of God. (John 1:9-13)

JTB, baptizing people in the Jordan River, sees Jesus approaching and unknowingly gives those around him a glimpse of the future purpose Jesus was to play here on earth by declaring, "Behold! The Lamb of God...!" Jesus will eventually be revealed as the "Sacrificial Lamb," sent from God. Given in order to provide a means by which we could all experience forgiveness for our sins.

> The next day John saw Jesus coming toward him, and said, *"Behold! The Lamb of God who takes away the sin of the world!"* This is He of whom I said, "After me comes a Man

> who is preferred before me, for He was before me. I did not know Him; but that He should be revealed to Israel, therefore I came baptizing with water."
> (John 1:29-31)

JTB also clearly differentiates between baptism with water and baptism with the Holy Spirit. In essence, Jesus came to be a vessel to impart the Holy Spirit, the power of God, to all who believe. Lastly, JTB leaves us no doubt who Jesus was by his personal admission, "I have seen and testified that this is the Son of God."

> And John bore witness, saying, "I saw the Spirit descending from heaven like a dove, and He remained upon Him. I did not know Him, but He who sent me to baptize with water said to me, 'Upon whom you see the Spirit descending, and remaining on Him, *this is He who baptizes with the Holy Spirit.' And I have seen and testified that this is the Son of God."* (John 1:32-34)

> I indeed baptize you with water unto repentance, but He who is coming after me is mightier than I, whose sandals I am not worthy to carry. He will baptize you with the *Holy Spirit and fire.* (Matthew 3:11)

Jesus later confirms JTB's testimony when he enters the temple and is surrounded by the Jews, who ask Him in John chapter 10 verse 24, "How long do You keep us in doubt? If You are the Christ, tell us plainly." In verse 30, Jesus leaves no doubt by responding to their question with a very direct response: "I and My Father are one." Of course, the Jews present that day did not expect to hear Him say this.

The Jews surrounding Jesus that day appeared to want the truth. But, were questioning Jesus' authority and attempting to discredit His ministry. Along with everyone at the time, the Jews had been watching the miraculous works being done by Jesus, but were not willing to accept His works were from God. They couldn't handle the truth!

Today we should embrace the truth, Jesus considers us His sheep and will never abuse His power or authority. Jesus is protecting us from S.I.N., a force that wants to keep us from our eternal destiny.

> Jesus answered them, "I told you, and you do not believe. The works that I do in My Father's name, they bear witness of Me. But you do not believe, because you are not of My sheep, as I said to you. My sheep hear My voice, and I know them, and they follow Me. And I give them eternal life, and they shall never perish; neither shall anyone snatch them out of My hand. My Father, who has given them to Me, is greater than all; and no one is able to snatch them out of My Father's hand. *I and My Father are one.*" (John 10:25-30)

> The Jews answered Him, saying, "For a good work we do not stone You, but for blasphemy, and because You, being a Man, make Yourself God." (John 10:33)

Our societies are not so different today, in that many of the world religions continue to reject Jesus' own admission that He was God by having us believe He was just a good man, a prophet or a teacher. S.I.N.'s deception in this line of thinking should be obvious to anyone and everyone. Jesus could not be a good anything if He was lying about being God.

Even some skewed Christian beliefs are floating around wanting us to think that we have become like Jesus in the sense that we too are God. S.I.N.'s deception in that belief should be obvious to anyone and everyone as well. When we invite God into our hearts we in essence become one with God, but we are not God.

Ladies and gentlemen, I ask you, "Are you ready to hear the truth?" Jesus was not just one with God, He was God in the flesh and His Word came alive by the power of His Holy Spirit, the Light. To lend proof to this point, we learned earlier in the book of John, that God intentionally came down from the throne room of heaven to earth in bodily form.

> *And the Word became flesh and dwelt among us,* and we beheld His glory, the glory as of the only begotten of the Father, full of grace and truth. John bore witness of Him and cried out, saying, "This was He of whom I said, He who comes after me is preferred before me, for He was before me." (John 1:14-15)

I have heard many preachers over the years challenge their congregations with the question, "Could you have put your son on that cross as a sacrifice for everyone's sins?" One pastor said, "I don't know about you, but I don't think I would allow my son to be hung on a cross as a sacrifice for all you yahoos," and of course, we all roared with laughter. Truth is, not one person sitting in the audience that day would want to see their son beaten close to death and hung on a cross naked as a sacrifice for anyone.

How could we ever know the magnitude of agony Christ endured at that point in time as he took on the sins of all humanity past, present, and future? That day, I sat listening in the audience asking myself, "Could you allow one of your sons to take Jesus' place on that cross?" Then the Lord revealed something to me – It was God Himself on that cross – God had allowed Himself to be hung on the cross. It wasn't just a decision whether to allow His Son to be sacrificed–it was a decision for God in the flesh to personally endure the pain of our sin by letting Himself be hung on that cross.

Out of God's love for humanity, He bore our iniquity, granting us access into His eternal kingdom. However, I, like everyone else, had been separating the Triune God at the time of His ultimate sacrifice. I was only seeing Jesus on that cross.

The next question that came to my mind seemed confusing, "But Lord, there was clearly separation because Jesus asked, 'My God, My God, why have you forsaken Me?' so what do you mean it was you on the cross?" I sensed God respond by revealing that He had truly forsaken Jesus Christ, Himself in the flesh, by withdrawing His Holy Spirit, thus allowing the weight of sin to rest fully on Christ's physical shoulders, His shoulders.

> And about the ninth hour Jesus cried out with a loud voice, saying, "Eli, Eli, lama sabachthani?" that is, "My God, My God, why have You forsaken Me?" (Matthew 27:46)

God through His flesh, Jesus Christ, had become the sacrificial lamb John the Baptist had professed three years earlier and that Isaiah had prophesied approximately 800 years earlier.

> But He was wounded for our transgressions, He was bruised for our iniquities; The chastisement for our peace was upon Him, And by His stripes we are healed. (Isaiah 53:5)

That was the day God bore our iniquity and defeated S.I.N. in the physical realm!

> And Jesus cried out again with a loud voice, and yielded up His spirit. (Matthew 27:50)

The Godhead

I offer the following definitions for the three parts of the Trinity from reliable and verifiable sources. So not to appear that I alone am attempting to sway your judgment or give the impression that I have some new revelation with respect to the concept of the Godhead. It is intended that these definitions help to provide you with a firm foundation on which to base your analysis and open your mind to the reality of God's divine nature.

Since we know by definition the Trinity is represented as "The union of three persons (the Father, the Son, and the Holy Ghost) in one Godhead," let us delve deeper into the meanings of God's three divine personalities.

The Father

> The supernatural being conceived as the perfect and omnipotent and omniscient originator and ruler of the universe; the object of worship in monotheistic religions [syn: God, Supreme Being] 2: any supernatural being worshipped as controlling some part of the world or some aspect of life or who is the personification of a force [syn: deity, divinity, immortal] (7)

God is *Omnipotent*, powerful – Able in every respect and for every work; unlimited in ability; all-powerful; almighty; as, the Being that can create worlds must be omnipotent. (8)

> Ah, Lord GOD! Behold, You have made the heavens and the earth by Your great power and outstretched arm. There is nothing too hard for You. You show lovingkindness to thousands, and repay the iniquity of the fathers into the bosom of their children after them—the Great, the Mighty God, whose name is the LORD of hosts. (Jeremiah 32:17-18)

God is *Omnipresent*, flesh – Present in all places at the same time; ubiquitous; as, the omnipresent Jehovah. (8)

> Where can I go from Your Spirit? Or where can I flee from Your presence? If I ascend into heaven, You are there; If I make my bed in hell, behold, You are there. If I take the wings of the morning, And dwell in the uttermost parts of the sea,

> Even there Your hand shall lead me, And Your right hand shall hold me. If I say, "Surely the darkness shall fall on me," Even the night shall be light about me; Indeed, the darkness shall not hide from You, But the night shines as the day; The darkness and the light are both alike to You.
> (Psalm 139:7-12)

God is *Omniscient*, Spirit – Having universal knowledge; knowing all things; infinitely knowing or wise; as, the omniscient God. (8)

> God is Spirit, and those who worship Him must worship in spirit and truth. (John 4:24)

God the Son is all spirit, but came to us in the physical form by way of the flesh. God the Holy Spirit is all spirit, but intercedes through our emotional being, convicting our conscious minds.

> Who, being in the form of God, did not consider it robbery to be equal with God, but made Himself of no reputation, taking the form of a bondservant, and coming in the likeness of men. (Philippians 2:6-7)

> But the Helper, the Holy Spirit, whom the Father will send in My name, He will teach you all things, and bring to your remembrance all things that I said to you. (John 14:26)

God is a perfect organizer; after all, he created perfectionism. Think of the most successful company in the world. What is the administrative order or organizational structure of that company? At the helm, there is usually a CEO, President, and then various officers. The CEO sets the vision, the President builds and leads the team and the team carries out the vision. God sets the vision for all creation, Christ assembles and leads the team, and the Holy Spirit carries out the vision. See any similarities? God created our universe with His divine vision for humanity and saw that it was good. In Genesis 1, we read the account of God's creation and His continual assurance that what He created was good.

THE TRINITY

> In the beginning God created the heavens and the earth. The earth was without form, and void; and darkness was on the face of the deep. And the Spirit of God was hovering over the face of the waters. (Genesis 1:1-2)

The Spirit of God was hovering over the face of the deep, ready to carry out God's plan as stated by His word, which we have already shown is Jesus Christ. God already had the vision and Jesus was ready to speak that vision into being by the power of God's Holy Spirit.

> Then God said, "Let there be light"; and there was light. And *God saw the light, that it was good*; and God divided the light from the darkness. God called the light Day, and the darkness He called Night. So the evening and the morning were the first day. Then God said, "Let there be a firmament in the midst of the waters, and let it divide the waters from the waters." Thus God made the firmament, and divided the waters which were under the firmament from the waters which were above the firmament; and it was so. And God called the firmament Heaven. So the evening and the morning were the second day. Then God said, "Let the waters under the heavens be gathered together into one place, and let the dry land appear"; and it was so. And God called the dry land Earth, and the gathering together of the waters He called Seas. And *God saw that it was good*. Then God said, "Let the earth bring forth grass, the herb that yields seed, and the fruit tree that yields fruit according to its kind, whose seed is in itself, on the earth"; and it was so. And the earth brought forth grass, the herb that yields seed according to its kind, and the tree that yields fruit, whose seed is in itself according to its kind. And *God saw that it was good*. So the evening and the morning were the third day. Then God said, "Let there be lights in the firmament of the heavens to divide the day from the night; and let them be for signs and seasons, and for days and years; and let them be for lights in the firmament of the heavens to give light on the earth"; and it was so. Then God made two great lights: the greater light to rule the day, and the lesser light to rule the night. He made the stars also. God set them in the firmament of the heavens to give light on the earth, and to rule over the day and over the night, and to

divide the light from the darkness. And *God saw that it was good.* So the evening and the morning were the fourth day. Then God said, "Let the waters abound with an abundance of living creatures, and let birds fly above the earth across the face of the firmament of the heavens." So God created great sea creatures and every living thing that moves, with which the waters abounded, according to their kind, and every winged bird according to its kind. And *God saw that it was good.* And God blessed them, saying, "Be fruitful and multiply, and fill the waters in the seas, and let birds multiply on the earth." So the evening and the morning were the fifth day. Then God said, "Let the earth bring forth the living creature according to its kind: cattle and creeping thing and beast of the earth, each according to its kind"; and it was so. And God made the beast of the earth according to its kind, cattle according to its kind, and everything that creeps on the earth according to its kind. And *God saw that it was good.* (Genesis 1:3-25)

Now imagine for a moment if the universe were out of balance. What would our world look like? One could rightly assume there would be complete chaos. Without natural order, the planets would not orbit correctly, the earth would not maintain its axis, seasons would not exist, and natural law would be void. Realistically speaking, we would not be here.

But, we are here, and since everything in the universe has functioned effectively as long as any of us here on earth can remember, we can accurately assume that God, being the Creator of the universe is also still in balance. However, many people still ask the question, "Who created the universe?" I once heard a self-professed atheist ask, "If God is real, show me His universe factory?"

These are seemingly good questions, but no one seems to be able to answer them with complete certainty, because they are unknown to us except through what we read in scripture. To answer those questions void of scripture, one is faced with a continuum void of time and space and if honest, the only answer then becomes a black hole. Black holes are real by the way, one only has to explore the universe. Just because we can't see them, doesn't mean they don't exist.

God's universe factory exists as well. Just because we can't see it, doesn't mean it isn't real. He is a powerful force that cannot be willed away.

With that said, how can we put God in a box? How do we define such a God? How in our finite wisdom do we begin to define an infinite God?

Many scholars have tried over the years. But, I ask, how can the created fully understand the Creator?

No matter how hard we try, we will never fully understand God. To support this point, just ask the astronomers how fast the universe is expanding and they will tell you that they are still trying to figure it out, but that they don't have a clue!

> Using the Hubble telescope, two international teams of astronomers are reporting major progress in converging on an accurate measurement of the universe's rate of expansion—a value that has been debated for over half a century. These new results yield ranges for the age of the universe from 9-12 billion years and 11-14 billion years, respectively. However, after all of these years there is still doubt about how fast the universe is growing and where it had its beginning. (9)

His power is infinite, His substance is infinite, and His life-giving spirit is infinite. God's order was set in motion from the beginning of the universe. Where is God's universe factory? It is all around us, all-powerful, all-encompassing, and all-knowing.

For this reason, one can rightly assume that God has always been in control and is still in control of all His creation. After all, there is no denying natural order exists and contrary to what some would have us believe, the overall food chain has not been interrupted and the seasons do come and go. Our world was created out of His perfect natural order, and His universe continues to be in balance. His perfect order is found in His triune character, which is evident in the natural process of creation. *He is God the Father.*

The Son – Jesus Christ

> A male human offspring; "their son became a famous judge"; "his boy is taller than he is" [syn: boy] [ant: daughter,] 2: the divine word of God; the second person in the Trinity (incarnate in Jesus) [syn: Son, Word, Logos] (7)

> A prophet of the first century (circa 8 BC - 29 AD); to Christians he was both God and man--the Messiah sent to save the human race from the sin it inherited through the Fall of Man [syn: Jesus, Jesus of Nazareth, Jesus Christ, Christ,

Savior, Saviour, Good Shepherd, Redeemer] 2: any expected deliverer [syn: messiah] (7)

God manifested Himself in the fleshly form through the man we know as Jesus Christ, and He did so in three parts: spirit, soul and body. God's creation of man has not changed since He created Adam and Eve in the garden; He has always created man in three parts. Therefore, just like Adam, man is capable of unity with God through those three parts.

> Now may the God of peace Himself sanctify you completely; and may your whole spirit, soul, and body be preserved blameless at the coming of our Lord Jesus Christ.
> (1 Thessalonians 5:23)

Life is birthed, nurtured and matured in that men and women marry, birth children, raise those children, and eventually release those children into the world. Following God's example, we are not to leave them nor forsake them, but we are to have continued fellowship with them and provide love and support for them.

> Let your conduct be without covetousness; be content with such things as you have. For He Himself has said, "I will never leave you nor forsake you." (Hebrews 13:5)

Like Jesus Christ, we have been made in the likeness of God. We are not three separate beings, but one being. Like Jesus, we are physical, emotional, and spiritual. Man is a spiritual being and has substance in the form of a physical body. Our soul or spirit has been given life, which allows us to have understanding.

> But there is a spirit in man, And the breath of the Almighty gives him understanding. (Job 32:8)

Earlier in this writing, John revealed to us that God the Son is the Word. Thus, God continues to dwell among us and is available to us by and through His Word, whether we choose to acknowledge His Word or not.

Have you ever walked into a room that is pitch black and before your eyes could adjust, bumped into the furniture? That is how most of us walk through life. We walk around in the dark, our eyes unadjusted to the sin around us, and we keep bumping into the challenges in life without a clue how to navigate through the world's obstacles.

God is longing to reveal His truths and guide us in life. If we want to know who created the universe and how to locate His so-called universe factory, one only has to go to His Word, the Bible, for the answers. His word testifies to Himself. In fact, when Moses asked God, "What shall I say to them?" God's only response was, "I AM Who I AM." How can anyone give testimony about the ultimate Creator, but the Creator Himself?

> And God said to Moses, "I AM WHO I AM." And He said, "Thus you shall say to the children of Israel, I AM has sent me to you." (Exodus 3:14)

> The Hebrew word used for I AM here is hayah; to exist, ie. be or become, come to pass (always emphatic, and not a mere copula or auxiliary)(10)

Hebrew scholars consider this to read "I Be that I Be" because the ancient Hebrew language has no past, present or future tense, but rather has a grammatical aspect with reference to time that is either imperfective or perfective.

If one is in agreement with the Hebrew scholars, the imperfective aspect in this statement might leave the impression that God is, has always been, and will always be in existence with no definitive answer toward completion. The perfective aspect would be an indicator of God's claim that He is still being and will finish what He has set in motion.

Therefore it should come as no surprise that God manifested Himself in the flesh through Christ and continues to live on in our physical world by virtue of His Word found in the Holy Scriptures.

> Jesus said to them, "Most assuredly, I say to you, before Abraham was, I AM." (John 8:38)

Jesus was putting Himself on par with God by claiming the same name God had given Moses. The Greek word for "AM" in John 8:58 is "eimi"—I exist (used only when emphatic): am, have, been. (6) Jesus, by His own admission, was emphatically stating that he was God.

Jesus Christ was God incarnate and came to earth in order to experience our world in the flesh and carry out His vision for humanity. We mentioned earlier that the CEO sets the vision and the President assembles the team in order to carry out that vision. God set the vision and He came to earth through Jesus Christ in order to assemble the team, a team that consisted of 12 original members.

> And when it was day, He called His disciples to Himself; and from them He chose twelve whom He also named apostles. (Luke 6:13)

These 12 apostles were the ones that Jesus chose to spend his earthly ministry. He imparted God's word in their hearts, pouring into them the vision set forth by the Father. God the Son didn't speak on His own authority, but by the authority given to Him by God the Father. Jesus was God's physical vessel.

> Then Jesus answered and said to them, "Most assuredly, I say to you, the Son can do nothing of Himself, but what He sees the Father do; for whatever He does, the Son also does in like manner." (John 5:19)

The Disciples became members of Christ's team, ordained to provide the example and teaching for all to follow. Multiplication if you will, in order to carry out God's vision for all humanity. The Holy Spirit moved through them, empowering them to speak the Word with boldness.

> And when they had prayed, the place where they were assembled together was shaken; and they were all filled with the Holy Spirit, and they spoke the word of God with boldness. (Acts 4:31)

Have you ever been approached by anyone with a multi-level marketing scheme? Ever wonder why so many of these capture our attention? God created multi-level marketing! It is a spiritual principle that has been distorted by the enticement of riches and glory, luring us through our lustful natures. Most often these schemes originate for dishonest gain or for the benefit of a few, and the only people that truly capitalize long-term on these schemes are the originators. God's multi-level marketing campaign started with one man, Jesus Christ, has been around for over 2000 years, and is still thriving today.

> In the year 2001, there were 159,514,000 self-described Christians in the continental United States. (11)

> Most assuredly, I say to you, he who believes in Me, the works that I do he will do also; and greater works than these he will do, because I go to My Father. (John 14:12)

Christ is still with us and though we can't see Him, He empowers us to carry out His Father's vision. Like His disciples, when we accept Him He imparts His power to us so that we will do greater works. *He is God the Son.*

The Holy Spirit

> The third person in the Trinity; Jesus promised the Apostles that he would send the Holy Spirit after his Crucifixion and Resurrection; it came on Pentecost [syn: Holy Ghost, Holy Spirit] (7)

> Air set in motion by breathing; breath; hence, sometimes, life itself. (4)

As created beings, we should intelligently assume that we are all connected in some fashion through God's life-giving spirit and rightly assume that we have access to an inheritance from our triune God: we should assume that we are heirs through Christ.

> Now I say that the heir, as long as he is a child, does not differ at all from a slave, though he is master of all, but is under guardians and stewards until the time appointed by the father. Even so we, when we were children, were in bondage under the elements of the world. But when the fullness of the time had come, God sent forth His Son, born of a woman, born under the law, to redeem those who were under the law, that we might receive the adoption as sons. And because you are sons, God has sent forth the Spirit of His Son into your hearts, crying out, "Abba, Father!" Therefore you are no longer a slave but a son, and if a son, then an heir of God through Christ. (Galatians 4:1-7)

Anyone who has played a part in the birthing process has knowledge of God's incredible creation. Through the birthing process, we in essence become co-creators with God of our own children. Don't we long to leave them an inheritance? Throughout mankind's time here on earth, the inheritance has been left to the children. One always leaves an inheritance to their children, unless of course, they have rejected their children or their children have rejected them.

God has not rejected His children, which is obvious in the scriptures we have read. Instead, He loves us so much that He gave His physical life for us and continues to give us free will to either accept Him or reject Him. He stands knocking "at the door" to our hearts, longing to have fellowship with all who invite Him in. He longs to bless us with "everlasting life."

> Behold, I stand at the door and knock. If anyone hears My voice and opens the door, I will come in to him and dine with him, and he with Me. (Revelation 3:20)

> For God so loved the world that He gave His only begotten Son, that whoever believes in Him should not perish but have everlasting life. (John 3:16)

Many of us today are confused about what happens when we die. Many think life as we know it ends and there are no other available options. I challenge you to consider that your spirit is infinite just as God's Holy Spirit is infinite. God is a God of the living, not of the dead.

> I am the God of Abraham, the God of Isaac, and the God of Jacob? God is not the God of the dead, but of the living. (Matthew 22:32)

It is foolish to automatically assume that once you die, the Spirit breathed into your substance also dies. How can man ever keep up with God's creation in order to fully understand that creation? After all, what is the determining point for the beginning of the universe? With the universe growing at an infinite pace, would it not be accurate to assume that the universe has been in existence infinitely? Therefore, no one will ever be able to pinpoint the beginning of existence or predict the ending of existence. Eternity reigns whether we like it or not, whether we want it to or not.

> I am the *Alpha* and the *Omega*, the Beginning and the End, says the Lord, who is and who was and who is to come, the Almighty. (Revelation 1:8)

> In the most widely accepted current model of the Universe, there is no starting place or time in the conventional sense of human experience. Space, as now defined and constrained by the outer limits of the *observable* Universe, did not yet exist; also, sequential events, embedded in a temporal continuum, had not begun. The observable Universe is just the visible or detectable part extending to the outermost reach of the Universe where objects or sources of radiation have sent signals traveling at the speed of light over an elapsed time not greater (usually somewhat less) than the time (age) of the start of expansion. Since now most cosmologists feel some confidence that there is something beyond the observable Universe be it the unseen parts of our Universe or some other Universe(s), that unobserved part plus the observed part is sometimes spoken of as the Cosmos. (12)

> The Cosmos - Pertaining to the universe, and having special reference to universal law or order, or to the one grand harmonious system of things; hence; harmonious; orderly. (8)

Since God's creation knows no beginning and no ending, how can one's spirit created by God have an ending? Our beginning was with God, because in Him and through Him all things were made; we were made in His image, according to His will and to His eternal vision. We were made into substance through birth and given life by His spirit.

The Bible, in the book of Luke, speaks of a beggar named Lazarus that sits at the gate of a wealthy man's home. He is content, we are told, to gather the crumbs from the man's table. Lazarus and the wealthy man die, the beggar went to be with God, and the wealthy man went to hell. The wealthy man sees "afar off" the beggar with Abraham and asks Abraham to send Lazarus to him in order to cool his tongue, but Abraham reminds him of the reward he had while on earth. The wealthy man could see Abraham and Lazarus in the distance. Don't you find it fascinating that all three men were dead, yet all three men were alive?

> There was a certain rich man who was clothed in purple and fine linen and fared sumptuously every day. But there was a certain beggar named Lazarus, full of sores, who was laid at his gate, desiring to be fed with the crumbs which fell from the rich man's table. Moreover the dogs came and licked his sores. So it was that the beggar died, and was carried by the angels to Abraham's bosom. The rich man also died and was buried. And being in torments in Hades, he lifted up his eyes and saw Abraham *afar off*, and Lazarus in his bosom. Then he cried and said, "Father Abraham, have mercy on me, and send Lazarus that he may dip the tip of his finger in water and cool my tongue; for I am tormented in this flame." But Abraham said, "Son, remember that in your lifetime you received your good things, and likewise Lazarus evil things; but now he is comforted and you are tormented." (Luke 16:19-25)

Could this possibly support the theory that our physical man perishes, but our spiritual man lives for all eternity? If I were a gambling man, my bet would be on the belief that our spirit man is not going to perish. Therefore, I am going to accept God, the infinite Creator, who is manifest in three parts. In fact, I had better accept that in His universal form He is all-knowing, all-powerful and all-encompassing, because if I bet the other direction…that He is not all-knowing, all-powerful, and not all-encompassing, I might very well take up residence with the wealthy man in the biblical parable. *He is God the Holy Spirit.*

> And do not fear those who kill the body but cannot kill the soul. But rather fear Him who is able to destroy both soul and body in hell. (Matthew 10:28)

How could an all-encompassing God of Love allow such a chasm or separation between the eternal realms of heaven and hell? Could it be that the order was established from the infinite beginning of time?

Free will says it is our decision to accept or reject God for who He is and who He says He is. The wealthy man in the parable had that opportunity before he died; unfortunately, he didn't embrace the reality of heaven and hell until after his death. He then embraced the truth, but as we read, it was too late. Lazarus died, his judgment was complete and because God's natural order was already in place, not even Abraham could reverse his fate.

I challenge that the eternal order was established in the very existence of God, because it is a part of who God is. Nothing can ever be truly separated from God. However, when we choose not to have a fellowship with God and not to acknowledge His ultimate authority, then we, like Lazarus, separate ourselves from God.

> And as it is appointed for men to die once, but after this the judgment. (Hebrews 9:27)

God understands creation because He is creation—from the beginning of time up to the time He takes us home for all eternity. It is a time that no one knows, and a time out of His goodness He hasn't even revealed to the host of heaven. Why? If man and woman knew when God planned to return, they might falsely believe that they could live without biblical accountability until the appointed time of His return.

That would be nice, wouldn't it? Live without any real cares, act any way we wanted, taste the deceitful sweetness of S.I.N. knowing all we had to do is straighten up at the appointed time. For that reason, no one knows, so if anyone claims to know, you had better question your source.

> But of that day and hour no one knows, not even the angels of heaven, but My Father only. (Matthew 24:36)

God has always been a triune God, a God in three parts from the beginning of creation. He set the vision, spoke the world into existence, and gave substance and life to the world. Creation is not a concept birthed by man or out of man's understanding of Christianity or any other religion, for that matter. God is eternal: past, present, and future.

> Jesus Christ is the same yesterday, today, and forever. Do not be carried about with various and strange doctrines. For it is good that the heart be established by grace, not with foods which have not profited those who have been occupied with them. (Hebrews 13:8-9)

We are taking a big chance if we make the decision to reject God. Not only are we rejecting Him here on earth in our physical form, we are also rejecting Him for all eternity in our spiritual form.

In essence, we are rejecting Him in three ways. First, we reject His divinity, then we reject His substance, and lastly we reject His spirit. There is no escaping the triune God of the universe. Just think how incredible God is: An infinite God pauses within His creation to reach out to us in physical form in order for each one of us to join Him in His spiritual kingdom—a kingdom that has no boundaries, no limitations, no exclusions, and is infinite in scope.

Furthermore, God has given His Word, His promise, and His covenants to all who will believe. God is so simple, yet so profound, that the intellectual human has a hard time understanding the infinite character of God. Out of ignorance, many have and will continue to discount His awesome power and His truths and stand destined to live eternally separated from His awesome presence.

In the second chapter, we will expose "Satan's Intended Notion" and show that he desperately longs for everyone to be separated from God for all eternity, just as he became separated because of his rejection of God. Hell is a lonely place, and Satan's torment because of his separation from the Creator is still too much for him to bear alone.

> How you are fallen from heaven, O Lucifer, son of the morning! How you are cut down to the ground, You who weakened the nations! For you have said in your heart: "I will ascend into heaven, I will exalt my throne above the stars of God; I will also sit on the mount of the congregation On the farthest sides of the north; I will ascend above the heights of the clouds, I will be like the Most High." (Isaiah 14:12-14)

How then can one be sure that he/she will spend eternity with God the Creator? Open your eternal eyes and invite God into your heart by accepting His divine Lordship in three parts: Father, Son & Holy Spirit. He will reveal to you His manifold presence, because just as His universe is in perfect order, so is His word in perfect order: He cannot lie.

> And if I go and prepare a place for you, I will come again and receive you to Myself; that where I am, there you may be also...Jesus said to him, "I am the way, the truth, and the life. No one comes to the Father except through Me."
> (John 14:3,6)

Chapter Two

Satan's Intended Notion

From the beginning, mankind has been deceived. Out of our ignorance and naiveté, we have been led down a destructive path; a path we have continued to follow throughout generations, beginning with Adam. We are no different than the day man first encountered sin. We continue to be deceived by our curious nature to attain some higher spiritual calling that is not within our grasp, but already innately a part of our created being.

We sit back and continue to allow our cultural degradation and our moral failures, casually passing them off as propagating forces that have naturally evolved because of man and woman's inherent lust for a more fulfilling life. We have become complacent and callous; allowing Satan to have his way by falling prey to sin's deceptions, accusations and temptations.

It is time we understood and uncovered S.I.N. for what it really is, "Satan's Intended Notion," and we learn through his deceptive tactics that it has become *Societal in Nature*. We know from the Bible that Satan was cast out of Heaven, so it should come as no surprise that he has an intended notion or evil desire that he is trying to achieve through natural processes. His intention is to accomplish this through the infiltration of our societal structures and by using men and women with ill-intended hearts. Since Adam and Eve, S.I.N. has been out to steal, kill and destroy.

> So the great dragon was cast out, that serpent of old, called the Devil and Satan, who deceives the whole world; he was cast to the earth, and his angels were cast out with him.
> (Revelation 12:9)

And He said to them, "I saw Satan fall like lightning from heaven." (Luke 10:18)

The thief does not come except to steal, and to kill, and to destroy. I have come that they may have life, and that they may have it more abundantly. (John 10:10)

In this chapter, we will start by defining society, pose some thought provoking questions and then examine how the deceptive process works. We will examine how Satan has infiltrated our society through the principle of *gang formation* and show how the birthing of a gang or group is based on a spiritual concept supported in scripture. We will explore the true intentions of men's hearts by citing three examples supporting the principle. Two of the examples were birthed by men whose hearts or notions were bent on control of their respective societies, the third example shows a leader who was bent on saving mankind.

SOCIETY DEFINED

Climactic in nature / spiritually immature. The totality of social relationships among humans. A group of humans broadly distinguished from other groups by mutual interests, participation in characteristic relationships, shared institutions, and a common culture. The institutions and culture of a distinct self-perpetuating group. (13)

CLIMACTIC IN NATURE

- Is your life a series of mountaintops?
- Is your life a series of valleys?

It had been my first mission trip with an international ministry organization. Forgive me if I don't tell you the name of the country, because it is still bound by communism. We arrived in the country's main city and boarded a bus, which took us into the interior. We drove up into the mountains to what at one time had been an exclusive resort. The next day we had trouble securing rental cars, which made us late setting out to visit outlying towns where appointments had already been set-up to receive us. I carpooled with a retired couple, full-time missionaries supported by members from their local church in Arkansas. One of the local pastors volunteered to drive us each morning to the towns where we would be working and pick us up each evening to return us to the hotel.

Every morning, we dropped the couple off in the town they had been assigned to and drove another hour to the town to which I was assigned. Our mission was to share the love of Christ by meeting and forging relationships with the townspeople. The couple I had been assigned to were wonderful people. The father was a minister and the mother a pediatrician. I would like to note that their combined monthly income was less than twenty dollars.

I was the first American to visit their village, a village I might add that had no paved streets, rarely running water, and intermittent electrical power. Batteries were used as backup power for refrigerators, so when the government turned the power off, what little food they had would not spoil. We spent a week traveling the countryside meeting in homes, sharing our life experiences, praying for one another, and saw many people make a decision to allow Christ into their hearts. It was both a mountaintop and a valley experience.

Upon arrival in my assigned town that first night, I attended a church service where I quickly learned I was the main attraction. With the assistance of a translator, I shared my life testimony and thanked them for allowing me to visit. When finished I felt like a man on fire, full of power, ready to take on all the spiritual forces. I was on top of the mountain!

The attending pastor asked me what I wanted to do next, so I suggested we ask if anyone in the audience needed prayer. The first person to raise her hand was a woman in her thirties, and she asked me to pray for her son who was deaf and dumb. The second person asked me to pray for her father who had cancer in his body. The third asked me to pray that her son's leg would be healed from the crushing blow he had sustained from a horse. The prayers for healing kept coming until I was so overwhelmed that I must have appeared in shock to those in attendance. I felt about as low and spiritually unprepared as one could possibly feel. I mustered all my strength to pray for everyone who had a request, and we closed out the service in worship.

On the long drive home, I was crushed. It felt like the weight of the whole world rested on my shoulders. Later that night, upon returning to the hotel, I shared the experience with my roommate. I told him, "If none of my prayers are answered they will consider me a fake—I can't return to that town because they will tar and feather me!" Those were not the words of a spiritual giant. I was in the valley!

Of course, when I returned the next day, it was just the opposite: everyone embraced me and welcomed me into their homes. I don't know if any of those prayers were answered, only God and the people of that town know for sure. It would have been nice to witness a supernatural move of God.

Looking back, that is exactly what I witnessed, because of the relationships that were built. I had been to the mountain, but soon found myself in the valley. The valley is where the real work gets done, and if we are honest, it is where we spend the majority of our lives. Through that valley experience, I forged a loving relationship with a whole town that still touches my heart. I hope to return one day, and I'm sure, I will hear how God answered our prayers.

Spiritually Immature

- Are your relationships spiritually mature?
- What determines maturity?

I attended college at a school in the southern part of Texas, and if I told you the name you would merely pass this story off by saying that's par for someone from that university. Therefore, to keep all you Texas fans guessing, I will not mention the name of the institution. I had a friend from Dallas who was a member of my fraternity. He owned an old red army Jeep. You remember them, don't you? The ones just like you used to see on the TV show *MASH* with Alan Alda. No top, a windshield that folded over on the hood and an indestructible body. He loved to hunt; in fact, he loved to hunt so much that instead of attending class, if he wasn't sleeping, he would be hunting. He would commune with nature, and for him that was about as spiritual as it got.

I remember both of us living in the fraternity house, and it seemed like every day he would ask me to go on an adventure with him. It was so tempting, because he was always in such a good mood and just fun to be around. Of course, none of us corrected or encouraged him to change; after all, it would have spoiled the fun. We lived vicariously through his adventures and couldn't wait to hear his stories.

We were not acting in a mature fashion, and we sure didn't cover him spiritually. Mainly because none of us had a spiritual relationship with the Lord at that point in our lives. We didn't love him enough to correct him. We were too self-centered and immature to realize that as his brothers, we had an obligation to speak into his life. We were bound by the oath of the fraternity, even if we weren't bound by the oath of God's Word. We had committed to be instruments of virtue, diligence and brotherly love.

Instead, we were satisfying our own lusts by enjoying his self-destructive behavior. Unfortunately, his parents didn't share our passion and were not really excited when he flunked out. Soon he was back in Dallas without a college degree, left with only regrets and insecure feelings, and we were heartbroken because we missed his adventurous spirit. As a result of our spiritual immaturity as well as our manly immaturity, (there is really no difference), we had let our brother down.

A GROUP OF HUMANS BROADLY DISTINGUISHED FROM OTHER GROUPS BY MUTUAL INTERESTS

- Are we drawn to other people by mutual interest?
- Does it matter if those interests are healthy or not?
- What is the climate of your social circles?
- Are they healthy, loving and life building?

While attending the same school, I remember inviting my friends from all over the state to the second annual Willie Nelson Fourth of July picnic. My house became a campground for our visitors, and I borrowed a pick-up truck in order to shuttle everyone to and from the picnic.

We were drawn together by mutual interest and interacted with several thousand other people at the Texas Motor Speedway. Together, we celebrated our independence: our freedom to drink, run wild and pick up girls. In fact, I had such a good time I got a tour of the local jail from one of the State highway patrol officers working the event. Fortunately, I had a friend that worked part-time at the jail who called some of my true friends to come make a donation on my behalf so I could rejoin my guests, who, by the way, had eaten, taken naps, showered, and returned to the Speedway without me.

Let me tell you, this experience was not healthy, loving, and most definitely, not life building! I know many of you reading this probably can't relate, because you grew up in a different setting or made better choices. However, don't be deceived.

There are people you know living this sort of lifestyle, only in a more private setting. For example, I had a friend tell me about a group of men who travel to Mexico each year on a hunting expedition with their so-called friends. They leave their wives at home even though they grew up listening to the refrain of a Beach Boy's song, "It's not right to leave the best girls home on a Saturday night." Of course, they tell their wives it would be boring for them, because it will just be a bunch of guys sitting around the campfire telling lies. Truth be told, they don't spend much time around a campfire. Instead, they rent expensive hotel rooms and invite a variety of young women to keep them company at night. Though they have mutual interests, these social circles are not healthy, loving, and life building.

THE INSTITUTIONS AND CULTURE OF A DISTINCT SELF-PERPETUATING GROUP

- Do you believe that like attracts like?
- Do you believe people in general are followers or leaders?
- Do you think certain groups are concerned about right or wrong, good or bad?

I had the pleasure of spending time with a group of incredible men from my son's Boy Scout troop. Most of the fathers were successful in their own right, but their true success was found in the investment of time and information poured into the young men that were members of the troop. Most of those young men joined the troop because they had a friend attending; in other words, they had a common bond. Their fathers spent countless hours behind the scenes planning weekend camping trips, preparing events and speakers, conducting merit badge classes, and assisting the young men in getting their Eagle Scout.

They had their priorities straight, they were leaders and they deposited good into those boys who eventually became leaders. They poured what they had learned in life into a group of fine young men destined for greatness. As a result, the troop is still successful to this day, and my guess is that it will be for years to come.

PRINCIPLE OF GANG FORMATION

One only has to study the psychology behind the principle theory of *gang formation* to understand the deceptive reality we are faced with in our current society. It is common knowledge that most gangs start by two people getting together and talking, but it is not until someone else joins and offers support and encouragement that momentum begins to build and others are invited to join their ranks.

> Definition of Gang: A group or association of three or more persons who may have a common identifying sign, symbol, or name and who individually or collectively engage in, or have

engaged in, criminal activity which creates an atmosphere of fear and intimidation. (14)

People join with others for a variety of reasons: to find acceptance, for intimacy, for approval, for a sense of identity and/or pressure from peers.

> A variety of factors have been cited as causes for involvement in gangs. Social problems associated with gang activity include poverty, racism, and the disintegration of the nuclear family. Some critics claim that gangs are glamorized in the media and by the entertainment industry. On a personal level, adolescents whose families are not meeting their emotional needs turn to gangs as substitute families where they can find acceptance, intimacy, and approval. Gangs can also provide the sense of identity that young people crave as they confront the dislocations of adolescence. Teenagers also join gangs because of social pressure from friends. (15)

Law enforcement understands that one person's boasting, however serious, is not something to be overly concerned about. When law enforcement learns that two people are talking about a destructive act, they will monitor the parties for fear they might take action. However, when they learn that three or more are meeting and talking about a plan of destruction, they will move on that information and take action to ensure the safety of our society. After the 9/11 terrorist attacks, our government put a major initiative in place in order to monitor various sectors and connect enforcement agencies in order to deter possible threats to our national security.

> The National Infrastructure Protection Plan (NIPP) provides the unifying structure for the integration of critical infrastructure and key resources (CI/KR) protection into a single national program. The NIPP provides an overall framework for programs and activities that are currently underway in the various sectors, as well as new and developing CI/KR protection efforts. This collaborative effort between the private sector; State, Territorial, local, and tribal governments; nongovernmental organizations; and the Federal Government will result in the prioritization of protection

initiatives and investments across sectors. It also will ensure that resources are applied where they offer the most benefit for mitigating risk by lowering vulnerabilities, deterring threats, and minimizing the consequences of terrorist attacks and other incidents. (16)

I think we can agree that gangs on the whole do not have good intentions, but are bent on some destructive behavior counterproductive to society. All we have to do is pick up our local newspaper and turn to the "Metropolitan" section to see the affect gangs have on our society. Many become perpetrators of selfish agendas in order to entice and lure additional members into their ranks. The goal is to assume power, and once in power, they will do anything to preserve that power.

In history, there have been many men who have ruled nations using this concept. Who are some of the men that have been able to influence whole societies with their personal agendas? Fidel Castro, Idi Amin Dada, Dr. François Duvalier, Adolf Hitler, Saddam Hussein, Abd al-Majid al-Tikriti, Slobodan Milosevic, Robert Gabriel Mugabe, Augusto José Ramón Pinochet Ugarte, Saloth Sar (Pol Pot), Mobutu Sese Seko, and Joseph Stalin.

The following study is from the National Gang Crime Research Center. Along with what has been learned through gang research, these men could be labeled as the "Super Predators" of the world.

THE FACTS ABOUT GANG LIFE IN AMERICA TODAY: A NATIONAL STUDY OF OVER 4,000 GANG MEMBERS

The term "Super Predators" refers to "The most violent of the violent criminal offenders operating in the United States today."

OVERALL PROFILE SUMMARY OF THE SUPER PREDATOR

Based on the analysis reported in this chapter we can now provide an overall profile summary of the "super predator" based on a large-scale national sample that is also very recent (i.e., collected in 1996) and therefore not dated.

- More likely to have the attitude "I get what I want even if I have to take it from someone."
- Younger, thus also less likely perhaps to have completed high school degree or the GED.

- More likely to have been a bully in school.
- More likely to engage in activities in which they might be injured.
- More likely to "demand" that their needs be fulfilled.
- More likely to have been sexually abused.
- More likely to have been from a mother-only family.
- More likely to have sold crack cocaine; as nine out of ten have been involved in organized drug dealing.
- Less likely to be deterred by stiff prosecution measures.
- *Less likely to believe in God, more likely to purport to be on Satan's side.*
- More likely to know an active gang member who works in a criminal justice capacity.
- More likely to continue their behavior behind bars: more disciplinary reports, more fighting, more weapons carrying, more attempts to smuggle illegal drugs into the institution, and more threats against facility staff or officers.

Summary And Conclusion

At first glance the concept of *super predator* may appear to some as just another "label" that stigmatizes the offender population. It is similar to the issue of *monsters* in the gang arena. Gang members cry out that they do not want to be regarded as "monsters". But thousands of victims and those who work in criminal justice know that there are such persons who really exemplify by their conduct a designation to that effect. In human history there have been such "monsters": gangsters, serial killers, etc. So the idea of super predator is not presented here as another way to add a negative label to gang members. The way the present research defined the super predator illustrated that it truly is a very small segment of the overall offender population in the United States (6.2%). Thus, it bears repeating here that the overwhelming majority of most offenders in the United States (93.8%) are not defined as super predators in the analysis reported here. This chapter tends to demonstrate with strong evidence that this small group constituting only about 6% of the offender population definitely accounts for a disproportionately high amount of crime and violence. (17)

As stated in the conclusion to this study, the so-called *super predators* don't make up the majority in the gang population, but they are the most feared and ruthless. These men or women will do anything to gain power and control their respective environments. The study states, "In human history there have been such 'monsters': gangsters, serial killers, etc." The research shows that the super predator is *"Less likely to believe in God, more likely to purport to be on Satan's side,"* thus they are really nothing more than Satan's instruments, pawns, if you will, of S.I.N. Out of spiritual ignorance, these men will most likely spend an eternity with Satan in the lake of fire as a consequence of the destruction they have brought on millions of people.

> But the cowardly, unbelieving, abominable, murderers, sexually immoral, sorcerers, idolaters, and all liars shall have their part in the lake which burns with fire and brimstone, which is the second death. (Revelation 21:8)

Many good companies and institutions have been formed or birthed from the same principle: one, two, then three or more coming together, ultimately building entities that are positive, and have a profound impact on the world. Yes, many good organizations have been formed based on the principle of *gang formation*, we just don't refer to them as *gangs*.

Two wonderful examples that have had a tremendous impact on the world are first, Bill Hewlett and Dave Packard, who started Hewlett Packard and second, Steve Jobs and Stephen Wozniak, who started Apple. Both companies were started with two men in a garage. Wozniak actually worked for Hewlett Packard before joining Jobs. However, it wasn't until others were enlisted that these companies began to grow and take shape.

It is extremely important to understand that the reason this principle works is that it is based on a *SPIRITUAL PRINCIPLE*, a principle that can be found in Ecclesiastes in the Bible.

> Two are better than one, Because they have a good reward for their labor. For if they fall, one will lift up his companion. But woe to him who is alone when he falls, For he has no one to help him up. Again, if two lie down together, they will keep warm; But how can one be warm alone? Though one may be overpowered by another, two can withstand him. And a *threefold cord* is not quickly broken. (Ecclesiastes 4:9-12)

The reason this scripture is powerful, as we will learn in more detail later in the book, is because the *threefold cord* is present in the TRINITY: God the Father, God the Son, and God the Holy Spirit. The power manifests itself when Christians bound by truth and love use this principle and acknowledge the Holy Spirit as the third cord, the cord that allows God and Christ to join them.

When building relationships, there is power spiritually. When we acknowledge and invite the Holy Spirit as the third cord, we invite the Holy Spirit to join in and bless the union. However, since this principle is present in the spiritual realm, whether we choose to acknowledge it or not, it is effective when employed in the secular realm. Therefore, the use of the principle isn't reliant on the understanding of scripture.

Thus, one might ask, "What is the difference between the men and women who build entities that are healthy for society and the men and women who build entities to control society?" The answer to this question is found in the next section.

INTENTIONS OF THE HEART

The difference is found in the true nature of the heart of those leaders. Do they truly want what is best for society, or are they perpetrators that are ill intended and bent on satisfying their own selfish desires and controlling society?

We must be careful, because even the most well-meaning people can have a hidden agenda. The real question we should be asking is, "What is the spiritual condition of their heart?" not "What is their intended desire?" The spiritual condition of their heart will reveal the intention contained therein.

For our purposes, I am going to cite three different examples where the principle of *gang formation* has been used. I will intertwine parts of the definition of society into these examples to support how the principle has been integrated into the societies in which we live. The first two are modern day examples birthed from leaders with ill-intended hearts, hearts set on destruction. The third example, however, is birthed from a leader with a well-meaning heart, a solid spiritual connection with the Father, and an agenda to save all mankind.

It was September 11, 2001 when radical extremists attacked two of our largest cities, bringing devastation on our nation as a whole. Their destruction was not brought about by one person paying lip service to the act of terrorism, but a concerted deceptive effort by a group. They were joined together by *mutual interests, participation in characteristic relationships, shared institutions, and a common culture.*

The leaders convinced members of the group that to die committing an act of terrorism would actually give them a blessing in the afterlife. We will explore later in the book that one of Satan's primary weapons is deception. That being said, should it come as any surprise that these terrorist were themselves *set-up* by S.I.N. and as a result, the whole world is still paying consequences for their ignorance and sinful behavior?

These men and women desired a relationship; their contentious behavior was birthed out of the pain caused by the societal influence on their lives. It didn't matter if that influence was right, wrong, good or bad.

Governments will even debate the right or wrong issues based on their own cultural backgrounds before making a unified effort to combat the destructive behavior and guard against future terrorist attacks. The struggle we are faced with politically is that different cultures define terrorist aggression in different ways. For the terrorists of 9/11 the act of terrorism was not birthed out of truculence, but a valid statement supported by the idea of jihad.

> *jihad* - A religious war against infidels or Mohammedan heretics; also, any bitter war or crusade for a principle or belief. (8)

The hierarchy behind the jihad appeals to the contentious spirit within their followers because S.I.N. exists in the hearts of men and women.

> As charcoal is to burning coals, and wood to fire, So is a contentious man to kindle strife. (Proverbs 26:21)

These men and women appeal to the weak and the ignorant, those easier influenced—the followers, not the leaders. Ignorance is no excuse, but it is alive and well in the hearts of those who have been birthed and raised in a society of hate and violence. Where I live in America, it is hard to grasp their reality. We are sheltered from the type of hate and anger they have been surrounded with their whole lives, which has been passed down from generation to generation. These men and women joined together and became *broadly distinguished from other groups by mutual interests,* and in hindsight we know what those interests were: crash two planes into the Twin Towers at the World Trade Center, one into the Pentagon, and it is thought a fourth plane, which crashed into a field near Shanksville in rural

Pennsylvania, was targeting either the United States Capital or the White House.

The leaders had planned this event over years, infiltrated our society and secretly trained up until 9/11. They recruited others to join in their cause, because they needed people to raise money, secure housing, and secure jobs with the airlines. But most importantly, they deceptively recruited them to give their lives for a false eternal promise. They had become a *distinct self-perpetuating group* bent on destruction and death to further their cause and force their ideals on the world.

For our second example, one only has to look to Cuba—90 miles south of Florida—to see how a whole society has been wronged because of the idealistic view of one man. Fidel Castro admittedly lied to everyone when he started talking about revolutionizing Cuba. He misled his fellow Cubans and the world to think his intentions were pure.

> Inflammatory rhetoric inflamed the public mood and provided the condition for more inflammatory rhetoric. Many Cubans shuddered, not knowing what to think or do. Perez goes on to quote Juan Arcocha, from his Los muertos andan solos (1962), "Carmen delighted to the orations of Fidel Castro. So young and so intelligent, and he said such magnificent things." (18)

Castro led them to believe that he was going to overthrow General Fulgencio Batista's dictatorial government in favor of a democratic form of government. He was able to convince everyone because at the time, Batista was himself a self-serving dictator who oppressed the weaker populace in order to achieve personal goals and finance a lavish lifestyle. Batista's deception was not different from other self-serving government leaders. The system in place allowed him to operate Cuba the way he saw fit.

Castro, after taking control, admitted he had studied Marxism in college and adhered to the socialistic ideals crafted by such men as Vladimir Lenin, Friedrich Engels, and Karl Marx. He was incensed by the oppression of the political engine holding office in his country and saw an opportunity to control it using Marxist principles. In 1961, he declared Cuba a socialistic state and allied himself with the Soviet Union. In reality, Cuba became Castro's personal property; one might even go so far as to say his personal playground. I would challenge that his methods were *climactic in nature.*

Castro was successful in his quest because Cuba at the time lacked a democratic foundation; the corrupt were taking advantage of the lack of legal authority to export Cuba's resources. They had no interest in developing her people. Myer Lansky and the mafia saw an opportunity in Cuba; it seemed an oasis separated from legal authority where they could set-up gambling, prostitution, and drug running with little or no opposition. Batista welcomed their money, power, and influence. As a result of their greed, Castro decided to radically alter the course of history by imposing his own socialistic ideals. Castro understood the system of communistic social identity and how one could exert ultimate control over a group of people.

In the beginning, Castro was joined only by his brother Raul, but he was able to convince others to join his cause. It wasn't until another well-educated revolutionary joined him, Ernesto Che Guevara, that plans were carried out to overthrow Batista. Guevara was not from Cuba, but was enamored by Castro and shared his Marxist ideology. Guevara was born in Argentina and studied medicine at Buenos Aires University.

Now there were three united *by a common cause, mutual interests, participation in characteristic relationships, shared institutions, and a common culture.* Together they garnered support.

They led the Cuban people to believe that the new government would allow them to take back control of their homeland and rule according to the wishes of the whole, not just the wealthy and educated. Castro knew what to say, because he knew the cries of the people. He also understood historically the change that could be brought about if he could get enough people united behind him. He rallied the support of other nations, the United States being one.

History has revealed that the true nature of his heart was never democratic, but self-serving: to take control and ultimately dominate. Castro, by setting up the allegiance with the Soviet Union and declaring his dominance, encompassed and defined the *totality of social relationships* within the country.

> Batista's dictatorial rule fueled increasing popular discontent and the rise of many active urban and rural resistance groups, a fertile political environment for Castro's 26th of July Movement. Faced with a corrupt and ineffective military--itself dispirited by a U.S. Government embargo on weapons sales to Cuba — and public indignation and revulsion at his brutality toward opponents, Batista fled on January 1, 1959. *Although he had promised a return to constitutional rule and democratic elections along with social reforms, Castro used his control of the military to consolidate his power by repressing*

all dissent from his decisions, marginalizing other resistance figures, and imprisoning or executing thousands of opponents. An estimated 3,200 people were executed by the Castro regime between 1959-62 alone. As the revolution became more radical, hundreds of thousands of Cubans fled the island.

Castro declared Cuba a socialist state on April 16, 1961. For the next 30 years, Castro pursued close relations with the Soviet Union and worked in concert with the geopolitical goals of Soviet communism, funding and fomenting violent subversive and insurrectional activities, as well as military adventurism, until the demise of the U.S.S.R. in 1991. (19)

In these first two examples, the men involved would argue that their intentions were pure and guided by what they thought was best for their nation. We've all heard the expression, "The road to hell is paved with good intentions." For the most part, people are well intended. However, a misguided intention can have an effect on a nation and ultimately the world. If those intentions are birthed out of a deceptive spirit, anyone or anything that tries to thwart their effort will become their enemy. Any attempt at exposing the truth or to bring about a peaceful resolution will be faced with opposition. Those attempts will be twisted and turned in such a way that the masses will question the intentions of those trying to bring about a peaceful resolution. Deception is as alive today as it has been since the beginning of time.

Accusation and deception are two of the enemy's primary weapons, and we will look at them in detail later in the book. Thus, stronger personalities are able to dominate and intimidate weaker personalities. Often at that juncture, a plan that began as simple boasting, criticism or an expression of one's personal belief is stimulated into action.

We are creatures of our surroundings and, in the case of these two examples, a *distinct self-perpetuating group.* For a group to be perpetuating there has to be a catalyst and a continuation of action. That catalyst in society is a common or agreed upon mindset that is stimulated to action by forces joining together by *mutual interests.* In essence, by the very definition of *Society,* they have separated from the mainstream population and formed their own society, attempting to impose their beliefs on the rest of the world.

One can easily see that the movements in these two examples were headed by *Super Predators* and were built knowingly or unknowingly on the principle of *gang formation* in the most extreme sense. The entities were unhealthy, and their members had a sick sense of common identity, however they were accepted and became part of a family.

Our third example was birthed by a leader with a well-meaning heart, a heart bound by truth, and His mission was to save all humanity from the grip of S.I.N. This leader still remains true to His people and to His Creator. His name is Jesus Christ.

> And she will bring forth a Son, and you shall call His name JESUS, for He will save His people from their sins. So all this was done that it might be fulfilled which was spoken by the Lord through the prophet, saying: "Behold, the virgin shall be with child, and bear a Son, and they shall call His name Immanuel," which is translated, "God with us."
> (Matthew 1:21-23)

> Therefore the Lord Himself will give you a sign: Behold, the virgin shall conceive and bear a Son, and shall call His name Immanuel. (Isaiah 7:14)

Jesus Christ didn't have the methods of communication we have today or the methods cited in our previous two examples. He didn't need our modern methods to build His ministry and carry His message to the entire world. Instead, he chose a few very unassuming men to walk with Him, learn from Him, and ultimately represent Him to carry out His plan of salvation for all humanity.

Jesus' ministry didn't start until He was 30 years of age, when He stood up in the synagogue, quoted Old Testament scripture, and basically declared Himself the Messiah.

> Now Jesus Himself began His ministry at about thirty years of age, being (as was supposed) the son of Joseph, the son of Heli. (Luke 3:23)

> So He came to Nazareth, where He had been brought up. And as His custom was, He went into the synagogue on the Sabbath day, and stood up to read. And He was handed the book of the prophet Isaiah. And when He had opened the book, He found the place where it was written: *"The Spirit of the LORD is upon Me, Because He has anointed Me To preach the gospel to the poor; He has sent Me to heal the*

> brokenhearted, To proclaim liberty to the captives And recovery of sight to the blind, To set at liberty those who are oppressed; To proclaim the acceptable year of the LORD." Then He closed the book, and gave it back to the attendant and sat down. And the eyes of all who were in the synagogue were fixed on Him. And He began to say to them, "Today this Scripture is fulfilled in your hearing." (Luke 4:16-21)

The people in his village were perplexed and felt threatened, because they knew him only as the son of Joseph and Mary, a common couple in the community. Prior to this day, the people of the town thought he was a carpenter, which surely gave no one cause for alarm.

> So all those in the synagogue, when they heard these things, were filled with wrath, and rose up and thrust Him out of the city; and they led Him to the brow of the hill on which their city was built, that they might throw Him down over the cliff. Then passing through the midst of them, He went His way. (Luke 4:28-30)

We learn that it wasn't until this time of declaration that the religious and political leaders began to take notice, and the people became angered, intending to throw Him out of the city.

In chapter one, we saw how another man, John the Baptist (JTB), came on the scene before Jesus, stirring up the masses and confronting the religious authorities of the time. JTB was receiving people to be baptized and hearing their confessions of sin. He was becoming a threat to the authorities, and of course, it didn't help things when JTB called them a "brood of vipers."

> In those days John the Baptist came preaching in the wilderness of Judea, and saying, "Repent, for the kingdom of heaven is at hand! For this is he who was spoken of by the prophet Isaiah, saying: 'The voice of one crying in the wilderness: Prepare the way of the LORD; Make His paths straight.'" Now John himself was clothed in camel's hair, with a leather belt around his waist; and his food was locusts and wild honey. Then Jerusalem, all Judea, and all the region around the Jordan went out to him and were baptized by him in the Jordan, confessing their sins. But when he saw many of the Pharisees and Sadducees coming to his baptism, he said to

them, *"Brood of vipers!"* Who warned you to flee from the wrath to come? (Matthew 3: 1-7)

Of course, they had no idea that JTB was paving the way for Jesus, who was ready to begin His ministry and claim His *God ordained authority*.

However, Jesus was alone at the time and didn't have any followers. In fact, we just learned His own people had thrown Him out of town with an attempt to kill Him. So how did Jesus assemble His team?

> Again, the next day, John stood with two of his disciples. And looking at Jesus as He walked, he said, "Behold the Lamb of God!" The two disciples heard him speak, and they followed Jesus. Then Jesus turned, and seeing them following, said to them, "What do you seek?" They said to Him, "Rabbi" (which is to say, when translated, Teacher), "where are You staying?" He said to them, "Come and see." They came and saw where He was staying, and remained with Him that day (now it was about the tenth hour). (John 1:35-39)

Suddenly, Jesus had two followers join Him, and, we learn as a result of their membership, there would soon be three more men ready to join and follow Jesus.

> One of the two who heard John speak, and followed Him, was Andrew, Simon Peter's brother. He first found his own brother Simon, and said to him, "We have found the Messiah" (which is translated, the Christ). And he brought him to Jesus. Now when Jesus looked at him, He said, "You are Simon the son of Jonah. You shall be called Cephas" (which is translated, A Stone). The following day Jesus wanted to go to Galilee, and He found Philip and said to him, "Follow Me." Now Philip was from Bethsaida, the city of Andrew and Peter. Philip found Nathanael and said to him, "We have found Him of whom Moses in the law, and also the prophets, wrote—Jesus of Nazareth, the son of Joseph." And Nathanael said to him, "Can anything good come out of Nazareth?" Philip said to him, "Come and see." Jesus saw Nathanael coming toward Him, and said of him, "Behold, an Israelite indeed, in whom is no deceit!" Nathanael said to Him, "How do You know me?" Jesus answered and said to him, "Before

> Philip called you, when you were under the fig tree, I saw you." Nathanael answered and said to Him, "Rabbi, You are the Son of God! You are the King of Israel!" Jesus answered and said to him, "Because I said to you, 'I saw you under the fig tree,' do you believe? You will see greater things than these." And He said to him, "Most assuredly, I say to you, hereafter you shall see heaven open, and the angels of God ascending and descending upon the Son of Man." (John 1:40-53)

Jesus didn't put out advertisements or solicit His followers. Instead, He appealed to their curiosity and, ultimately, their hearts. In all, He assembled a team of twelve who were set apart to join his inner circle and were ready to become *distinguished from other groups by mutual interests, participation in characteristic relationships, shared institutions, and a common culture.*

He began to teach them; His influence and ideas became the foundation of belief and the basis for their actions. They in turn began to organize events attracting multitudes of people who were being oppressed by the political and religious establishment. At the time, the religious authorities started to become concerned, anxious, and finally threatened, knowing that action needed to be taken for fear of a rebellion. Thus, they devised and carried out a deceptive and accusatory scheme to have Him arrested, tried, and ultimately killed.

> And they began to accuse Him, saying, "We found this fellow perverting the nation, and forbidding to pay taxes to Caesar, saying that He Himself is Christ, a King." (Luke 23:2)

Their initial fears were fueled by Jesus' own admission that He was a king and their secular misconception that He was speaking about becoming the ruler of a physical kingdom. However, Jesus was referring to Himself as a spiritual king, a king that would ultimately rule a spiritual kingdom for eternity.

They ignorantly assumed that He was declaring himself king in order to birth a movement, all part of a dangerous ploy to overthrow their political system. The hierarchy of that political system feared for their lives. Why? Because they knew the abuses they were placing on society: taxation to the point where people had no choice but to live in poverty. Those abuses existed to support the lavish lifestyle of the political and religious authorities. If the people could be unified by an opposing group intent on exposing the truth of their oppression, the political and religious authorities knew all too well that they could be ousted from office. Thus stripped of power and denied the lavish lifestyle to which they had become accustomed.

However, it wasn't until Jesus was joined by others that the movement became a threat to those leaders. Does this example of how Jesus birthed His ministry sound any different from the two previous examples we explored? The same principle of *gang formation* was at work. As previously stated, the principle is based on scripture and is established in the spiritual realm. Spiritual principles are effective, not just in the heavenly realm, but also when employed in the secular realm. That is why many organizations and companies today that have been formed unknowingly using spiritual principles are successful; we just don't refer to them as *gangs*.

We showed in each of our examples that to the establishments in power, the movements seemed to be a threat to society. I ask you then, what was the difference? The difference was exposed when we acknowledged the true nature of the hearts of those in leadership. The true nature of the hearts of men and women involved in any rebellion will always define the underlying principles and ultimately guide the course of that rebellion.

> Brood of vipers! How can you, being evil, speak good things? For out of the abundance of the heart the mouth speaks. A good man out of the good treasure of his heart brings forth good things, and an evil man out of the evil treasure brings forth evil things.
> (Matthew 12:34-35)

> Therefore judge nothing before the time, until the Lord comes, who will both bring to light the hidden things of darkness and reveal the counsels of the hearts. Then each one's praise will come from God. (1 Corinthians 4:5)

> The heart knows its own bitterness, And a stranger does not share its joy. The house of the wicked will be overthrown, But the tent of the upright will flourish. There is a way that seems right to a man, But its end is the way of death. Even in laughter the heart may sorrow, And the end of mirth may be grief. The backslider in heart will be filled with his own ways, But a good man will be satisfied from above.
> (Proverbs 14:10-14)

> Let us draw near with a true heart in full assurance of faith, having our hearts sprinkled from an evil conscience and our bodies washed with pure water. (Hebrews 10:22)

History supports my theory, because there is no doubt that in our first two examples, the people involved did not have good intentions. In fact, by their own admission, their intentions were to take control of their surroundings and enforce with violence their idealistic principles on the masses. However, in our third example, history has proven that Christ had good intentions, and his intentions were birthed out of a love for all humanity. His was a message of repentance and forgiveness of sin and was guided by love. The only thing He asks us in return is that we love Him.

> You shall love the LORD your God with all your heart, with all your soul, and with all your strength.
> (Deuteronomy 6:5)

We are all influenced by those around us, and stronger personalities have a way of dominating and setting the course or direction of our society. It is the nature of man to unite in a common cause. The common cause is at the core what makes up the various cultures that our societies support; cultures distinctly different, but at the core are bonded by what they stand for.

Here in America, we have people of different cultural backgrounds from all over the world: Africans, British, Eastern Europeans, French, Germans, Hispanics, Indians, Italians, Spaniards, etc. These are in essence subcultures, but once they become citizens, they are asked to willingly buy into our overall culture. Their cultural groups may remain distinctively different, but once united into the overall culture, the common bond becomes our inalienable rights granted by our country.

Many of us have joined causes that were birthed in a similar way, we just haven't thought about them in these terms. One man or woman begins talking, another joins in, and soon a company, group or movement is birthed. These entities gain momentum, money is raised, and the strength of their numbers gives them influence to affect their surroundings. Sometimes to affect political policy. Society on a whole will be affected right or wrong by those influences or policies; in essence, we all become influenced by their belief systems, whether we agree with them or not.

The fact is we live in a society that was actually created using the principle of *gang formation*. However, we should be thankful that the leaders were bound by truth and love and that the intention of their hearts was to create a new society that would be free from colonial rule. They were all joined by *mutual interests, participation in characteristic relationships, shared institutions, and a common culture*. We know from history that the people had become tired and burdened by the British concept of "taxation without representation." However, it wasn't until a few men began talking and meeting that the people became united and were able to give serious consideration to the possibility of gaining independence from the British.

Our Founding Fathers understood firsthand that people were going to disagree about how the country should be organized and ultimately governed. They knew that it is human nature to try to convince everyone else that your way is the best way. So rather than be suspicious of everyone with differing opinions, they set-up our government's structure to deal with this inevitable reality of human behavior. They created three separate but unified branches of government: the legislative, executive, and judicial.

> "They proposed a strong central government made up of three branches: legislative, executive, and judicial; each would be perpetually restrained by a sophisticated set of checks and balances." (20)

Our forefathers didn't attempt to control, manipulate or change who we are at the core, but rather established a system whereby there would be checks and balances. Their intention was to safeguard the nation from one person or one group's ideals that could, if not held in check, influence and overturn the core principles and beliefs the country was built on.

Our Founding Fathers were intent on preserving those principles and beliefs, yet at the same time honoring the free will of the people. They knew the hearts of men were deceitfully wicked and that at any given time they might choose the evil intentions over the good intentions within their heart. They didn't attempt to change the hearts, for this would have been similar to what the British were doing to them. No, they merely implemented a system that kept the hearts in balance.

Our country was built on the idea of free will, where people were given a say in the direction of the country by and through a system that allowed them to elect leaders. Once elected, those leaders are expected to represent the interests of the people. Today, we see how these elected officials are influenced by lobbyists representing special interest groups that don't always respect the will of the people. Sometimes these groups are well intended, but many times they are deceptive and selfish. One thing is sure, the elected officials are influenced whether we like it or not, and as a result, we are affected. Thus, we should thank our Founding Fathers for their wisdom in creating a system of checks and balances.

We study history as a reminder of times past. It helps us understand and not forget the reason our forefathers came to this country in the first place, and why they laid the foundation on such solid ground. Our country is made up of many groups, culturally different, but at the core united in the free society our country offers each one of its citizens. Within each one of us there is a desire to be heard, a desire to change, a desire to make a difference, a desire to be great, and a desire to be accepted. Unfortunately, our intentions are not always pure and don't always have the interest of everyone in mind.

Oftentimes, our intentions are birthed out of our own upbringing and the abuses we have been subjected to from childhood. To some, those intentions are not misdirected, but necessary to bring about change, and to reverse the pain of the past. We assume that everyone must share in our cause; that somehow they should understand our pain and the abuses we have endured. They become convinced they are right because others join their cause, bringing strength and conviction to their belief.

Every rebellion from the beginning of time has begun using the principle of *gang formation*. Unfortunately, it is not until we look back upon history and specific events that, as a whole, we realize the danger and the destruction wrought by individual ideals that have been imposed on the masses.

We all want to be a part of something bigger than ourselves. Inherently, we want our lives to count, we want to be accepted, and we want to be united in a common cause. After all, we were all created to be part of something bigger than ourselves. Jesus Christ was placed here on earth by God, and God's intention all along was to build His church.

Like our Founding Fathers, Jesus knew the hearts of men and the destruction that their evil intentions have brought on so many. He didn't come to us demanding change. Jesus came, experienced life with all its hardships and offered His love, while respecting our free will. Jesus Christ is "The head of the body, the church" which is made up of His followers. However, it was and still is intended for everyone.

> *He is the image of the invisible God, the firstborn over all creation.* For by Him all things were created that are in heaven and that are on earth, visible and invisible, whether thrones or dominions or principalities or powers. All things were created through Him and for Him. And He is before all things, and in Him all things consist. And *He is the head of the body, the*

church, who is the beginning, the firstborn from the dead, that in all things He may have the preeminence. For it pleased the Father that in Him all the fullness should dwell, and by Him to reconcile all things to Himself, by Him, whether things on earth or things in heaven, having made peace through the blood of His cross. (Colossians 1:15-20)

The following are radical scriptures by most standards prognosticating a deceptive enemy—an enemy preying on people with hearts that are well-meaning and bound by truth and love; the simplicity that is in Christ.

Be sober, be vigilant; because your adversary the devil walks about like a roaring lion, seeking whom he may devour.
(1 Peter 5:8)

But I fear, lest somehow, as the serpent deceived Eve by his craftiness, so your minds may be corrupted from the simplicity that is in Christ. (2 Corinthians 11:3)

Satan's intended notion, S.I.N., has not changed and will never change. The devil is an evil spirit and has infiltrated our societal structures in order to cause us to self-destruct by adhering to unbiblical doctrines.

Doctrines which are fraught with lies from the men and women who sometimes knowingly and many times unknowingly, have joined his gang and declared war on God's elect. Their hearts have become tainted and the intentions of their hearts have come parallel with his destructive intentions. Which have resulted in many devastating injustices that our society on the whole has suffered.

Furthermore, as a result of S.I.N., our nation as we know it today has become divided over numerous secular issues. For that reason, I challenge you to ask:

- Is the society I am surrounded by healthy?
- Are my personal relationships life giving?
- Am I perpetuating negative influences?
- Is there anything holding me back?
- Am I growing in a positive manner?
- What is the condition of my heart?
- Most importantly, am I open to examination and change?

Unless we are willing to ask ourselves these questions, we are at risk to stagnate in our spiritual growth. I am not posing these questions as an outline for the book, but rather as thought provoking questions in order to open your minds to the material presented in the book. It is my intention to get you thinking, to challenge you to examine your own life by answering those questions, and in doing so be open to what your heart is telling you.

Chapter Three

The Set-Up

Recently in the news, there was a story about a toddler that had been found on the side of the road strapped in his child protective seat. He had apparently been thrown from the window of a moving vehicle. The article went on to say, the child had been dead before being thrown from the car, the cause of death being a crushing blow to the head. Who could orchestrate such an atrocity? Wouldn't the pain of conviction be too great? How could something so terrible happen in our country?

Another story reads that a mother left her children in an apartment with little food while she traveled to Europe to marry a man she had met on the Internet. Fortunately, the authorities intercepted her as she got off the plane. However, in the long-term, what about those kids? What kind of life are they destined to have? I relate these stories to say this—the enemy is alive and at work. But folks, I have a news flash for you—the enemy resides in each one of us from the beginning of our lives!

Society has shaped generations beginning with Adam, the formation beginning in the womb, and we are born into this world into a society not of our choosing. When a woman becomes pregnant, her abdomen begins to grow, and as the infant develops in the womb, the activities, lifestyles, conversations and people around the mother influence the infant. The baby's life course is being determined from the first heartbeat.

Imagine, if you will, the mother on heroin, each time she gets high, the baby gets high. Imagine the mother who is being beaten, the baby flinching at each blow. Now imagine the mother determined not to spoil her seed, the baby resting comfortably in the womb. Imagine the mother playing classical music; the baby is soothed by the melody. You might be thinking at this moment, "There are exceptions and uncontrollable events; after all, life is hard." All true for sure, regardless, does it change society's hold on our destiny? Let us explore how we are all born into sin and how society on the whole has been "Set-Up."

SATAN'S ROLE IN HISTORY

> Lucifer was the second entity in all of heaven and his name means *"bearer of light" or "morning star."* (21)

> How you are fallen from heaven, O Lucifer, son of the morning! How you are cut down to the ground, You who weakened the nations! (Isaiah 14:12)

> And no wonder! For Satan himself transforms himself into an angel of light. (2 Corinthians 11:14)

Lucifer was a created being that, by his God given nature, illuminated heaven. However, we learn in the Bible that the power associated with the position evidently went to his head. He must have become discontent being number two, he desired more, and as a result, he set out to unseat God, and take His throne. Why did he snap? Scripture does not address that question, thus we really don't know. However, we do know that Lucifer had a will, and along with that will, he also had a choice. Let that resonate in your thoughts for a moment.

God gives all His creation a free will; if not, he would be a dictatorial God. Just because Lucifer was an angel and a member of the heavenly host, that did not preclude him from being granted free will. In a perfect world there is always a choice, otherwise how could it be perfect? We will cover God's creation in more detail later in the book, but I think it is important to note that God gave Lucifer and the entire heavenly host free will. Because of this free will, evil came into being and was birthed as a direct result of Lucifer's rebellion. It was Lucifer's notion or idea to overthrow God and assume His throne.

> For you have said in your heart:
> I will ascend into heaven,
> I will exalt my throne above the stars of God;

> I will also sit on the mount of the congregation
> On the farthest sides of the north;
> I will ascend above the heights of the clouds,
> I will be like the Most High. (Isaiah 14:13-14)

At the time of his rebellion, society consisted only of God and the heavenly host. Lucifer's influence at the time was strong and deceptive. We learn in scripture one-third of the angels in heaven bought into his treason and ultimately were cast out with him for all eternity. They too were deceived!

> And war broke out in heaven: Michael and his angels fought with the dragon; and the dragon and his angels fought, but they did not prevail, nor was a place found for them in heaven any longer. So the *great dragon* was cast out, that serpent of old, called the *devil and Satan*, who deceives the whole world; he was cast to the earth, and his angels were cast out with him. (Revelation 12:7-9)

Lucifer was now referred to as the *"great dragon...called the devil and Satan."* God, in His goodness, could not and would not allow Lucifer to remain in His presence because of the evil plot to birth sin. Which I have declared to be S.I.N., Satan's intended notion, a notion birthed out of his rebellion. Satan's fall from grace was never God's desire, but as a result, became God's way of creating a climate of free will. You might be thinking, "Why didn't God just stop Satan in his tracks, say 'poof' and in so doing be done with him? After all, if God is all powerful, it wouldn't have been much of a burden for Him to zap Satan?" The truth of God's goodness is evident in the answer to this question.

God didn't expect or intend for Lucifer to rebel any more than He expects or intends for us to rebel against Him today. It was Lucifer's choice, his free will decision. Behind that decision was his pride, jealousy, arrogance, and ultimate ignorance that caused his downfall. Think for a moment, if God did not allow free will, how could he be a loving God? Is it the nature of a loving God to force everyone to love Him? How could He love us unconditionally unless He gives us a choice to love Him unconditionally?

Several years ago, I owned a dog named Brandy. She was a mixture of collie, spaniel, and quite possibly a little German Sheppard made its way in as well. She was not only beautiful with her golden fur, but also smart to boot. Brandy didn't like being tied up, so every chance she got as a puppy, she would bolt for the door. Of course, if she made it out the front door, both my children would start yelling and run after her in an attempt to catch her, and bring her back. She thought it was a wonderful game and loved having everyone chase her through the neighborhood.

I learned early in my training of her that it wasn't going to work to just keep her locked up and then expect her to stay once released. I started giving her liberties by letting her escape out our back door into the fenced yard where she could run loose without fear of being hit by a car. However, on those occasions, I instructed the kids not to chase her or yell at her. We didn't engage in playing her game of chase. Soon she became curious as to why no one was chasing her and became lonely out back all by herself. After a fair amount of time had elapsed, I would stand at the door and call her. Eventually, she would come running, I would reward her with treats, and lavish praise on her every time she obeyed.

Later, when Brandy was a little older, the kids had a trampoline in the backyard and spent countless hours jumping on it. So eventually, the backyard became a place of action for Brandy. She didn't see the backyard as a place of confinement, but instead embraced it because of the company the kids provided as they played. As she got older and more mature, we could let her out in the front yard or take her with us on road trips without any fear of her running off. All we had to do was call her name and by her own free will, she came running to receive her praise.

Heaven is a place where God resides and the heavenly hosts reside out of their own free will. Those whom reside with God do so because He has allowed them to choose between Himself and Satan. God's love is not based on conditions. His love is unconditional and offered freely to any and all who choose to accept it. When Satan was cast from Heaven, he was well aware of God's love, God's nature, and God's plan for man. What Satan saw as God's weakness actually revealed God's goodness and God's greatness.

We have already established that unfortunately for Satan, God is omnipotent, omniscient, and omnipresent, meaning he is all powerful, all knowing, and can be in all places at all times. Satan, however, a created being, can only be in one place at one time. Having that knowledge, he knew he was going to have a fight on his hands. His first action was to deceive and recruit supporters; in other words, he had to influence the society of heaven with his tempting lies and deceptive nature in order to gain the support of his peers. In so doing, he set in motion a destructive pattern that we still face today.

> You were perfect in your ways from the day you were created,
> Till iniquity was found in you. (Ezekiel 28:15)

We previously read in Revelation 12:7-9 that a mighty battle ensued in the heavenly realm between God's archangel Michael and his angels and Satan and his angels, with Michael ultimately the victor, and Satan being cast down to earth. One might be thinking, "But, why not just kill Satan and all of his rebellious angels? Wouldn't that make more sense?" Maybe the answer to that question lends credence to our previous study of the Holy Spirit; Satan is spirit and spirits don't die, but live on in the eternal realm. Thus, spirits are not bound by the same space and time continuum that we know and live by.

Satan, being an eternal spirit, had to live somewhere, just not in heaven with God. I guess God could have sent Satan to some far away planet like Mars, Jupiter or elsewhere in the universe never to be heard from or seen again. We really have no way of knowing. What we do know, however, as we will continue to explore later in this chapter, Satan hatched a plan, that plan I refer to as *the set-up*. Unfortunately for Satan, it was that very plan that turned on him and gave God the impetus to execute his eternal purpose. As stated earlier, God in his goodness could not allow evil to exist much less reign in heaven, so when Satan rebelled, he and his followers were cast out of heaven. However, Satan became God's opportunity! Why not use him to save humanity?

Satan and his cronies would become the deceivers by which each of God's creations would be able to exercise their free will. Either accept God as their Father or to reject God, and live apart from God for all eternity along with Satan. I challenge, that it was for this reason, that God cast him to earth and gave him permission and the power to reside on earth, instead of relegating Satan to some far away planet. How frustrated do you think it made Satan to be relegated to earth having previous knowledge of God's plan to create man and give man dominion over earth?

> Then God said, "Let Us make man in Our image, according to Our likeness; *let them have dominion* over the fish of the sea, over the birds of the air, and over the cattle, *over all the earth and over every creeping thing that creeps on the earth.*" (Genesis 1:26)

Given the above scripture, I think it is safe to assume that God communicated His intention to create the universe, heavens and earth to all the community of heaven. Given God's nature of love, He must have also expressed His excitement about the creation of man. Remember, this is the man that would rule over earth. Everything was going to be put under him and entrusted to his care.

> So God created man in His own image; in the image of God He created him; male and female He created them. Then God blessed them, and God said to them, "Be fruitful and multiply; fill the earth and subdue it; have dominion over the fish of the sea, over the birds of the air, and over every living thing that moves on the earth." (Genesis 1:27-28)

Therefore, I ask again, "How frustrated do you think this made Satan?" If he was jealous of God's power and stature in heaven, how much more jealous would he be of man's power and rule on earth? God had been his competition in heaven, but now he had another competitor: man. This must have been too much for him to bear.

Satan, as stated earlier, is not omnipresent, so he had to figure a way to multiply himself in order to taint God's plan of creating a perfect garden where man could dwell and rule. Given this limitation, he came up with what he thought would be a foolproof plan, a plan we are still battling with today. Satan's set-up was to plant his evil seed into the heart of every human being through the natural birthing process. Satan's scheme started in the Garden of Eden with Adam and Eve.

As we analyze his plan, keep this in mind: God is all knowing and all things work together for good to those who love God. Thus supporting my claim that Satan would ultimately be God's opportunity to allow all of His creation the choice to execute free will.

> And we know that all things work together for good to those who love God, *to those who are the called according to His purpose.* (Romans 8:28)

ORIGINAL SIN

Let me take you back to the year 1940 in Chicago. There was a man named Alphonse Capone who used the principle we looked at in the previous chapter, gang formation, to build an empire in the heart of the city. He recruited a following among other thugs and eventually built an army of soldiers dedicated to his cause.

He deceived a city into thinking he was a good guy, because he provided them with the much desired alcohol they were being denied during prohibition. He ran prostitution, numbers, and capitalized on everyone's weakness, all the while growing stronger and stronger. In his mind, he had become invincible and no one dared challenge him. Capone had an evil reputation and embodied all the characteristics of Satan himself.

Did you ever see the movie *The Untouchables?* Alphonse Capone was played by Robert De Niro, and there is one scene in the movie that gives us a clear visual of Capone's evil. Capone's captains have been brought to Chicago and are sitting at a large, round dinner table. Capone is delivering a speech as he paces around the table behind his captains.

He begins by saying, "Life goes on, a man become pre-eminent he is expected to have enthusiasm; enthusiasms, enthusiasms, what are mine, what draws my admiration, what is that which gives me joy?"

At that moment Capone pauses, casually turns, lifts a baseball bat from a table and then continues pacing and answers the question: "Baseball."

He keeps walking and further states, "A man, a man stands alone at the plate. This is the time for what, for individual achievement? There he stands alone. But in the field, what? Part of a team!" Capone says this last sentence with emphasis and the entire table begins to chant "Teamwork."

Capone continues, "Looks, throws, catches, hustles part of one big team, bats himself the live long day, Babe Ruth, Ty Cobb, and so on. If his team don't field what is he? Follow me? No? One sunny day the stands are full of fans what does he have to say? I'm going out there for myself, but I get nowhere unless the team wins."

Now moving more slowly, Capone pauses and looks down on one of his captains, the man has his back to Capone and is puffing on a big cigar while shaking his head in agreement saying, "Team, team."

Suddenly, Capone raises the bat and beats the man over the head repeatedly, blood squirting all over the table splattering on those around him. All the captains are in shock to say the least, and his message to them is clear: no one double-crosses Alphonse Capone!

Unfortunately for Capone, he underestimated a man named J. Edgar Hoover, head of the FBI at the time. Hoover wasn't impressed with Capone's antics or diatribes. J. Edgar didn't care for Capone or the likes of Capone. He enlisted a young FBI agent and moved him to Chicago with one purpose and one purpose only—take down Capone's empire. Elliot Ness was his name and as we know by our history books, Ness became Capone's nemesis. He became a thorn of offense in Capone's backside. Ultimately, Ness brought the empire crumbling down, sending Capone to prison. By the planting of Ness in Chicago, the government was able to bring down one of the most ruthless gang leaders that America had known up to that time.

One might ask, "Why did God allow Capone to reign?" To which I offer another question, "Why did God allow Satan to reign?"

We all are born into sin and subject to its vices. God doesn't intervene in His ordained nature of creation that was set in motion when he spoke the world into existence. That order already set in motion existed in Capone's day and still exists today.

Ultimately, God would place a man on earth who would become Satan's nemesis; a man who would ultimately defeat Satan's plan, bring down his evil empire, and send Satan to prison. Prison for all eternity!

> And He said to me, "It is done! I am the Alpha and the Omega, the Beginning and the End. I will give of the fountain of the water of life freely to him who thirsts. He who overcomes shall inherit all things, and I will be his God and he shall be My son. But the cowardly, unbelieving, abominable, murderers, sexually immoral, sorcerers, idolaters, and all liars shall have their part in the lake which burns with fire and brimstone, which is the second death."
> (Revelation 21: 6-8)

More on that later, but for now turn with me again to the beginning of Genesis, and let us take a look at how Satan tried to exploit his Godly knowledge, always thinking he could achieve his original plan to unseat God from His throne. As stated earlier, originally his name was Lucifer, the number two entity in heaven, and he made a choice to rebel—having no excuse—because he knew full well the true nature of God.

> Then God said, "Let the earth bring forth grass, the herb that yields seed, and the fruit tree that yields fruit according to its kind, whose seed is in itself, on the earth"; and it was so.
> (Genesis 1: 11)

Here it is confirmed, "God said" so it is accurate to assume that in his position, Lucifer was listening as God spoke creation into existence. Thus, he most likely had prior knowledge of God's plan to create the garden. He sensed the excitement in God's voice as He spoke about creating Adam and his intention to grant Adam dominion over the earth. Lucifer hatched his plan out of jealousy; he could not stand that man would vie for God's affection.

In the above scripture, Lucifer also knew there would be trees in the garden. However, Lucifer probably didn't know at the time that God was going to name one of those trees "the tree of the knowledge of good and evil." Why, you might ask? How would he not know this? I challenge that it was because good and evil did not exist until his rebellion. Lucifer was becoming jealous, but had not yet rebelled! Quite possibly his jealousy was birthed out of a misdirected love for God; he didn't want anyone competing with him for God's affection. He obviously could not stand the thought that man might one day be greater than him.

Now are you starting to get a feel for the anger and resentment that was building in Lucifer? Eeverything was good before Satan's rebellion. But, evil was birthed as a result of his rebellion, and sin was birthed after his fall from grace. Yes, evil was birthed when Lucifer deceived the heavenly host and coerced one third of the angels to join him.

He hadn't planned on losing the battle against Michael, much less being relegated to earth for eternity with all his angel cronies. We refer to them in present terms as demons. He knew that earth was the very place God created with the intention of giving man full dominion. God had not intended or planned for Satan to fall, but He was not going to be denied His creation as a result of Satan's rebellion. Satan was never a threat to God or His created order. God went ahead with His plan to create man, giving Him full authority to name all the animals and every living thing.

> Out of the ground the LORD God formed every beast of the field and every bird of the air, and brought them to Adam to see what he would call them. And whatever Adam called each living creature, that was its name. So Adam gave names to all cattle, to the birds of the air, and to every beast of the field. But for Adam there was not found a helper comparable to him. (Genesis 2: 19-20)

At this time, God noticed it wasn't good for man to be alone, so He decided to give Adam a helpmate. Now, be truthful, all you men out there: aren't you glad God created woman? No matter what you might be thinking, the creation of woman had to be one of God's greatest achievements. God is a good God!

> And the LORD God said, "It is not good that man should be alone; I will make him a helper comparable to him."
> (Genesis 2:18)
>
> And the LORD God caused a deep sleep to fall on Adam, and he slept; and He took one of his ribs, and closed up the flesh in its place. Then the rib which the LORD God had taken from man He made into a woman, and He brought her to the man. And Adam said: "This is now bone of my bones And flesh of my flesh; She shall be called Woman, Because she was taken out of Man."
> (Genesis 2: 21-23)

How did God create woman? We learn from scripture that while Adam was asleep God took one of Adam's ribs and created Eve. Now, here is where it gets heated. Can you imagine Adam's surprise when he wakes up and finds God's created beauty resting at his side? Tell me he wasn't just a little bit excited! What a woman Eve must have been! I am sure, when Adam woke up and saw Eve, he wasn't giving any thought to the pain in his side!

Now there were two humans in the physical realm comprising the societal order in Eden. Satan's reign over earth was and is different from man's dominion over earth. Satan's reign is of a spiritual nature, thus unseen, and man's dominion is of a physical nature, thus visible. The body is physical and the works of the body are visible, but Satan is spiritual and the works of the spirit are not visible. You are thinking, "Wait a minute, are you saying that Satan's evil is not visible?" Hold that thought and keep reading. I will show that Satan, though spiritual, works through and is manifested in the physical realm.

> The LORD God planted a garden eastward in Eden, and there He put the man whom He had formed. And out of the ground the LORD God made every tree grow that is pleasant to the sight and good for food. The tree of life was also in the midst of the garden, and the tree of the knowledge of good and evil. (Genesis 2:8-9)
>
> And the LORD *God commanded the man,* saying, "Of every tree of the garden you may freely eat; but of the tree of the

knowledge of good and evil you shall not eat, for in the day that you eat of it you shall surely die." (Genesis 2:16-17)

God provided instruction to Adam in the garden, commanding him not to eat from the tree of "the knowledge of good and evil." You see, God meant for man to have a choice from the very beginning. It wasn't His intention or notion to create a dictatorial society where everyone and everything would be in bondage to Him.

As noted earlier after Lucifer rebelled, God in His goodness chose to see the rebellion as an opportunity. God simply took what Satan had meant for evil and created a system of free will by which man could exercise his free will: choosing to obey and enjoy God's perfect creation, or choosing not to obey and suffer the consequence of a spiritual death. God did not go into a lengthy explanation with Adam about the death he would suffer if he ate from the tree; no, Adam was to trust God and obey.

He simply instructed Adam that if he ate of the tree he would surely die. Physical death just separates us from the rest of society, but God was speaking to Adam about spiritual death. When you die in your sin, you become spiritually separated from God. In God's goodness, He cannot allow lawlessness to exist in His presence with any of His creation. Satan's fall from heaven is our first evidence of this fact.

Now I hope it is clear why God decided to create and name one particular tree "the tree of the knowledge of good and evil." The tree represented a choice, a choice that would determine the true nature of man's heart. The same choice still exists today. God doesn't always give us a lengthy explanation; we too are supposed to trust God and obey.

It is my belief that Adam did not have knowledge of Satan's fall from grace. In fact, nowhere in scripture does it say that Adam and Eve had knowledge of Satan's fall. In the last chapter, we looked at Luke 10:18, *"And He said to them, I saw Satan fall like lightning from heaven,"* where we learned that in the New Testament Jesus is the only documented eyewitness of Satan's fall from heaven.

For this reason, it is also my belief that Satan was on the earth before God created the garden and before He created Adam. Having this inside information, what did Satan do after falling from heaven, knowing at some point that God was going to create Adam?

Remember there were no other humans for Adam to relate to until God created Eve. The society in Eden consisted only of the beasts of the field, which Adam later would name. Satan took the form of one of those beasts, a serpent. I believe that Satan stayed a good distance away as God created man. After all, God had already thrown him out of heaven. I don't think Satan was going to push his luck at that juncture. Instead he held back, looking for an opportunity to execute a plan with the goal of conquering God and taking dominion.

We don't know why he chose a serpent, but one could assume he did so in order to crawl around unnoticed, watching and waiting to hatch a plan, and then to put that plan in motion. Adam and Eve were obviously comfortable around all of God's creation at the time, so the serpent posed no visible threat. They knew no fear. Therefore, as Satan was crawling around incognito, he probably overheard God's command to Adam that he was not to eat from the one tree in the garden.

It is also accurate to assume that Satan was aware of man's curious nature. After all, I am sure Satan watched Adam's reaction when he awoke from God's operation and found Eve lying by his side. Satan probably noticed the curiousness of Adam's behavior. It very well could have been at that moment Satan saw his opportunity, an opportunity that would allow him to fulfill his ultimate plan to upset God's created order. His plan in the garden now became clear: plant the seed of S.I.N. into every human shell.

Because of man's curious nature Satan saw an opportunity to trick him into rebelling against God. Satan, knowing Eve was created from Adam, must have also known this would make her the more vunerable of the two, and the more easily influenced. Armed with that knowledge, Satan was ready to befriend Eve, play on her curious nature, test her resolve and trick her into rebelling against God.

> Now the serpent was more cunning than any beast of the field which the LORD God had made. And he said to the woman, "Has God indeed said, 'You shall not eat of every tree of the garden'?" And the woman said to the serpent, "We may eat the fruit of the trees of the garden; but of the fruit of the tree which is in the midst of the garden, God has said, 'You shall not eat it, nor shall you touch it, lest you die.'" Then the serpent said to the woman, "You will not surely die. For God knows that in the day you eat of it your eyes will be opened, and you will be like God, knowing good and evil."
> (Genesis 3:1-5)

The serpent communicated with Eve, thus putting into motion the ultimate "set-up." Satan, the deceiver, twisted the truth to make evil sound appealing. The evil he was tempting Eve with in this portion of scripture was disobedience to God's command. Eve was naïve and innocent and, as a result, easily influenced by Satan's deceitfulness. However, as we know all too well, being naïve and innocent are no excuse for ignorance.

Adam had to have communicated to Eve not to eat from the tree, because she was not present when God commanded Adam. We have no textual support that Adam miscommunicated God's instruction. In the scripture we just read, she informed the serpent that she and Adam were not to eat from the tree, but she went so far as to add onto God's Word by saying, "nor shall you touch it, lest you die." She must not have been paying full attention to Adam, and because she was ignorant of God's word, she was all the more vulnerable to sin's attack. Sin always seeks a companion and does so through deception. Satan first tempted Eve in sight, then in thought, appealing to her curious nature.

> So when the woman saw that the tree was good for food, that it was pleasant to the eyes, and a tree desirable to make one wise, she took of its fruit and ate. She also gave to her husband with her, and he ate. (Genesis 3:6)

Now to all you men who are thinking, "Wow, if it hadn't been for that woman..." Let me tell you men, Eve was not to blame; Adam was to blame. Let me enlighten you on the most important mistake that has ever been made: Adam was present with Eve when she ate from the tree. "And she gave also to her husband *with her, and he ate.*" Adam did not exercise his headship, which was his God ordained responsibility.

Think about the sin in your life today. How does it manifest itself? Does it start with some kind of visual temptation? Once you give in to the visual, does it move into the mind and play on your curious nature? When sin is finally conceived, it is because you acted on the visual temptation by making a conscious decision to entertain the act. Once you have acted on the sin, you have separated yourself from God. This is the same spiritual death that Adam and Eve experienced. It is not a physical death, but a spiritual death.

> Then, when desire has conceived, it gives birth to sin; and sin, when it is full-grown, brings forth death. (James 1:15)

Now, you might question whether Adam was really present at the time Eve ate or if he walked up right after. I challenge that it doesn't matter; he still didn't exercise his God-given authority. However, since it is somewhat unclear where Adam was and all we know from the scripture is that, "her husband with her," let me present you with the only two options that could have been exercised by Adam, which would have been pleasing to God.

For the first option, let us assume that Adam was with her before she had a chance to eat and was able to stop her by saying, "No, Eve, we can't eat the apple. God has commanded us not to eat any anything from that tree, and we are going to obey his command. Hand me the apple." Then, imagine Adam taking the apple from her hand, rearing back and throwing it as far as he was humanly able, and then picking up the serpent and slinging him out of the garden as well.

For the second option, let us assume Adam walks up right as Eve is biting into the apple and then she offers it to Adam. But, instead of following suit, Adam exercises his God-given authority by saying, "I will not eat from the tree and furthermore I am tossing all three of you out of the garden: you, this apple, and this cunning serpent!" Then imagine him putting his bare foot on her behind and booting her out of the garden, throwing the apple after her, and then grabbing the serpent by the tail and hurling him through the air.

What would have been different in the garden? What would life be like today? Could it be that God's plan for an eternity void of evil could have been preserved? Could all the pain and suffering in the world today have been avoided?

There is no way of knowing the answer to those questions, because Adam made the decision to disobey. However, one could rightly assume that the world would look a whole lot different and our lives would be radically improved! Instead, Adam's ignorant rebellion is still haunting us and ultimately opened the door for division in our relationships and promotes desolation in the societies in which we live.

Today, Satan still uses Adam's rebellion to his benefit and we play right into his hand. Men are not exercising their spiritual headship, and as a result, the women in our society are no more covered than Eve was in the garden. We continue to eat from the *"tree of the knowledge of good and evil."*

God commanded Adam, not Eve! Adam was to protect and cover Eve, not because she was inferior, but because she had been created from Adam's rib. Think about our ribs. How strong are they? What happens when you punch someone hard in the side? Broken ribs cannot be treated; they only heal with time.

> Husbands, love your wives, just as Christ also loved the church and gave Himself for her, (Ephesians 5:25)

> Nevertheless let each one of you in particular so love his own wife as himself, and let the wife see that she respects her husband. (Ephesians 5:33)

God intended for Adam to exercise authority in the garden and to spiritually cover Eve, to protect her, stand up, and be the man God created him to be. Adam let us all down because he did not obey God, but gave in to temptation.

As a result, Satan was able to carry out his plan: evil was birthed and S.I.N. was planted into the heart of man. Adam became Satan's pawn and would forever be known as the *Father of Sin*. Satan knew very well what came next. Every time Adam and Eve conceived and birthed a child, S.I.N. would be planted in the baby's heart. The laying of an evil foundation had been Satan's intention all along, or better yet his "intended notion."

> Behold, I was brought forth in iniquity, And in sin my mother conceived me. (Psalm 51:5)

God had warned His children that they would die if they ate from the tree. They experienced death all right; God's warning was now a reality. Their eyes were open to good and evil. Sin always results in guilt, cover up and eventually death—spiritual death!

> Then the eyes of both of them were opened, and they knew that they were naked; and they sewed fig leaves together and made themselves coverings. And they heard the sound of the LORD God walking in the garden in the cool of the day, and Adam and his wife hid themselves from the presence of the LORD God among the trees of the garden. Then the LORD God called to Adam and said to him, "Where are you?" So he said, "I heard Your voice in the garden, and I was afraid because I was naked; and I hid myself." And He said, "Who told you that you were naked? Have you eaten from the tree of which I commanded you that you should not eat?" Then the man said, "The woman whom You gave to be with me, she gave me of the tree, and I ate." And the LORD God said to the woman, "What is this you have done?" The woman said, "The serpent deceived me, and I ate." (Genesis 3:7-13)

They died to the unadulterated nature of being made in God's image. They died to perfection. Adam and Eve died to a perfect existence in a perfect place that was void of pain, suffering, war, and destruction of any kind. Now, all mankind to follow was cursed, because Adam obeyed the voice of his wife instead of the instruction of God.

> So the LORD God said to the serpent: "Because you have done this, You are cursed more than all cattle, And more than every beast of the field; On your belly you shall go, And you shall eat dust All the days of your life. And I will put enmity Between you and the woman, And between your seed and her Seed; He shall bruise your head, And you shall bruise His heel." (Genesis 3:14-15)

For that reason, all serpents should be mad at Satan.

> To the woman He said: "I will greatly multiply your sorrow and your conception; In pain you shall bring forth children; Your desire shall be for your husband, And he shall rule over you." (Genesis 3:16)

For that reason, all women should be mad at Satan.

> Then to Adam He said, "Because you have heeded the voice of your wife, and have eaten from the tree of which I commanded you, saying, 'You shall not eat of it': Cursed is the ground for your sake; In toil you shall eat of it All the days of your life. Both thorns and thistles it shall bring forth for you, And you shall eat the herb of the field. In the sweat of your face you shall eat bread Till you return to the ground, For out of it you were taken; For dust you are, And to dust you shall return." (Genesis 3:17-19)

For that reason, all men should be mad at Satan.

> Then the LORD God said, "Behold, the man has become like one of Us, to know good and evil. And now, lest he put out his hand and take also of the tree of life, and eat, and live forever"—therefore the LORD God sent him out of the garden of Eden to till the ground from which he was taken. So

> He drove out the man; and He placed cherubim at the east of the garden of Eden, and a flaming sword which turned every way, to guard the way to the tree of life. (Genesis 3:22-24)

For that reason, Satan's *set-up* had been put into motion.

WE ARE BORN INTO SIN

> Now Adam knew Eve his wife, and she conceived and bore Cain, and said, "I have acquired a man from the LORD." Then she bore again, this time his brother Abel. Now Abel was a keeper of sheep, but Cain was a tiller of the ground. (Genesis 4:1-2)

After God declared His judgment on Adam and Eve for their rebellion, we learn in scripture that Adam "knew Eve," or had intercourse with Eve. She bore him Cain and Abel, who became the first sons the world had ever known. We also learn that Cain was a farmer and worked the land, and Abel was a rancher and herded sheep.

> And in the process of time it came to pass that Cain brought *an offering* of the fruit of the ground to the LORD. Abel also brought of *the firstborn* of his flock and of their fat. And the LORD respected Abel and his offering, (Genesis 4:3-4)

Cain brought a portion of his produce to God as a gift, but Abel gave the first of his flock to God as his gift. We learn that God was pleased with Abel's gift, but not with Cain's gift.

I am sure many of you have read this or heard this scripture and might have thought it was pretty cold of God to look down on Cain's gift. God gave his best to mankind, not expecting anything in return. However, when the gifts were exchanged, God knew the hearts of the givers. He didn't need the gifts; He desired the hearts of the givers. Cain showed that his heart was sinful by not giving the first fruits of his produce. Thus, God spoke to Cain, asking him why he was upset.

> So the LORD said to Cain, "Why are you angry? And why has your countenance fallen?" (Genesis 4:6)

God then spoke an eternal truth to Cain, a truth, which is just as applicable today as it was at the beginning of time: *"Sin lies at the door. And its desire is for you, but you should rule over it."* Cain did not choose to heed God's advice, humble himself and get back on track. In fact, we learn that he went on to murder his brother out of jealousy.

> If you do well, will you not be accepted? And if you do not do well, sin lies at the door. And its desire is for you, but you should rule over it." Now Cain talked with Abel his brother; and it came to pass, when they were in the field, that Cain rose up against Abel his brother and killed him. Then the LORD said to Cain, "Where is Abel your brother?" He said, "I do not know. Am I my brother's keeper?" And He said, "What have you done? The voice of your brother's blood cries out to Me from the ground. (Genesis 4:7-10)

God asked Cain, *"Where is Abel your brother?"* To which Cain snidely replied, *"How should I know. Am I my brother's keeper?"* God then said something that few of us really pay much attention to, *"The voice of your brother's blood cries out to Me from the ground."* I ask you if Abel was dead how is it that his blood was still alive? I challenge you to think and pray about God's statement. I challenge you to think just possibly it was Abel's spirit calling out to God through his blood, which further substantiates our claim in the first chapter that the spirit is eternal.

What happened next to poor Cain? There is always going to be a consequence for our actions. God cursed Cain; the work of his hand. Cain responded by saying, *"My punishment is greater than I can bear."* Cain was in agony and feared for his life, because he was feeling the ultimate effect of sin—separation from His Creator!

However, God still loved him, as evidenced by the fact he spared Cain's life and placed a mark on Cain that acted as a warning to anyone else who would try to take his life. God, in his goodness, had no choice but to discipline Cain, but in His grace, God spared his life. God hasn't changed, He deals with us in much the same way today.

> So now you are cursed from the earth, which has opened its mouth to receive your brother's blood from your hand. When you till the ground, it shall no longer yield its strength to you. A fugitive and a vagabond you shall be on the earth." And Cain said to the LORD, "My punishment is greater than I can

bear! Surely You have driven me out this day from the face of the ground; I shall be hidden from Your face; I shall be a fugitive and a vagabond on the earth, and it will happen that anyone who finds me will kill me." And the LORD said to him, "Therefore, whoever kills Cain, vengeance shall be taken on him sevenfold." And the LORD set a mark on Cain, lest anyone finding him should kill him. (Genesis 4:11-15)

Cain's separation came as a consequence of his sinful disobedience. My friends, our blood too will cry out, and our souls too will live on, after our natural body has gone back to dust. Where do you suppose our spirit will reside? The Bible tells us there is only one heaven and there is only one hell. I have news for you: there are no other options. It is either heaven and eternity in union with God or hell and eternity separated from God.

I am He who lives, and was dead, and behold, I am alive forevermore. Amen. And I have the keys of Hades and of Death. (Revelation 1:18)

Remember the game show *Let's Make a Deal?* There were three doors to choose from and behind each of those doors was a prize. However, only one door held the coveted prize, the more valuable prize. Well, in this life there are only two doors, not three. Which of those doors do you want to choose?

Death, we have shown, is S.I.N. and ultimately brings separation from God. Now look at the effects that S.I.N. has on our society as a whole and how it taints the family structure. We just explored the very first family and the dysfunction that ensued because of Adam's sin. The children were conceived by man and woman after sin had been birthed in their hearts. Sin brings confusion, jealousy, and pain and suffering. Cain and Abel became competitors within the family, and instead of being unified in love, they were divided by Satan's deception brought about by Cain's disobedience to God the Father.

The very first family was dysfunctional and our families today are still dysfunctional. Do you know anyone who has grown up in a completely functional family environment? I challenge you to show me one family you consider void of dysfunction. How could we really know what determines functional if society sets the functional and dysfunctional standard? There can't be a truly functional family that exists in the sense that God intended before sin was birthed.

However, inherent in every human being there is a God-given ability to discern right from wrong, good from evil. Thus, Satan's plan is to distort our thinking, so that we become confused by what our inherent nature tells us. It has been a slow process in our society and don't be fooled: Satan has not given up.

> And these are the ones by the wayside where the word is sown. When they hear, Satan comes immediately and takes away the word that was sown in their hearts. (Mark 4:15)

Do you remember growing up and hearing "Children are to be seen and not heard?" Those of us who grew up in the 60s and 70s remember this statement well. It was echoed every time we were to be around adults. What message did this convey? Initially it was intended that children be disciplined and know their place, to respect their elders. In fact, during those days, children didn't dare disrespect their parents or elders. It was automatic thinking: you were the child, and they were the parent or elder.

Unfortunately, few of us remember the instruction, because it quickly became a way adults controlled the behavior of their children. They seemed to be communicating, "Do as I say, not do as I do." Children were to keep silent and remain in the background. However, what they should have been conveying was obedience, as we find in the following scriptures from the Old Testament and the New Testament. We are specifically instructed to obey the father's instruction or command and the mother's law or teaching.

> My son, hear the instruction of your father, And do not forsake the law of your mother. (Proverbs 1:8)

> My son, keep your father's command, And do not forsake the law of your mother. (Proverbs 6:20)

> Children, obey your parents in the Lord, for this is right. (Ephesians 6:1)

When I was growing up, my mother stayed at home and raised my two brothers and myself. The responsibility was on her shoulders to lay down the law of the house. When my father came home, he supported her in order to reinforce the law, but his duty was also to instruct us accordingly, and to warn us of future consequences.

To bring clarity to this spiritual principle, let me relate a personal experience. I so admired the older kids who played sports. I used to wait outside the locker room and admire the players as they walked by dressed in their letter jackets. I admired those letter jackets so much so that I talked or coerced my mother into buying one for me.

One day, I stood near the pantry in our kitchen, proudly wearing my new letter jacket. This day, I remember being rather upset at my mother and wasn't having much success gaining her attention. So I started striking matches, blowing them, out and throwing them into the trash. My mother scolded me verbally, "Stop that this instant. You will start a fire." Of course, this just motivated me more, and I struck another match. Only this time when I threw the match, it was not fully extinguished, and, suddenly, flames started to appear. My mother casually walked to the pantry, instructed me to take off my letter jacket, and proceeded to put out the fire...with my jacket! To this day, I run matches under cold water to make sure the flame is extinguished before discarding them in the trash.

Of course, when my father returned home, he asked if I understood why my mother had asked me not to play with matches. I was also instructed by the pain of his belt, and as a result, I became instructed about the dangers of fire. Because of my Mother's teaching, I learned a valuable lesson that day. Because of my father's instruction, I learned that playing with fire was not only dangerous, but boy, did it hurt my backside. Not to mention the most painful consequence—no more letter jacket.

Unfortunately, after World War II, many men and women like my parents were working to rebuild our country. Many women were left to raise the children and manage the affairs of the home. As a result, many men failed to fulfill their role in the home, resulting in the mothers providing not only the law, but also the instruction. This is not what God designed mothers to do. With the absence of the Father to support the teaching/law and no adequate command/instruction, there was no balance in the home. This resulted in a generation that was not properly instructed according to biblical principles. Men seldom hugged each other, much less expressed love to their family. "I love you" was not a common statement heard from fathers. Society was changing and taking on a different form; a foundation was being formed.

In today's society, we are classified by how we are raised, where we were raised, and the socio-economic level attained. Societal levels determine your place, like it or not. In order to rise above one's roots, one must have a strong sense of purpose, clarity of vision, and personal determination. Even with the right formula, the picture is not always clear or easy to attain.

Not all families are functional by definition, and not all family environments are healthy. However, we are still taught to honor and respect our parents. Does this mean that we endure abuse, hardship, and domestic violence? NO. There are exceptions, no absolutes, but spiritually, we are still called to honor and respect. We've already discussed that we all deal with two realities of life: one is seen, but the other is unseen. It is that unseen world that exists to bring hardship and agony on all God's creation.

Since God is good and out of His goodness, He will not control our thoughts, Satan is able to create havoc on earth. He plants evil thoughts intended to deceive even the strongest and most well-meaning individuals into thinking, "If God is good, why allow all this destruction?" We end up blaming God for Satan's evil acts.

Are you starting to see the picture of how evil creeps in through the seed of S.I.N. already present in our hearts? Remember, he can only be in one place at one time. Well, guess what? His plan was well executed, because today, sin is in the heart of every human being!

We saw from the story of Cain and Abel and the events in the garden of Eden, whenever a baby is conceived by the joining together of a man's sperm and a woman's egg, sin is birthed. The baby is a product of Adam's curse, and S.I.N. is birthed. Satan's intended plan is a plan still very much alive today.

> Therefore, just as through one man sin entered the world, and death through sin, and thus death spread to all men, because all sinned. (Romans 5:12)

We are all sinners until the day we die, but we are also children of God until the day we die. The problem is simple—crossed wires. Electrically speaking, when two exposed wires cross, you have the potential for a short circuit. Life is much the same way. When we cannot separate the two realities of life, we have the potential of a spiritual short circuit.

Christ loves us and wants us to spend eternity in Heaven with Him, and Satan despises us and wants us to spend an eternity separated from God. Our societal upbringing has molded our lives, beliefs, and values. What we learn growing up conditions us and becomes the basis for our expectations in life. If we were raised in a healthy home, we grow up with a better understanding of marital values, family unity, and what love is meant to be. However, if we are raised in an unhealthy home, we grow up without the proper understanding of marital values, and seldom are unity and love taught or modeled. However, no home as we previously discussed, is completely functional. By virtue of our upbringing, we buy into society's rules.

In life, from an early age, we are taught to fend for ourselves. Many children today grow up without the influence of a father. In many homes, the mother works and the children come home to an empty house. Sin takes its root in our heart in the form of Satan's seed; that seed germinates and sprouts, and then begins to take root in our lives. The extent of the growth is determined by how it is watered; the water being the influences we are exposed to growing up. It also manifests itself in our decisions in life. Once we become teenagers, we start making bigger decisions, and along with those decisions come life's temptations.

One wrong decision can change a life. For instance, a young couple decides to have sexual relations and pregnancy occurs, or a young man decides to drink at a party and has an accident on the way home. We want to blame God for our poor decisions, but our bad decisions are often the cause of these evil results.

Furthermore, the innocent are affected by other people's poor decisions, and as a result, they pay a price for someone else's sin. The real culprit is Satan himself, because of the seed he planted in each one of us. The seed of S.I.N. is in each of us, and as long as we continue to make the decision for sin to rule in our hearts, we perpetuate Adam's curse.

As a result of that seed, society has been tainted and generations have been improperly trained. From a standpoint of revelation, we need to see S.I.N. for what it is: a destructive force created by Satan to control us, hold us back, disqualify us and, ultimately, destroy us.

Instead, we continue to justify our actions. What is birthed in the heart will ultimately direct our actions and our minds will be quick to justify what is in our hearts. *Satan's intended notion* is *societal in nature*. Why not wake up and acknowledge the fact that he is trying to control our behavior by the way he has so molded our society? We have played right into his hand.

It's like spinning a top; once you yank that cord, the top starts spinning. Unfortunately, we are the tops. Satan keeps yanking our cords, and as long as we are spinning, he has complete control of our lives. It's not until we finally stop spinning and regain our bearings of the true nature of Jesus Christ that we come to realize all the negativity, lies and degradation all around us.

> For as by one man's disobedience many were made sinners, so also by one Man's obedience many will be made righteous. Moreover the law entered that the offense might abound. But

> where sin abounded, grace abounded much more, so that as sin reigned in death, even so grace might reign through righteousness to eternal life through Jesus Christ our Lord. (Romans 5:19-21)

S.I.N. is death, which leads to hell here on earth, because it causes us to separate from God. We bring it upon ourselves as we give into "the lust of the flesh, the lust of the eyes, and the pride of life." In reality, we are just tops spinning in Satan's playroom. All the while he is just laughing at us, playing with us, and attempting to lead us into eternal separation from God.

> For all that is in the world—the lust of the flesh, the lust of the eyes, and the pride of life—is not of the Father but is of the world. (1 John 2:16)

Chapter Four

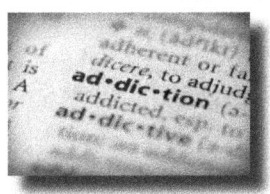

Societal Addiction

Today, we have unknowingly become addicted in our societal upbringing in the same way some become addicted to a substance. The sad truth is we are glorifying Satan on a daily basis through the decisions we make. Satan has been molding whole societies since the beginning of man's tenure here on earth. He has set the standard measurement for how people within those societies should live.

In the last chapter, we learned that everyone is born into S.I.N. and, I challenge, an addictive society. For example, we have all grown up hearing about the American dream, but what has become the difference in how society defines that dream and how God defines that dream? Society says, "You can have everything in life right now!" God says, "You can have everything in life for all eternity!"

The world's definition of *everything* is found in material possessions: the houses we live in, the cars we drive, and the amount of money in our bank account. Nevertheless, God's definition of *everything* is grounded in a relationship with Him, which leads to eternal salvation. Christ promises us an eternal place in God's house.

> Let not your heart be troubled; you believe in God, believe also in Me. In My Father's house are many mansions; if it were not so, I would have told you. I go to prepare a place for you. (John 14:1-2)

Satan wants to confuse us with the lure of material possessions. After all, he knows we have needs, and let's be honest, those needs are real. But Satan has his own best interests at heart. God, on the other hand, wants us to know that He understands that we need certain material possessions, but those possessions are not to take the place of our relationship with Him.

> Therefore do not worry, saying, "What shall we eat?" or "What shall we drink?" or "What shall we wear?" For after all these things the Gentiles seek. For your heavenly Father knows that you need all these things. But seek first the kingdom of God and His righteousness, and all these things shall be added to you. Therefore do not worry about tomorrow, for tomorrow will worry about its own things. Sufficient for the day is its own trouble.
> (Matthew 6: 31-34)

God intends for us to keep a proper balance and order by entering into a right relationship with Him. As a result, He will bless us in ways we can't imagine. However, when we choose the world's blessings first without acknowledging God, we have already been deceived and are outside His will. In John 10:10 we learn God's desire for us, "I have come that they may have life, and that they may have it more abundantly."

In other words, the true *American Dream* is really about the freedom God has given us to worship as we please, to exercise our faith in accordance with free will, and to enjoy an abundant life. These are the unalienable rights He provides everyone in His creation. Our Founding Fathers understood the importance of seeking God's blessing. Because of their wisdom, we live in one of the greatest countries on earth.

> IN CONGRESS, July 4, 1776 - We hold these truths to be self-evident, that all men are created equal, that they are endowed by their Creator with certain unalienable Rights, that among these are Life, Liberty and the pursuit of Happiness.
> (22)

Unfortunately, because of the addictive nature of our society, we have forsaken those rights, and don't acknowledge from where they truly came. The society we live in encourages, "Just roll up your sleeves, work hard, and in time you too will be successful." This is true, but more and more, we have put ourselves first. Many of us are secretly telling ourselves, "I'm going to get mine, after all, everyone else is!"

Society teaches the opposite of what God teaches. This has been Satan's intended notion from the beginning. At the core, this is deception, and deception is one of Satan's primary weapons (we will discuss this in more detail later in the book). Deception causes us to doubt ourselves, doubt others, and ultimately doubt our Creator. Inserting deception into the societal equation is like injecting a cancer cell into the blood stream; it goes undetected until one day you awake to find your body being eaten away by the infectious nature of the cancer, in this case, our societal addictions. Let's be truthful, aren't we all addicted to something?

> *Addiction by definition:* 1. A physical or psychological need for a habit-forming substance, such as a drug or alcohol. In physical addiction, the body adapts to the substance being used and gradually requires increased amounts to reproduce the effects originally produced by smaller doses. 2. A habitual or compulsive involvement in an activity, such as gambling. (23)

Oh, you might be thinking, "Not me, I am constructive, successful, whole, complete, lacking nothing. Look at my resume, look at my kids, look at my family, we don't have any problems. Well, maybe just a few, but isn't that to be expected?"

Society's teachings are not God's teachings. The sooner we come to realize this fact, the better off we will be. Our lives are patterned by the world around us. This world is: things we are taught as we grow up, the things we are influenced with by our peers, and the things we put into our system.

Addiction comes in many forms, flavors and sizes: people, work, money, materialism, exercise, sex, pornography, food, drugs, and alcohol, to name a few. There are roots attached to these addictions that run deep into our souls. Because most of us don't think we have any form of addiction, we have fallen prey to one of the biggest deceptions in our society today.

> The heart is deceitful above all things, And desperately wicked; Who can know it? I, the LORD, search the heart, I test the mind, Even to give every man according to his ways, According to the fruit of his doings. (Jeremiah 17:9-10)

Everyone in our world today has some form of addiction. Of course, many of those addictions you can live with and they won't cause you to ultimately live under a bridge somewhere. We have been conditioned and in effect desensitized by our surroundings and the moral decay that is so prevalent today. The concept *trash in—trash out* which, simply stated, means the more trash we put into our minds the more trash that will be produced by our minds, is at work on a daily basis in our lives. By the very nature of our societal environment and its influences, we are loading up on trash.

Just think, every time you read a newspaper, every time you look at or listen to the media, and every time you drive down the street where you subliminally take in the billboards lining the roads. There has been a lot of trash deposited over the years, and just where is that trash deposited? I challenge that it is not only in the recess of our minds, but also in the recesses of our hearts. Jesus said to his disciples that it isn't the trash that defiles; it is the heart that defiles. Why? Because S.I.N. has been deposited there from birth. The trash that comes in co-mingles with the trash that is already present and when the two collide, there is real trouble.

> When He had called all the multitude to Himself, He said to them, "Hear Me, everyone, and understand: There is nothing that enters a man from outside which can defile him; but the things which come out of him, those are the things that defile a man. If anyone has ears to hear, let him hear!" When He had entered a house away from the crowd, His disciples asked Him concerning the parable. So He said to them, "Are you thus without understanding also? Do you not perceive that whatever enters a man from outside cannot defile him, because it does not enter his heart but his stomach, and is eliminated, thus purifying all foods?" And He said, "What comes out of a man, that defiles a man. For from within, out of the heart of men, proceed evil thoughts, adulteries, fornications, murders, thefts, covetousness, wickedness, deceit, lewdness, an evil eye, blasphemy, pride, foolishness. All these evil things come from within and defile a man." (Mark 7:14-23)

We have deceived ourselves into thinking that we can entertain the lusts of this world and at any time "take out the trash," and that somehow we are in control. We don't acknowledge the addictive nature of our society and the hold it has on our lives.

Why? Because, doing so would mean that we need to change our behavior and our response to the lusts of this world. We might have to dig deep into our soul to find out why we are so easily lured by Satan's deceptive tactics disguised in our material possessions. We might not get to enjoy the pleasures of S.I.N. if this revelation occurs.

ROOTS OF ADDICTION

There are underlying roots of these addictions and they become manifested in a variety of ways: insecurity, loneliness, depression, rejection, loss of hope, pain, various hurts, and sometimes the abuse of loved ones, friends and coworkers. The addictions themselves are not the real problem. The addictions are usually the manifestations of the real problem. The real problem is found in the roots of those manifestations— some of which go deep into our souls.

What do those roots stem from? Some examples might be: mental abuse, physical abuse, sexual abuse, parental influence, sibling rivalries, death of someone close, divorce, missed opportunities, unrealized dreams, wrong expectations, a failed past, and in some cases, all of the above.

Those roots are fed by the trash deposited over time into our minds and our hearts. Because of the sinful nature of our hearts, we react, manifesting specific behaviors as we grow and mature. Look at the societal vehicles by which the addictive process sets its course in each of our lives: our surroundings, parental behavior and influence, teachers, role models and father figures, peer relationships, movies, television, radio, internet, and music. The list is endless.

We have more external influences on us today because of the media than at any time in the history of man. We live in such a fast-paced world that has been fueled by technology. In just 100 years, we have gone from Henry Ford's one color choice in automobiles (black) to a plethora of colors, styles, and ranges of power. We have traveled into space, searched the depths of the universe, and cured a multitude of diseases. We can travel anywhere in the world within a matter of days, sometimes even hours.

> Currently, two-thirds of adults have Internet access from home (67%), up 34% since 2000. In fact, among the fastest-growing technologies in America is high-speed Internet access, which has nearly doubled since 2003. (24)

Wrong choices stimulate the roots of our addictions. The root of Eve's addiction was her ignorance of God's word and was manifested when she ate of the apple. Adam gave into her addiction by partaking of the same. This in itself is where the cycle of addiction could have been broken. As stated in the first chapter, if Adam had simply said to Eve, "We will not partake of the fruit of the tree of Good and Evil, we must honor God and all that he has given us," the cycle might have been squelched at that very moment. But, we know how the story turned out—we are all living remnants of that first sin.

Our world is in the midst of the greatest turmoil mankind has ever known. Wars are being waged daily all over the world. Even in peaceful countries, the war is fought on the streets, in the back alleys, in crack houses, in abortion clinics, among gangs, in business, and in the home. The true enemy does not care how the battle is fought or where the battle is waged, only that the battle is waged, and ultimately carried to victory. Satan's victory, which is happening all around us—his intended notion—has permeated our society.

I want to share a story, which paints an extreme picture. But, makes my point about the widespread infiltration of addiction into our society. Clearly demonstrating how we have become entrapped by Satan's deceptive plan. Most of us will be able to relate to this story, because it has become so prevalent in our society and most will probably know someone who has been affected in the same way.

I received a call at three in the afternoon from a dear friend whose name will remain anonymous for obvious reasons. The caller proceeded to tell me he was trying to kill himself and my first thought was, "He's going to shoot himself." However, almost reading my mind, he said, "I'm not going to shoot myself. I got rid of my guns several weeks ago because I was afraid I might do something stupid. No, I am trying to drink myself to death. I checked into a motel two weeks ago and have been drinking a half-gallon of scotch every day, praying to God that I would not wake up."

That phone call would ultimately be his lifeline and the end of a culmination of events that had transpired over a lifetime. His addiction was rooted in childhood events not in his control, but events nonetheless; he had to deal with in his life. Those events, ultimately created a sense of hopelessness, and a feeling of low self-esteem.

In high school, he started drinking with his friends. The drinking seemed to be innocent enough, after all, he had grown up with alcohol in the home and had not experienced anyone abusing it. However, the drinking soon became a way for him to escape his low self-esteem and falsely gave him a sense of power and control over his emotions. He soon became the *life of the*

SOCIETAL ADDICTION

party and was well liked by all who came in contact with him. Unfortunately, as time wore on, his drinking progressed to such a level that no one wanted to be around him.

What had started as seemingly innocent fun ended up causing him strained relationships with family, friends, and took years from his life. He became addicted to the substance of alcohol. Some of you may by thinking, "He should have quit drinking when things began to progress, owned up to his childhood, and sought counseling." The truth is he tried that remedy, but the addiction had a hold on his life. He didn't understand this hold, and no one around him understood it either.

He even tried to substitute cocaine for the alcohol, thinking, "If I could only stop drinking, everything would be okay." So it is important to note an important fact at this time—alcohol is a drug. Therefore, when I am talking about alcohol I could just as easily be talking about cocaine, heroin or any of a multitude of barbiturates or stimulates. Hello, the painkillers in the medicine cabinet of most American homes qualify! They are all mind-altering substances and when abused will at some point take control of one's life.

The destruction which results is the same: first separation from God and, ultimately, separation from everyone else. It is my hope as you read this, that you are smart enough to know, the stronger the substance, the more harmful the effect and the ultimate destruction on the person's life, and those around them. However, the main thing I want you to understand is the spiritual blindness these substances bring to the lives of the people affected by them. Why? Because S.I.N., knows that spiritual blindness will keep you in the cycle of your chosen addiction. It keeps the roots of those addictions hidden.

One could argue that the cycle of addiction begins by way of introduction. Like my friend, we might grow up with alcohol in the home and observe our parents and/or other adults drinking. We are certainly introduced to alcohol by the media that surrounds us daily and by our peer groups. In the case where we grew up with it in our home, it might be easier to embrace drinking as a way of adult life. However, it doesn't really matter if we grew up with it or not, because society has taught us through advertising, that drinking is an integral part of adulthood and something to enjoy.

Seldom do you see advertisements showing people getting drunk and being loud and abusive, only to later throw up in the street. No, we see commercials with pretty woman and men indulging their primal instincts, and having fun. The commercials seem innocent enough, but what is the subliminal message being portrayed? If you indulge, then you too will be surrounded by pretty men and women having fun.

Furthermore, included disclosures do not promote abstinence because that would hurt sales; instead, we are warned to drink responsibly and not to drink and drive. Since it is a legal substance, we have laws governing the legal drinking age, but the industry is self-regulated in terms of their ability to advertise. We have bought into these lies, not realizing that Satan is the originator of those lies, that the advertisers are merely his pawns.

The drinking laws are meant to protect the public and to protect minors from the dangers of alcohol. Of course, we know that not everyone matures at the same rate, so just because someone turns 21 overnight doesn't mean they are going to drink responsibly or that drinking won't lead to more serious issues. They rarely have the proper experiential knowledge of the long-term dangers of alcohol. Therefore, the enemy has been able to use this substance and its effects to bring about the destruction of millions of people. This dates back to the Old Testament, remember Lot's drunkenness?

> Come, let us make our father drink wine, and we will lie with him, that we may preserve the lineage of our father.
> (Genesis 19:32)

The amount of any drug we start consuming depends not on our level of education, but on the level of our self-control, and the root issues in our life. Let's be honest. Most everyone hears the warnings at some point, because is it mandatory that our schools teach the damaging effects alcohol and drugs can have on people. However, not everyone has the same self-control, and not everyone is experiencing the same issues in life, thus some begin consuming more than others.

> In 2005 17.6 percent of adolescents between the ages of 12-17 admitted using alcohol in the past month, 11.1 percent admitted to binge drinking (binge drinking means 5 or more drinks at a time) and 2.6 percent revealed heavy alcohol use. Binge drinking was prevalent in 28.1 percent of seniors within the last two weeks, 21 percent of tenth graders and 10.5 percent of eighth graders. Males are slightly higher in the older categories and close to even for eighth graders. Overall, 47 percent of seniors, one third of the tenth-graders and about 17 percent of the eighth-graders admitted to using alcohol in the past month. (25)

Let me relate the story of another friend. It was late one night, and my friend was driving home from a bar where he had been drinking. At the same time, a man was changing a flat tire on the side of the road, but because of the vehicle's location, it was hard for the oncoming traffic to see him. My friend hit the back of the car, the man ended up in the hospital, and my friend ended up in jail.

The man lost his leg that night, and as a result of the accident, my friend ended up in prison for two years. He had no way of knowing that his behavior prior to that night had set him up, that a battle had been raging in the spiritual realm for years—a battle that ultimately would cost him two years of his life. He was deceived by an enemy, and in this case, the enemy disguised itself in the form of a liquid.

Now let me ask you a question, "How many times have you driven home after consuming a few drinks?" What makes you any different from my friend?

> Over half of all drivers arrested for driving while intoxicated, and almost two-thirds of drinking drivers who were fatally injured, had a blood alcohol content higher than 0.15. This is nearly twice the legal limit in most states. Drinking drivers make approximately 950 million trips each year and about 21 percent of American drivers admitted they had driven after drinking in the past year. (26)

In the case of alcohol and drugs, we may initially like the way they make us feel. For some it is euphoric, but for many it is a sedative used as a way to wind down from a difficult day or from a difficult situation. In the case of addiction, the drinking or drug use is fueled not by a feeling of euphoria, but as an escape from the root issues in life. Many of the issues that cause us to abuse substances may seem innocent on the surface (such as stress or fatigue), but in many cases, the issues are much deeper, and more painful.

The cycle continues because the effects of the substance eventually wear off, at which point one is faced with their issues. As with any mind-altering substance, the only way to avoid facing the issues of life is to keep abusing the substance. The problem we don't count on is since you can't sustain the feeling the substance generates, eventually your body develops a level of tolerance. It then takes more of the substance to escape your reality.

How does any abuse begin? It starts with the temptation to indulge, and as in the case of my friend, the temptation originates out of our innocent ignorance. We don't have the experiential knowledge to know the path that might lie ahead. We don't intend to become addicted or intend for the substance to adversely affect our lives. However, once we give in to the temptation to experiment, it is easier to indulge on a regular basis, and it escalates from there. Eventually, the more substance that is consumed, the greater the toll on the individual resulting in an unmanageable life.

I want to note that not everyone goes to this extreme. These two stories are severe examples, because I want you to understand how the enemy has used substances in our society to bring about division and destruction in individuals and their relationships.

I also want to point out that just because some people think they can consume large amounts and still be functioning members of society, they might be deceived or, better put, they might be lost. I ask you to think back over your life and be honest as you ask yourself this question. Has alcohol or any other mind-altering substance had a positive influence on your life?

When I was growing up, the 5 o'clock hour was referred to by adults as "the time to take their medicine," meaning time to take a drink. Of course, most of us remember the popular tune sung by Alan Jackson and Jimmy Buffet, *It's Five O'clock Somewhere*, which let us all in on the secret of how to get around this seemingly common sense principle and justify our drinking at any hour. The painful reality in the families where drinking was present is this: *How much better a job parenting could they have done if alcohol or other substances were not present in the home?*

Ultimately, the unforeseen affects these substances have had over time on lives within our society are unfulfilled expectations and the absence of the most important aspect of life—God's love. The enemy has used alcohol and drugs alone to kill more people than cancer and to bring more division than all other issues among families. With all of this said, at this very moment you might be thinking, "This guy quotes the Bible a lot. What about Jesus? After all he drank and the Bible is full of stories about wine." You would be right in your thinking, so let me share the story found in the book of John.

> Now there were set there six waterpots of stone, according to the manner of purification of the Jews, containing twenty or thirty gallons apiece. Jesus said to them, "Fill the waterpots with water." And they filled them up to the brim. And He said to them, "Draw some out now, and take it to the master of the feast." And they took it. When the master of the feast had tasted the water that was made wine, and did not know where it came from (but the servants who had drawn the water knew), the master of the feast called the bridegroom. And he

said to him, "Every man at the beginning sets out the good wine, and when the guests have well drunk, then the inferior. You have kept the good wine until now!" (John 2:6-10)

Jesus was not threatened by the wine, in fact, he produced the best quality wine, and as a result, the master of the feast was impressed. In fact, it was the first miracle Jesus performed. Jesus just didn't produce a couple of bottles; he produced some 120 to 190 gallons of wine. Wow! For a *teetotaler* that would be a little ignorant, don't you think? Jesus must have really been a sot and set out to get everyone drunk.

However, nowhere in that story did he condone the abuse of that wine, and we have no way of knowing how many were being served. That wine was to be enjoyed as part of the wedding celebration. I have heard it said that in the Jewish culture at the time, as the night wore on, the bridegroom would serve watered down wine in order to save money. In this story, the master of the feast was impressed because the bridegroom had apparently served the best at the end of the feast. God only gives us the best.

Let's be realistic. One glass of wine, one beer or one drink is not destructive, and the people that exercise that kind of self-control are not bound by the substance. However, when we become more enamored by the effects of the wine more than the wine itself, we become deceived by the spirit behind the wine.

The people who will take offense to my stance on this subject are the ones who are in denial. They would not be content to debate the possibility that they have a problem, because doing so would expose their ignorance and could threaten their indulgence. The fact remains that Satan himself has deceived them and is in control of their lives.

> Wine is a mocker, Strong drink is a brawler, And whoever is led astray by it is not wise. (Proverbs 20:1)

There is an old adage, *don't shoot the messenger.* For those of you who are ready to throw this book across the room remember I am not the bad guy here. So don't shoot me for sharing this scripture. It has been in the Bible for years. Societal addictions are real, and we can't escape their effects. They are deeply rooted in our culture and hidden away in our hearts because of past hurts and pains.

Addictive Erosion

Steeped in our worldly lust, we have become ignorant of what I call the addictive erosion that has been wrought on our society throughout time.

In order to prove this point, let me use a real life example about a product we consume on a daily basis, a product that is at the core of controversy in our current economic climate. Think about pulling into a gas station. Does anyone walk up and ask, "Would you like me to fill your tank, wash your windows and check your oil?" Of course not! Why, because service has become the exception, not the rule.

We have been slowly weaned to the point where now, if someone came up and asked us to fill our tank, we would be suspicious and think, "Does this vagrant want a handout?" Think about it. Gas stations started out only offering *full service*. You pulled into a gas station and the attendant would greet you at the window of your car, asking, "How may I help you?" You didn't even have to pay a premium to receive the service! However, over time, we were slowly weaned by the gas companies. Let me explain. Initially, they would fill your tank with however much gas you requested (yes, you didn't even have to fill up the tank), then they would check tire pressure, oil and washer fluid, and finally, wash your windows. When finished, they would actually say, "Thank you for your business come back and see us soon."

> Please Note: Some states have laws requiring that an attendant fill the customer's tank, but the service of old is still lacking.

As time passed, the stations changed. You were given a choice of *full service* or *self service*, however, you were now charged a premium for the full service. A little more time passed, and when you pulled into the station you didn't see an attendant, much less have anyone ask if you wanted full service. Oh, if you asked, it was available, but not because they were happy to do so. As more time passed, you pulled into the station only to find an attendant behind a glass booth or inside the station collecting money, and full service was no longer an option. Now the only choice you have are diesel or three grades of gasoline, depending on the octane level you desire for your automobile. It has been a weaning process companies have employed over time. The effects have been subtle, but they have been able to lower operating costs without jeopardizing sales.

These companies, possibly without realizing it, have employed one of the primary tactics Satan has used effectively over time. Our society as a whole has been weaned the same way. Think about the biggest and most obvious areas we have seen this concept at work: *our moral decline and moral decay.*

Our movie rating system has become lax to the point where we consider nudity on the screen as a normal and innocent medium to be enjoyed. We don't see it as a harmful example that could possibly be used as a tool of the enemy to lead us astray from proper moral and ethical behavior. We don't associate this content with the erosion of our health system, a contributor to sexually transmitted diseases.

One used to be forced to drive to an x-rated store or movie house in order to view this type of content.Now in the movies, on cable/satellite television or over the internet, anyone can watch all forms of pornography.

Just like in our gas station example, our younger generations are being weaned and in time will have limited or no knowledge of our past system of moral decency. The ethical and moral decline in our society has been a slowly eroding process and all the while has deceived us into thinking that these mediums are good.

For many, they feel a sense of entitlement; that no one has a right to censorship, everyone should be able to make his or her own decision about what is right or wrong, good or bad. After all, don't we deserve to have options in life? Don't we have the right to choose? Of course we do. Everyone has a choice or the option to act a certain way or to look at certain content, but not at the expense of others and the decay of society as a whole—especially the minor population that will one day be the ruling class of our society.

Freedom from Addiction

God provides the tools necessary to overcome these addictions and live free from the sinful nature of our heart. We do not have the strength to do it alone. The only way to be delivered from an addictive lifestyle is through the saving grace of Jesus Christ and obedience to His word. Oh, some seem to have an easier time breaking the cycles of addiction, but usually that is because there is some inherent genetic factor working in their favor.

Earlier we learned that Jesus gave the account, "I watched Satan fall from heaven like lightening." If we read the remainder of the scripture in Luke, we learn that not only has Satan fallen, but Jesus has taken back dominion from him and given us the authority—"over all the power of the enemy." In other words, Satan's reign of terror, though still evident in the physical realm, has been defeated in the spiritual realm. We need to claim this power through faith!

> Behold, I give you the authority to trample on serpents and scorpions, and over all the power of the enemy, and nothing shall by any means hurt you. Nevertheless do not rejoice in this, that the spirits are subject to you, but rather rejoice because your names are written in heaven. (Luke 10:19-20)

The battles in life will continue to be fought, but the war has been won. We have already shown that through Jesus Christ, God conquered death when he became incarnate through Mary, born by the very Spirit of God, and offered His life in exchange for our sins. We now have access to His Holy Spirit, which provides an opportunity for all of us to rest in His strength and His power. We have been so clothed in our intellectualism, so trained by society and so deceived by Satan that we have rested on ignorance in our determination of God's power.

Most of us have read the story of Job or at least heard his story. Job had lost everything: family, material possessions and all dignity. He had no choice but to put his faith and trust in God. All his friends accused him of sin, and his own wife suggested he curse God and die. Finally, still loyal to his faith, Job begins to question God. The following is God's response. This passage of scripture is long, I ask you to forgive me in advance. But I thought it was important in order to realize the full effect of God's wonderful glory and awesome power.

> Then the LORD answered Job out of the whirlwind, and said: "Who is this who darkens counsel By words without knowledge? Now prepare yourself like a man; I will question you, and you shall answer Me. Where were you when I laid the foundations of the earth? Tell Me, if you have understanding. Who determined its measurements? Surely you know! Or who stretched the line upon it? To what were its foundations fastened? Or who laid its cornerstone, When the morning stars sang together, And all the sons of God shouted for joy? Or who shut in the sea with doors, When it burst forth and issued from the womb; When I made the clouds its garment, And thick darkness its swaddling band; When I fixed My limit for it, And set bars and doors; When I said, 'This far you may come, but no farther, And here your

proud waves must stop!' Have you commanded the morning since your days began, And caused the dawn to know its place, That it might take hold of the ends of the earth, And the wicked be shaken out of it? It takes on form like clay under a seal, And stands out like a garment. From the wicked their light is withheld, And the upraised arm is broken. Have you entered the springs of the sea? Or have you walked in search of the depths? Have the gates of death been revealed to you? Or have you seen the doors of the shadow of death? Have you comprehended the breadth of the earth? Tell Me, if you know all this. Where is the way to the dwelling of light? And darkness, where is its place, That you may take it to its territory, That you may know the paths to its home? Do you know it, because you were born then, Or because the number of your days is great? Have you entered the treasury of snow, Or have you seen the treasury of hail, Which I have reserved for the time of trouble, For the day of battle and war? By what way is light diffused, Or the east wind scattered over the earth? Who has divided a channel for the overflowing water, Or a path for the thunderbolt, To cause it to rain on a land where there is no one, A wilderness in which there is no man; To satisfy the desolate waste, And cause to spring forth the growth of tender grass? Has the rain a father? Or who has begotten the drops of dew? From whose womb comes the ice? And the frost of heaven, who gives it birth? The waters harden like stone, And the surface of the deep is frozen. Can you bind the cluster of the Pleiades, Or loose the belt of Orion? Can you bring out Mazzaroth in its season? Or can you guide the Great Bear with its cubs? Do you know the ordinances of the heavens? Can you set their dominion over the earth? Can you lift up your voice to the clouds, That an abundance of water may cover you? Can you send out lightnings, that they may go, And say to you, 'Here we are!'? Who has put wisdom in the mind? Or who has given understanding to the heart? Who can number the clouds by wisdom? Or who can pour out the bottles of heaven, When the dust hardens in clumps, And the clods cling together? Can you hunt the prey for the lion, Or satisfy the appetite of the young lions, When they crouch in their dens, Or lurk in their lairs to lie in wait? Who provides

> food for the raven, When its young ones cry to God, And wander about for lack of food?" (Job 38:1-41)

Like Job, not one of us has ever caused the sun to rise, made the sun set, ever placed a star in the sky or a baby in the womb. God hasn't changed in the time that has elapsed since Job was alive, and He isn't going to change after you and I pass from this earth. Further testimonies of God's awesome power are found in the book of Isaiah.

> Have you not known? Have you not heard? Has it not been told you from the beginning? Have you not understood from the foundations of the earth? It is He who sits above the circle of the earth, And its inhabitants are like grasshoppers, Who stretches out the heavens like a curtain, And spreads them out like a tent to dwell in. (Isaiah 40:21-22)

Of course, some of our more *knowledgeable* citizens, or should I say, the "naysayers" of the world, would have us believe they have a better idea of how the world was created. So whose story of creationm are you going to believe: some sinful man or woman living in modern times, or the God of the universe speaking through a Job or an Isaiah living in ancient times before Christ was born? Are you going to believe the likes of Oprah, Tony Robbins or some other celebrity? Well, as for me and my house, we are going to believe God, who declared His creation on his own behalf!

> Now therefore, fear the LORD, serve Him in sincerity and in truth, and put away the gods which your fathers served on the other side of the River and in Egypt. Serve the LORD! And if it seems evil to you to serve the LORD, choose for yourselves this day whom you will serve, whether the gods which your fathers served that were on the other side of the River, or the gods of the Amorites, in whose land you dwell. *But as for me and my house, we will serve the LORD.* (Joshua 24:14-15)

We defined the Godhead at the beginning of the book, the entity that is capable of creation. We saw that there is no possible way to put a limit on that kind of power. We showed that as created beings we are not smart enough to know more than the Creator. Maybe a good question to ask at this point in our reading is this, "How would you have created the world?" God simply spoke it into existence! God created everything we physically have knowledge of in six of His days, and in doing so, formed the world through natural causes in order for the whole of mankind to have purpose. Are His six days like yours and mine?

> But, beloved, do not forget this one thing, that with the Lord one day is as a thousand years, and a thousand years as one day. (2 Peter 3:8)

Let's face the facts. Life is hard and no one promised you a rose garden. Well, except God, and look what we did to that garden: we took it for granted. Maybe it wasn't a rose garden, but I bet you would prefer it today to the community where you are now living!

He created us in His image. We were like Him in that we were given a free will to choose how to live, but what did we do with our free will, what did we choose? We chose to listen to Satan, and we ate from the tree of the knowledge of good and evil. We bought into the lie that if we ate from the tree, we would be like God. We were already created in God's image, so how could we be any more like God? No, Satan longed to be God, so he used his own lustful desires in his temptations of man.

Most intelligent people that don't have a revelation of God's Word will tell you, "The Bible is full of good stories, but they are not true, after all, we evolved." When you look at our evolutionary process, doesn't it strike you as odd that everything works together in perfect union except for what man has made? Take a breath and blow into your hand. Can you see the air? Of course not, but there is no denying its presence, because you can feel it. Speak a word. Where does the sound come from? Medically we can explain it, but what gives the voice life? Look at your fingertips and ponder the truth; no one else on the planet has that print and no one that has lived previously had the same print.

Forest fires are nature's way of pruning themselves in order to thrive. Seasons come and go, people are born and then they die. I could go on. Oh, but our society will define creation for us and we filter that information through our generational upbringing. I ask you this, knowing what you know about society as a whole, do you really want society to define creation for you?

Most of us have read about or have heard of Sherlock Holmes and thus remember his favorite phrase to his faithful assistant, "Elementary, my dear Watson." Life is elementary, but at the same time it is deeply profound, is it not? Our bodies are made up of approximately 60 percent water. We have a nerve network that would rival any electrical source on earth. We have a heart pumping blood carrying oxygen to every part of our body. We have a brain more efficient than any computer built with man's hands. And let us not forget our skin covering that holds all this in.

But we had no part in our creation. We aren't required to do anything. Life is a gift to us. How then do we explain what constitutes a life form based on evolutionary principles? The Bible tells us that we were created from the dust of the ground, and in the end, we will return to the dust of the ground. Where will the spirit of man return?

> And the LORD God formed man of the dust of the ground, and breathed into his nostrils the breath of life; and man became a living being. (Genesis 2:7)

> Then the dust will return to the earth as it was, And the spirit will return to God who gave it. (Ecclesiastes 12:7)

We think we can clone man, but who can clone the soul of a man? Who is the ultimate Creator? Do you believe in Him? If you don't, you are taking a mighty big chance; because His Word says that He is your Creator and that He created the world and the universe you live in. He states that there is a physical Heaven and a physical hell. Thus, if you make the decision not to believe in Him and He is real, then guess what? You will be living an eternity in a place separated from His presence. You are taking a tremendous gamble, because your eternal salvation rests on your decision.

Provided His word is true, then believers only have one place to look forward to for all eternity. God longs to bring us into His kingdom, so much so that He came to us in the form of man. This in itself should overwhelm you, because every religion other than Christianity requires that men and women go to their God.

I once had a friend (a very well-read friend of mine) tell me that Jesus was a great man, but that he had manipulated and staged the entire fulfillment of prophecy during his lifetime. Can you imagine a single man orchestrating the fulfillment of prophecy put down in writing over several thousand years prior to his birth? How long have you been alive? How many books have you read? How far have you traveled? Don't be afraid to answer. In Jesus' life, he did not have access to the resources you have today, and His ministry consisted of only a small geographic area because of the limitations on travel at the time. One only has to look at a map of all His journeys to see that He was geographically limited.

Let's assume that He didn't start His ministry until the age of 30 because He was memorizing the Torah and laying the foundation to fulfill all Old Testament prophecy. How would you go about it? Where would you start? Surely, my friend gave this some thought, or did he? Ignorance is like a cloud, a cloud that can shield the mighty flames of the sun, can snuff out the moon, and can bring darkness upon our lives. Those clouds shroud the revelation of Jesus Christ in our life regardless of how many books we have read, how many lectures, and seminars we have attended, or how many debates we enter into.

We need to wake up to the fact that society has so clouded our vision that we don't know who God really is, and we have become content to live lifestyles set in the clouds of addiction.

Take a moment and ask yourself these questions: What determines one's motivation? What determines one's drive? Where do we find the answers? Whom do we depend on for advice? How were you raised? What was your environment like? What was going on during your childhood? What effects did those times have on your future? Can you retrace your life with all its problems, deficiencies, successes, failures, and heartaches and somehow find joy, peace, and a future hope? The freedom comes from knowing there is an answer to all of these questions and it was placed inside you in your mother's womb.

> Then the word of the LORD came to me, saying: "Before I formed you in the womb I knew you; Before you were born I sanctified you; I ordained you a prophet to the nations." (Jeremiah 1:4-5)

Most have seen the famous painting by Leonardo da Vinci entitled *The Last Supper*, which depicts Jesus and His disciples sitting at a table ready to partake in the Lord's Supper. Many of us have also either read or heard the account from Matthew given in the scripture.

> And as they were eating, Jesus took bread, blessed and broke it, and gave it to the disciples and said, "Take, eat; this is My body." Then He took the cup, and gave thanks, and gave it to them, saying, "Drink from it, all of you. For this is My blood of the new covenant, which is shed for many for the remission of sins." (Matthew 26:26-28)

There have been numerous books written and movies made about this story. In fact, do you remember the movie *Indiana Jones and the Last Crusade*, in which Harrison Ford plays the main character? Jones is in search of the grail used by Christ at the last supper. In his quest, he comes to a place where the grail is being guarded by one of the knights of old. Unfortunately, to get to the grail he must cross a wide and deep chasm, a chasm so deep Indiana Jones couldn't see the bottom. Standing at what seems the dead end of his journey, he remembers his Father's notes where it is stated, "God will prepare the path," so he assumes that this must be the place his Father was referring to in his journal. Jones closes his eyes and steps off the ledge out over the chasm.

As we watched, our hearts pounded, anxiously awaiting the outcome of his leap of faith. Would he tumble to his death or would God prepare the path? As he lowers his foot, it comes in contact with a semi-invisible stone pathway. He proceeds ahead slowly at first, but as the path unfolds and becomes more visible, he rushes across to the other side. He then hesitates before continuing, picks up a handful of dust and throws it across the now invisible bridge, marking it for his return trip.

Aren't we all like Indiana Jones? Even when we take a leap of faith and God comes through, we continue to doubt our future path. We have all sensed the guiding of something bigger than ourselves from time to time. Sometimes we have even taken that same leap of faith only to turn around and question its existence. And in some different but symbolic way, we have thrown dust across the trail, hoping we could somehow sustain that feeling or know how to find it again in the future.

Freedom from addiction is accomplished once we accept the Lord into our hearts. God marks our path and orders our steps, regardless of our inferior plans.

> A man's heart plans his way, But the LORD directs his steps.
> (Proverbs 16:9)

We live in an addictive environment where dysfunction has become a functional reality. Why don't we see Satan for who he really is and see that he has used societal influences to distort our thinking, dampen our faith, and question God's intentions? Why not come out of denial, admit your shortcomings, begin life anew, and acknowledge the good news? God wants to direct your path toward an eternity with Him.

Chapter Five

Playing Life

We are all playing a game and that game is called *life*. Every day is a new day, a new adventure, and we tread on in anticipation. We robotically move through life, hoping that one day we will awaken to find that our lives had purpose and meaning. Unfortunately, many will awaken to find they have been playing this game by running with the herd. In essence, going along with everyone else in an attempt to get along.

This is as much of a problem in our churches as it is in the secular community. Many people have a tendency to pick portions of scripture that justify their lifestyle instead of fully embracing God's Word. Choosing to interpret scripture in such a way knowingly or unknowingly compromises Christian beliefs. Especailly when doing so is out of fear of being rejected or offending someone. Thus, blocking the ability to eradicate sin in individual lives.

Still others have a tendancy to pull away from anyone and anything that gets in their way or that reminds them of their past. When this is allowed to happen they are being kept in bondage, having fallen into the enemy's trap. Instead they continue to follow the herd and don't dare stop, because when they do stop, they are afraid their life will have no meaning.

It is time we came to the realization that many of us have been deceived or are in a state of denial. We are in a spiritual battle, and just like most contact sports, we must learn to put on the Armor of God in order to fully protect our spiritual beings. The enemy only has three primary plays in his playbook. When we study those plays and the many options he runs off those plays, we can expose his intended tactics and gain renewed hope. We must learn to react to S.I.N.'s offense with a different defense.

With God's covering, our eternal destinies are secure. We can rest assured that though we still have to play in this game called life, in the end, we are victors. God is with us, not against us; He is on our side!

Running with the Herd

I had the privilege of spending discipleship time with a good friend several years ago, and we discussed the difficulties of life—how some aspects just didn't seem fair. He was facing many challenges in the workplace, at home, and in his personal relationships. He was an incredible young man: athletic, good looking, smart, successful, and had a good career. However, he was not living a life worthy of blessing. He was more interested in chasing fame and fortune and living in the fast lane. Part of me wanted to shake him to receive revelation of how special he was to the Creator and how the Lord had blessed him.

One morning, in my quiet time with the Lord, I had a vision of a wild mustang running loose through an open field. Suddenly I sensed in my spirit that the Lord wanted me to share with him that he was like that wild mustang running loose through the open field. His mane flowing in the wind, strong legs flexing with every stride. His firm back arched, his head held high, and stride-for-stride faster than any of the other horses. He was in the lead, and the herd followed him wherever he desired.

This young man didn't realize the gifts and purposes God had for his life. Little did he know, as he assumed the role as leader in the home and workplace, that he was poised to fulfill God's purpose for his life. Unfortunately, the way he was living his life, anyone choosing to follow his behavior would be led astray and would pay a consequence. In other words, this beautiful creation had become a danger to those he professed to love and to himself.

In some way, all of us can relate to my friend, because we are like that wild mustang. We run loose through the open fields of life, and God looks down on us so proud of His creation. However, God knows that in order for us to accomplish the purposes He has for us, we must be reined in. Like that wild mustang, we can be of no use to anyone until we are broken. Interestingly enough, there is always a leader of the herd and the rest of the mustangs follow that leader, sometimes to a fault.

Do you see the parallel between my friend and Satan? Now, don't get me wrong, I am in no way implying that he was Satan. However, what I am implying is that the enemy wants us to parallel his behavior, not God's behavior. The enemy will always lead us astray, and if the he can command the loyalty of the leaders, it will be easy to command the loyalty of the followers. The Father's desire is that we would not just run with the other horses, but that we would lead the other horses.

> Plans are established by counsel; By wise counsel wage war. (Proverbs 20:18)

> The plans of the diligent lead surely to plenty, But those of everyone who is hasty, surely to poverty. (Proverbs 21:5)

> When the scoffer is punished, the simple is made wise; But when the wise is instructed, he receives knowledge. (Proverbs 21:11)

In all aspects of life, we have a tendency to go along with what everyone else is doing. Look at the world around your home, work, and church. We wake up, go to work, eat lunch, work out, eat dinner, and go to sleep, only to get up the next day and repeat it all over again. We listen to the same music, view the same movies, and become defined by the society in which we have become immersed. We look up to our parents, friends, bosses, celebrities, and other public figures. We have a tendency to dress like them, talk like them, and act like them.

We have become, in a sense, like those wild mustangs following the leaders, leaders who have been deceived and manipulated by S.I.N. They are leading us toward the edge of the cliff. The fall off that cliff leads to eternal death and separation from our Creator, and we are just allowing them to lead us right to it.

We must stop running toward the edge of that cliff, reassess our lives, and evaluate if we are running with the wrong herd. Are we simply weak and feel a need to follow something or someone, regardless of their intentions? Or are we exhausted to the point where we are just going along to get along? Are we preparing for the mission we were put here on earth to achieve? Have we become prey to complacency, where we run the risk or have a tendency to choose counsel that provides the easiest route in life, even if we sense it is the wrong route?

Think how much time has been wasted following the easiest path. The reality is this: God loves us, and no matter what route we take in life, if He is truly in our hearts, all routes will ultimately lead back to Him. So in essence, you will only be prolonging the inevitable cleansing of the Lord, to eradicate the sin in your life.

It's usually not until we take a step back and see ourselves as God sees us that we can rein in our emotions and actions in time for God to mold us into His beauty of creation. It is only then that we experience the Lord's brokenness and the preparation for life that it brings.

Have you ever felt frustrated with your life, as if you were hitting your head up against a brick wall, all the while expecting the wall to crumble? But the more you hit that brick wall, the more your head ached? Of course, the brick walls in life will stand firm. They are not fazed by our battering. The best thing to do is stop beating your head against that wall, take a step back, reevaluate the situation and ask, "Lord, is there a better way?" Like the mustang, God is still looking down on us, pleased with His creation. Don't you think it is time to let go of your own personal pursuit and give in to God's pursuit?

Pick and Choose to Suit

We take the Bible out of context and wonder why we are so confused in today's society. I was doing some research and came across a website written by a homosexual. He was using the argument of grace to defend his homosexuality. His argument, based on scriptural truth, was that no one could keep the laws of Moses, the Old Testament laws God gave the Hebrews. His point seemed to make sense. No one today could fulfill all the law; thus, being saved by grace, he should not be judged for his sexual orientation. The article went on to quote scripture after scripture, mounting a defense in favor of this belief.

Many people presented differing opinions using scripture, but he attacked every counterpoint that was offered. Looking at scripture we find Paul made it very clear that when we sin we have an advocate standing between us and God—Jesus Christ. Christ took our sin upon His shoulders.

> My little children, these things I write to you, so that you may not sin. And if anyone sins, we have an Advocate with the Father, Jesus Christ the righteous. (1 John 2:1)

> But now, it is no longer I who do it, but sin that dwells in me. (Romans 7:17)

> What shall we say then? Shall we continue in sin that grace may abound? Certainly not! (Romans 6:1)

However, Paul also made it clear that we do not go on sinning. His point is this: once you trust in Christ there will be conviction of sin, and if you truly made a heartfelt decision, you should follow the Word of God. Not manipulate it to justify your sinful nature. We all have a tendency to pick out those scriptures that suit our needs and discard the rest. We choose to believe what we want to believe, not realizing that at times we are doing so in order to justify some sinful behavior. Does this change God's perspective on sin?

When we continue our sinful behavior and hold out to our peers that it is holy behavior in God's eyes, are we not deceived by the enemy? Without this revelation, our hearts have become hardened, and we are destined to enter a wide gate leading us to eternal separation from God.

"Difficult is the way. But its end is the way of death." Below are two scriptures, one from the Old Testament and one from the New Testament. These scriptures do not condemn nor do they judge. Rather, they testify to the truth. If we choose to remain in willful sin, we are being deceived. In the end, the behavior will lead to destruction. How many times are we warned in scripture that this type of thinking and this type of response to scripture is wrong?

> Enter by the narrow gate; for wide is the gate and broad is the way that leads to destruction, and there are many who go in by it. Because narrow is the gate and difficult is the way which leads to life, and there are few who find it. (Matthew 7:13-14)
>
> There is a way that seems right to a man, But its end is the way of death. (Proverbs 16:25)

We are all familiar with the story of the woman caught in act of adultery whom the elders were ready to stone. According to Old Testament scripture, they were under authority to do so, and thus could fully justify their intention to stone her.

> Then they shall bring out the young woman to the door of her father's house, and the men of her city shall stone her to death with stones, because she has done a disgraceful thing in Israel,

> to play the harlot in her father's house. So you shall put away the evil from among you. (Deuteronomy 22:21)

Yet, as related in the scripture below, Jesus knew no one was capable of keeping the Old Testament law. He challenged the elders to first look into their own hearts and search out the seed of sin before bringing judgment. He was not negating the law but was establishing the concept of future grace, grace He would offer to all God's creation. He clearly did not condone the sin as evidenced when He instructed Mary to "Go and sin no more."

> Then the scribes and Pharisees brought to Him a woman caught in adultery. And when they had set her in the midst, they said to Him, "Teacher, this woman was caught in adultery, in the very act. Now Moses, in the law, commanded us that such should be stoned. But what do You say?" This they said, testing Him, that they might have something of which to accuse Him. But Jesus stooped down and wrote on the ground with His finger, as though He did not hear. So when they continued asking Him, He raised Himself up and said to them, "He who is without sin among you, let him throw a stone at her first." And again He stooped down and wrote on the ground. Then those who heard it, being convicted by their conscience, went out one by one, beginning with the oldest even to the last. And Jesus was left alone, and the woman standing in the midst. When Jesus had raised Himself up and saw no one but the woman, He said to her, "Woman, where are those accusers of yours? Has no one condemned you?" She said, "No one, Lord." And Jesus said to her, *"Neither do I condemn you; go and sin no more."* (John 8:3-11)

Jesus didn't say you can keep on sinning, go to the priest, make confession and all will be forgiven. No, He spoke on His own authority by saying, "Neither do I condemn you." In other words, Jesus was instructing her that once forgiven, all you have to do is quit sinning, and you won't have to deal with the issue ever again. Pretty simple, wouldn't you agree? Well, we have a hard time with anything that appears to be that simple, especially if we are not willing to give up the behavior.

The 613 "Mitzvos" are found in the Torah and are referred to as the Mosaic law. These laws God gave to Moses and are principles of law and ethical behavior—a road map for living—that if followed would lead all Jews on the narrow path referred to in Matthew. They are listed at the end of this book in the appendix, so look them over, see how they relate to our legal system today and then ask yourself, "Is the law negated just because we cannot or do not adhere to the law?"

Recently, I opened a piece of mail and discovered a ticket stating I had run a red light at a busy intersection. I was caught red handed; included within the notice were pictures of my vehicle at various points in the intersection, the light clearly red in the photos. I had a choice: pay the fine or not pay the fine. After all, no one was going to stone me if I choose not to pay the fine. However, the next time a law officer stopped me for a traffic violation and ran my driver's license through his computer, he would inform me of my offense and would probably arrest me.

I would not have a say in the matter. It would make no difference if I believed in the law or determined that I was no longer bound by the law; he could enforce the law. Fortunately, all I would have to do is admit my guilt, pay the fine, and everything would be forgotten. This can be likened to the Lord's grace. In Old Testament times my punishment would have been much more severe.

Our prisons are filled with men and women who claim their innocence, but regardless are still paying a price for their crime. We do not escape the final judgment of God, but through His son, we are offered grace and mercy, allowing us to fully know His love for us. Adam made a mistake that we are still paying for, but Christ, by suffering for our sins, cancelled Adam's debt. Of course, we don't get a "get out of jail free" card, but we still get to enter God's kingdom, "Eternal life through Jesus Christ our Lord."

> Therefore, as through one man's offense judgment came to all men, resulting in condemnation, even so through one Man's righteous act the free gift came to all men, resulting in justification of life. For as by one man's disobedience many were made sinners, so also by one Man's obedience many will be made righteous. Moreover the law entered that the offense might abound. But where sin abounded, grace abounded much more, so that as sin reigned in death, even so grace might reign through righteousness to *eternal life through Jesus Christ our Lord.* (Romans 5:18-21)

Scripture is to be taken in totality and read with an open mind toward God's revealing love. Love is revealed starting in Genesis with creation, then follows the course of mankind through Old Testament times. We are to savor the counsel of the Major and Minor Prophets, and press on to the instruction of Abraham and Moses. We are to learn from the mistakes of henotheistic men and women and see the effect their destruction has wrought on mankind. Some of which is still being played out today. We learn from the 40 years the Jewish people wandered in the wilderness when the promise land was within their grasp. We are to embrace the fact that Old Testament prophecies found in Isaiah and Jeremiah have been fulfilled by the Lord's coming.

> Who has believed our report? And to whom has the arm of the LORD been revealed? For He shall grow up before Him as a tender plant, And as a root out of dry ground. He has no form or comeliness; And when we see Him, There is no beauty that we should desire Him. He is despised and rejected by men, A Man of sorrows and acquainted with grief. And we hid, as it were, our faces from Him; He was despised, and we did not esteem Him. Surely He has borne our griefs And carried our sorrows; Yet we esteemed Him stricken, Smitten by God, and afflicted. But *He was wounded for our transgressions, He was bruised for our iniquities*; The chastisement for our peace was upon Him, And by His stripes we are healed. All we like sheep have gone astray; We have turned, every one, to his own way; And *the LORD has laid on Him the iniquity of us all*. He was oppressed and He was afflicted, Yet He opened not His mouth; He was led as a lamb to the slaughter, And as a sheep before its shearers is silent, So He opened not His mouth. He was taken from prison and from judgment, And who will declare His generation? For He was cut off from the land of the living; For the transgressions of My people He was stricken. And they made His grave with the wicked—But with the rich at His death, Because He had done no violence, Nor was any deceit in His mouth. Yet it pleased the LORD to bruise Him; He has put Him to grief. When You make His soul an offering for sin, He shall see His seed, He shall prolong His days, And the pleasure of the LORD shall prosper in His hand. He shall see the labor of His soul, and be satisfied. By His knowledge My righteous Servant shall justify many, For He shall bear their iniquities. Therefore I will divide Him a portion with the great, And He

shall divide the spoil with the strong, Because He poured out His soul unto death, And He was numbered with the transgressors, And He bore the sin of many, And made intercession for the transgressors. (Isaiah 53:1-12)

Behold, the days are coming, says the LORD, when I will make a new covenant with the house of Israel and with the house of Judah—not according to the covenant that I made with their fathers in the day that I took them by the hand to lead them out of the land of Egypt, My covenant which they broke, though I was a husband to them, says the LORD. But this is the covenant that I will make with the house of Israel after those days, says the LORD: I will put My law in their minds, and write it on their hearts; and I will be their God, and they shall be My people. No more shall every man teach his neighbor, and every man his brother, saying, "Know the LORD," for they all shall know Me, from the least of them to the greatest of them, says the LORD. *For I will forgive their iniquity, and their sin I will remember no more.* (Jeremiah 31:31-34)

Then it is on to the New Testament with the four gospel accounts, Doctor Luke's book of Acts, the thirteen Pauline epistles, the general epistles, and finally John's account of the end times found in the last book of the Bible, Revelation. All the while the Bible is flowing back and forth clearly in support of itself.

The homosexual man I referred to at the beginning of this writing is deceiving many by his teaching, and don't think he won't be held accountable. He can argue these points and try to convince us that we are wrong, but what if he is the one that is wrong? He is risking eternal separation from God and is ignorantly keeping many out of heaven. All because he is not willing to heed Paul's advice and admit that his lifestyle is a sin.

I think it is important to note at this time that my intention is not to judge this man, I am not against any kind of people. I am, however, against the sinful nature within all of God's people, first and foremost myself. We label ourselves with descriptive titles and attempt to separate ourselves from the rest of the world, but in God's kingdom, we are all His children. There can be no separation, and His judgment is unbiased.

> Do you not know that the unrighteous will not inherit the kingdom of God? Do not be deceived. Neither fornicators, nor idolaters, nor adulterers, nor homosexuals, nor sodomites, nor thieves, nor covetous, nor drunkards, nor revilers, nor extortioners will inherit the kingdom of God.
> (1 Corinthians 6:9-10)

> Flee sexual immorality. Every sin that a man does is outside the body, but he who commits sexual immorality sins against his own body. Or do you not know that your body is the temple of the Holy Spirit who is in you, whom you have from God, and you are not your own? For you were bought at a price; therefore glorify God in your body and in your spirit, which are God's. (1 Corinthians 6:18-20)

The above scriptures cover just about every kind of willful sin imaginable. So if we are honest, all of us have bought into the enemy's lies at one time or another. We can avoid putting ourselves at risk eternally by checking what anyone says against the scriptures. Even if what we are hearing is being delivered through a fellow child of God or from the pulpit of our church. Just like that ticket I received for running the red light. We will not be able to argue our innocence on judgment day by saying, "But, Lord so-and-so told me this behavior was okay, I didn't know you warned us about it in the scriptures."

If there is an area of sin in your life that God has revealed to be wrong through scripture you need to heed His warning. But, if you are manipulating scripture by claiming God's grace to justify the behavior and continuing in that act of sin, you are hypnotized under S.I.N.'s influence. You are at risk of spending an eternity separated from God.

How will you know if the behavior is sinful? Eventually, the true child of God experiences conviction of their sin, and the conviction weighs them down until the pain of that conviction becomes unbearable. Ultimately leading them to confession and repentance.

We are not to judge others of their sin, but remain focused on those areas in our own lives that are sinful. When we judge others, that judgment will ultimately reflect back on us to show unequivocally that we are as guilty or even more guilty than them.

> Judge not, that you be not judged. For with what judgment you judge, you will be judged; and with the measure you use, it

will be measured back to you. And why do you look at the speck in your brother's eye, but do not consider the plank in your own eye? (Matthew 7:1-3)

I challenge that God doesn't categorize sin. To Him, sin is sin, no matter what we want to believe. It is in His power to judge us for our sin, in His power to forgive us of our sin. He alone executes judgment and determines our eternal fate. How could we, in our intellectual pursuits of interpreting His Word, ignorantly think we can dictate to God what He intends or means in scripture?

For this reason, one must look at the Bible in totality and not just "pick and choose" scripture to suit a need or to mount a defense for intellectual debate. The center verse of the King James Bible is found in Psalm 118:8-9: "It is better to trust in the LORD than to put confidence in man. It is better to trust in the LORD than to put confidence in princes." Interesting, don't you think? God is a big God, an eternal God, and is not moved by our intellectualism. In fact, our intellects are a product of His creation. For that reason, He instructs us to look to Him, not man, in our quest for the truth.

Scripture will not always make sense to us, but just because we become confused or even deceived by someone's opinion or interpretation of scripture, it does not change God's love for us. He will bring conviction into the hearts of those who have rightfully chosen to believe and put their trust in His free gift of salvation. There will be mountains of consequence to circle until a conscious choice is made to receive conviction by revelation, confess our sin, repent, and turn away.

Isn't it time we quit picking and choosing God's Word to justify our sinful behavior? Isn't it time that we admit in our intellectual debate of scripture that S.I.N. has manipulated us in such a way that we are self-destructing? We think that by defining God's Word to fit our behavior we will be free from God's righteous judgment. When in reality we have become slaves to sin and are already being held in judgment.

To Pull or To Push

We need to know how the enemy attacks in order to defend those attacks. Once we identify the enemy's methods, we have a choice: use our own reaction or use God's reaction. It makes sense that we will be more successful if we react according to God's plan versus our own plan.

What I am basically saying is, why pull when you could push? Have you ever studied self-defense or the martial arts? One concept taught in self-defense is that there are normal responses and there are learned responses. Let me give an example to make this point. I was taking a tae-kwon-do course when I was younger, and my instructor was of Korean descent. His whole life had been dedicated to learning martial arts, and he was classified as a master in several disciplines. He stood approximately 5' 6" tall, was trim and limber, and he was able to stand flat-footed and bring one leg straight up against his body with the bottom of his foot pointing to the ceiling.

During one of our classes, all the students gathered around as he related a story about a woman being accosted by a large and muscular man. The man grabbed the woman by the arm and she struggled to pull away. However, being stronger, the man tightened his grip. Thus, overpowering her and pulling her into his arms. Our instructor then asked a male student and a smaller female student to get up and act out this scenario for the class. Before they started, he whispered something into the ear of the female student. Sure enough, as the larger male student tightened his grip and started pulling, the female student fell into the larger student, catching him completely off guard. She was able to break his hold and quickly move out of harm's way. Her normal instinct or impulse would be to pull away and try to break free in order to escape, but through instruction, she did just the opposite, and was victorious.

This is an interesting concept, push instead of pull. Pulling back in this example is what is called a natural response; a response that on the surface makes perfect sense. The attacker expects you to pull away, as in our examples, knowing he is bigger and stronger and will expect to overpower you. In fact, most bullies would welcome your response to pull away so they can prove their strength and dominance. What the attacker is not expecting is for you to do the opposite—push into him—thus using your weight against him and throwing him off balance. As he falls back, trying to regain his balance, he will relax his hold in an effort to stabilize. At that moment, you are able to break free, start running and hope you are faster. Thus, our natural response is not always the correct or best response.

On another occasion, our instructor asked a student to stand and attempt to attack him. The person made a move to attack, and for the next five minutes, as the instructor spoke to the class, the student twisted and turned every way he knew how in an attempt to break free. Every move he made the instructor countered, all the while casually engaging in conversation with his students.

In this example, the instructor was teaching us to initiate a learned response and avoid being trapped into utilizing a natural response. He was teaching a basic principle in self-defense, one I will not soon forget.

Sometimes we need to implement a learned response, one that may not feel very comfortable and might even seem crazy.

As shown in these examples, it is the learned response that will set us free. Life is the larger of the two in our example, and unfortunately, life's struggles can have much the same effect on us. They can be so powerful that we become overwhelmed by their hold and dominance over us. The world or S.I.N. would have us pull, intending for us to be hamstrung by our fear. But the Lord wants us to push in, break S.I.N.'s hold. By doing so, we learn that the source of our struggles is not what makes us afraid; it is our inability to cope with those struggles that grips us.

Fear of the unknown will keep you bound up and feeling trapped and insecure. But fear of the Lord is the beginning of wisdom. When we trust the Lord by pressing in and giving our fear of the unknown to Him, He will deliver and strengthen us. He is the only one to be feared.

> The fear of the LORD is the beginning of knowledge, But fools despise wisdom and instruction. (Proverbs 1:7)

Earlier, I quoted the scripture from Matthew 10:28: "And do not fear those who kill the body but cannot kill the soul. But rather fear Him who is able to destroy both soul and body in hell." So, whom are you going to fear? Or would you rather fall in the rank of fools as listed in the above proverb?

SATAN'S PLAYBOOK

In the first chapter, we learned that Satan leads a team, one third of the heavenly hosts. We know that in life for any team to be successful, they must have a strategic game plan made up of specific plays, and then they must execute those plays.

It is also important for any team to study their opponent. Satan's team continually studies us, looking for cracks in the foundations of our life in order to execute an advantage spiritually. What if we could turn the tables and peek into Satan's playbook? Would this give us an advantage in this game called life? Satan has a limited amount of plays in his playbook, and with access to those plays, it makes sense that we could mount a better defense against those plays.

In fact, the enemy only has three primary weapons that he has been using since that fateful day in the garden when he approached Eve. All his other weapons are option plays that stem from these three: Temptation, Accusation and Deception.

1. Temptation

We are all too familiar with the enemy's first play, temptation, which is usually brought about in the physical realm. Satan uses temptation in the physical sense by enticing us to lust after a person, place or thing.

Think for a moment of all the societal influences we are faced with on a daily basis. As we drive down the street, we are inundated with material on billboards tempting us in so many ways. Every time we open our email, the enemy tries to entice us to open up just one email that he knows will open the sinful door of our heart.

Temptation will come to us all, but our reaction to it is under our control. We can give into it, or we can avoid it. The power is within us, but first we have to believe in faith that we can overcome. Then we have to exercise that faith.

God spoke to Cain in the beginning, warning him of sin's impending danger and expressing that he had the tools within him to avoid its snare. Sin does not control us; we should control sin. We are to "Rule over it." The key to ruling over sin is found in these four words: "If you do well." These are four simple words we can all understand. This is not rocket science.

> So the LORD said to Cain, "Why are you angry? And why has your countenance fallen? *If you do well,* will you not be accepted? And if you do not do well, sin lies at the door. And its desire is for you, but you should *rule over it*."
> (Genesis 4:6-7)

How do we "do well?" The key to avoiding sin's grasp is to follow the Lord's commandments as found in His Word given to Moses on Mount Sinai. I find it interesting that the Lord gave Moses the tools for us to rule over sin on a Mount with sin in its name. The word Sinai in Hebrew is Ciynay, and The Hebrew word for sin is Ciyn. Mount Sinai is near the wilderness of sin.

> And they journeyed from Elim, and all the congregation of the children of Israel came to the Wilderness of Sin, which is between Elim and Sinai, on the fifteenth day of the second month after they departed from the land of Egypt.
> (Exodus 16:1)

There are Ten Commandments to ruling over sin, and sadly, most Christians could not recite them from memory. We need to imbed them deep within our heart so that we too can "Rule over it."

> And God spoke all these words, saying: "I am the LORD your God, who brought you out of the land of Egypt, out of the house of bondage. (Exodus 20:1-2)

THE TEN COMMANDMENTS
Exodus 20:3-17

#1 You shall have no other gods before Me.
#2 You shall not make for yourself a carved image—any likeness of anything that is in heaven above, or that is in the earth beneath, or that is in the water under the earth; you shall not bow down to them nor serve them. For I, the LORD your God, am a jealous God, visiting the iniquity of the fathers upon the children to the third and fourth generations of those who hate Me, but showing mercy to thousands, to those who love Me and keep My commandments.
#3 You shall not take the name of the LORD your God in vain, for the LORD will not hold him guiltless who takes His name in vain.
#4 Remember the Sabbath day, to keep it holy. Six days you shall labor and do all your work, but the seventh day is the Sabbath of the LORD your God. In it you shall do no work: you, nor your son, nor your daughter, nor your male servant, nor your female servant, nor your cattle, nor your stranger who is within your gates. For in six days the LORD made the heavens and the earth, the sea, and all that is in them, and rested the seventh day. Therefore the LORD blessed the Sabbath day and hallowed it.
#5 Honor your father and your mother, that your days may be long upon the land which the LORD your God is giving you.
#6 You shall not murder.
#7 You shall not commit adultery.
#8 You shall not steal.

> *#9* You shall not bear false witness against your neighbor.
> *#10* You shall not covet your neighbor's house; you shall not covet your neighbor's wife, nor his male servant, nor his female servant, nor his ox, nor his donkey, nor anything that is your neighbor's."

Temptation is inevitable, but we have indelible power, a power that is not affected by sin and therefore cannot be controlled by sin.

> And He said to them, "I saw Satan fall like lightning from heaven. Behold, I give you the authority to trample on serpents and scorpions, and over all the power of the enemy, and nothing shall by any means hurt you." (Luke 10: 18-19)

It is Satan's desire to lure us through his plays of temptation so that we give into our lustful desires. His hope is that we will become weakened spiritually. Satan does not want us following the Lord's commandments that enable us to draw upon the power available to us through the Holy Spirit.

> But if the Spirit of Him who raised Jesus from the dead dwells in you, He who raised Christ from the dead will also give life to your mortal bodies through His Spirit who dwells in you. (Romans 8:11)

Think how your sinful nature has manifested at times. Have you ever been drawn to something you knew in your heart to be wrong? Have you been drawn in to an area of sin innocently, only to linger long enough that later you felt further enticed to explore that area of sin in more depth? Where did it lead you?

For the men reading this, they can relate, because they are visual creatures and know what happens when they look at an image of sin. Our enemy is not just content with us looking at the image; S.I.N. wants us to act on that image in our flesh, which will result in separation from the very Spirit that has authority over S.I.N.

> And you know that He was manifested to take away our sins, and in Him there is no sin. (I John 3:5)

Jesus, being fully human, was tempted in all areas just as we have been tempted, but He did not sin, because there was no sin in Him. When did this temptation occur? Right after John the Baptist baptized Him in the

Jordan. The temptation of Christ is found in the Gospel accounts of Matthew and Luke (we will be looking at Matthew's account.)

In the first verse, we find, interestingly enough, that Jesus was led into the wilderness by the Holy Spirit, the same Spirit that protects and empowers us to rule over our flesh today.

> Then Jesus was led up by the Spirit into the wilderness to be tempted by the devil. (Matthew 4:1)

God knew that it is only through experience that one can truly understand what happens to man and woman when sin comes knocking on the door of their hearts. For this reason, He led Himself into the wilderness so that He could understand what it was like to be tempted in the flesh.

Now let's face it, God being the Creator of the universe had an advantage over Satan. In order to level the playing ground and make it more interesting, He denied Himself food for 40 days and nights.

Have you ever fasted from food? Try it sometime and see how your body and mind react. You will find that in your physically weakened state, your spiritual awareness will become heightened. Why do you think this is the case? God's grace carries us in our times of physical weakness by strengthening us in spirit.

God employed this concept as Jesus emerged from the wilderness. Satan correctly assumed that Jesus was at His weakest point, not having eaten in 40 days. What Satan did not factor in was the fact that Jesus, being one with God, had to totally rely on His spiritual nature. Which meant He was at His strongest point spiritually!

Paul came to this conclusion in second Corinthians, and the same holds true for us today that when our flesh is weak, our spirit is also strong.

> And He said to me, "My grace is sufficient for you, for My strength is made perfect in weakness." Therefore most gladly I will rather boast in my infirmities, that the power of Christ may rest upon me. Therefore I take pleasure in infirmities, in reproaches, in needs, in persecutions, in distresses, for Christ's sake. For when I am weak, then I am strong.
> (2 Corinthians 12: 9-10)

Jesus was going to need all the spiritual strength He could muster in fending off the enemy's attacks at the end of the 40-day period. Satan first tempts Jesus through his stomach, knowing he had to be hungry by this time.

> And when He had fasted forty days and forty nights, afterward He was hungry. (Matthew 4:2)

The enemy will always bring a temptation in the area where we are weak, but His intention goes deeper, as we learn in this scripture. His real intention in this first temptation was to trick Jesus into proving His authority.

> Now when the tempter came to Him, he said, "If You are the Son of God, command that these stones become bread." (Matthew 4:3)

Of course, Jesus is not moved by Satan's attacks and doesn't skip a beat when He responds.

> It is written, "Man shall not live by bread alone, but by every word that proceeds from the mouth of God." (Matthew 4:4)

The only way to thwart the enemy's attacks is through scripture. The Word is alive, and when spoken, brings us strength to overcome the obstacles that temptation tries to get us to stumble over. Satan was just getting wound up and in no way was ready to give up. So once again he tries to trick Jesus into defending who He was by tempting Him with angelic power by distorting God's Word.

> Then the devil took Him up into the holy city, set Him on the pinnacle of the temple, and said to Him, "If You are the Son of God, throw Yourself down. For it is written: 'He shall give His angels charge over you,' and, 'In their hands they shall bear you up, Lest you dash your foot against a stone.'"
> (Matthew 4:5-6)

One thing Jesus knew was the Word of God, and He did not hesitate when responding to the enemy's lie.

> It is written again, "You shall not tempt the LORD your God." (Matthew 4:7)

Satan, obviously frustrated at this point, makes one final attempt to lure Jesus into his clutches by attempting to get Jesus to worship him instead of God.

> Again, the devil took Him up on an exceedingly high mountain, and showed Him all the kingdoms of the world and their glory. And he said to Him, "All these things I will give You if You will fall down and worship me." (Matthew 4:8-9)

Jesus didn't dare fall to this temptation, because he knew all too well that He already owned everything through creation. Satan's rein and Christ's dominion are two totally separate things. Satan's reign is temporary and he only has it because God cast him out of heaven to earth. Christ's, however, is eternal. God granted Him all authority, and thus His dominion supersedes the earthly realm. Satan had no choice but to flee at the command of Jesus.

> Away with you, Satan! For it is written, "You shall worship the LORD your God, and Him only you shall serve." Then the devil left Him, and behold, angels came and ministered to Him. (Matthew 4:10-11)

Temptation is a strong and effective play in Satan's arsenal, and our defense against it needs to be strong as well. We must stay alert to his schemes so when the day comes that he runs that play of temptation, we are spiritually on guard. The Apostles learned this lesson the hard way in the garden of Gethsemane.

> Then He came to the disciples and found them sleeping, and said to Peter, "What! Could you not watch with Me one hour? Watch and pray, lest you enter into temptation. The spirit indeed is willing, but the flesh is weak." (Matthew 26:40-41)

The enemy has been using this play effectively for over 2,000 years. He is continuing to use it effectively on us today to keep us from our eternal destiny. We can give into temptation, or we can avoid temptation. The choice is ours because of the free will granted by our Creator. The Lord desires that we would rule over temptation, letting us know that when we do we are blessed, and by doing so will receive His crown of life.

> Blessed is the man who endures temptation; for when he has been approved, he will receive the crown of life which the Lord has promised to those who love Him. (James 1:12)

2. Accusation

The enemy's second play is accusation and is usually carried out in a more emotional way, by attacking our character. When Satan accuses you of something, he will do so by mixing just enough truth in with the lie in order for the outcome to be put in question. When Satan brings an accusation birthed out of deceitful intentions, it is an extremely dangerous play. Especially when left to another person's perception.

> Now Jesus stood before the governor. And the governor asked Him, saying, "Are You the King of the Jews?" Jesus said to him, "It is as you say." And while He was being accused by the chief priests and elders, He answered nothing. Then Pilate said to Him, "Do You not hear how many things they testify against You?" But He answered him not one word, so that the governor marveled greatly. (Matthew 27:11-14)

In Matthew Jesus was accused by the chief priests and elders of being the King of the Jews. Jesus knew better than to mount a defense. The truth, Jesus was a King, but not in the secular realm they were implying. Satan's play of accusation always attempts to get us to buy into his lie, because there appears to be a hint of truth in what he is saying. How did Jesus react? Jesus didn't feel the need to defend himself or argue with Pilate, but remained silent. Jesus knew who He was and also understood that the only one He was accountable to was God.

When anyone brings a false accusation against you, do not defend the accusation. The enemy doesn't care about right and wrong, he just wants you to engage him. For that reason, you do not want to defend yourself. In fact, you want to do just the opposite: remain silent and calm. S.I.N. is interested in stirring us up through the confusion birthed out of the accusation. This divides us and gets us to question one another and, quite possibly, ourselves. If we are truly innocent, God will mount a defense on our behalf. God knows your heart.

I was caught in a situation at my church where one of our women (a good friend and someone I had known for several years) falsely accused me of asking her an inappropriate question. She had been dating a man who was new at our church. One Sunday while sitting in the main sanctuary, he had her trapped in one of the chairs and raised his voice in anger. One of the men came and got me, saying she was in trouble, and she had been looking for me. I knew this man because he had attended a men's group I was co-leading, so I walked up and casually asked if I could speak to him in private.

There was another member of our men's group standing close by, so the three of us went into another area of the church and had a private conversation. I asked him what his intentions were with our sister in Christ. He related how much he cared for her, but felt he was losing her. I went on to tell him that the very thing he feared was coming to pass, that she was scared of him, and given her history, the only thing she knew to do was to pull back. I suggested he look at her as a sister, not a potential mate, treat her with the utmost respect, and honor her wishes to pull back. I went on to suggest that he humbly apologize without getting into a debate of right and wrong and let her go. The Lord willing, she could have a change of heart and he might have another opportunity to move forward with the relationship. He agreed, confessed that his behavior was inappropriate, and we ended the meeting.

After the service the woman asked me what had happened. Not wanting anyone to overhear, I asked if we could step into our prayer room. I related to her everything as it had happened and she indicated her relief. I then asked her, "Are you doing anything inappropriate with him?" She responded by saying yes. I merely cautioned her by saying, "I will tell you the same thing I tell the men in my group. The only way to honor God in a relationship is to abstain from physical contact. In turn God will protect you from making the wrong choice with respect to a mate."

Our conversation lasted all of two minutes, and we left the room. About 10 minutes later, I felt a tug on my arm and one of the elders in our church, who was obviously upset. He asked if I would follow him, saying, "The pastor and I need to talk to you."

He ushered me into the pastor's office and started accusing me of asking a woman in our church if she had engaged in sexual intercourse with another member. Then went on to say that, she had also told him that I was romantically interested in her. Needless to say I was flabbergasted, spellbound, and could not speak. He continued with his accusations, saying that I had no right to question a member of the opposite sex in this fashion.

Finally, I lashed out by saying, "I did no such thing and where is the person making this accusation? I don't see her sitting in this room." With that, I rose and said, "This meeting is over." To which the elder responded, "Why don't you just sit down, shut up, and listen for a change?" I looked at him coldly, got really quiet, and sat down. The pastor then responded by saying, "We can't resolve this now; I need to deliver the message, we will talk later."

I had been falsely accused and felt about as betrayed as one could feel. The enemy had won a temporary victory by effectively running the play of accusation against me. My first response had been to angrily defend. My second response was to pull away and flee.

Whenever we allow ourselves to be stirred to the point of anger and defend an accusation, our accusers will think that there must be some element of truth, otherwise why would we react in such a way? There just has to be a little bit of the truth mixed into the lying equation for the accusation to stick. Then there is a lot of back-peddling that our natural man feels is necessary to offset the lie.

In my case, I had asked her about being physical, but in no way implied that being physical meant sexual intercourse. When we are insecure with ourselves, our faith is weak, we are caught off guard, and the enemy scores a victory. When Jesus was accused by the chief priests and elders, He remained calm. He wasn't moved by Satan's lies, "He answered nothing." I could have easily done the same thing in the story I just related.

What if I had remained calm, listened to all their accusations, and when they were all played out said, "Really, bring her in and let's work this out." Had I not taken offense by letting my anger rule my emotions, had I not engaged the enemy's accusations, I could have further covered my sister in Christ. I could have saved us all a lot of grief.

You see, S.I.N. doesn't care about the right or wrong of an issue, it only cares about keeping us stirred up until eventually we want to pull away and divide. Once we flee, the enemy has accomplished what the play had originally been designed to do, bring division. We, in essence, self-destruct. But if we will press in, letting go of our natural tendency to defend, and instead apply our learned response, we have a much better chance of dispelling the accusation and letting God expose the truth.

Eventually I was exonerated; my sister in Christ, pastor, and the elder all apologized. God will allow accusations in life, fully knowing in the end we will be "perfect and complete, lacking nothing" when we enter His heavenly realm.

> And you shall know the truth, and the truth shall make you free. (John 8:32)

My brethren, count it all joy when you fall into various trials, knowing that the testing of your faith produces patience. But let patience have its perfect work, that you may be perfect and complete, lacking nothing. (James 1:2-4)

3. Deception

The third play the enemy deploys is deception, which is usually carried out in the form of a spiritual attack. Deception is probably one of the most ruthless weapons in Satan's arsenal. Satan will allow the truth to be told, but will inject a small enough lie so that the truth will be under suspicion. Thus, if we engage in his deceptiveness, we in essence are walking right into his trap and will start to doubt and question the truth.

For example, let us say you have known a person all your life and he is your best friend. In all the years you have known him, there has never been a time where he lost his temper or in any way retaliated against another person's attacks. However, one day you enter his house and hear what sounds like a gunshot. You enter a room and see your best friend holding a gun with a hint of smoke coming out of the barrel, straddling a dead body, blood oozing from a wound to the head.

As you take in this scene, you notice that a door leading outside is standing wide open. What would be your first impression? That your friend shot the man? That the perpetrator fled from the scene?

Let's assume that your friend is innocent. He came into the room, saw the man on the floor with a gun at his side, and was completely stunned. In disbelief, mesmerized by the atrocity that had been committed, he picked up the gun, and stood over him. Would you believe him? No matter how well you knew your friend, there is enough visual evidence to cause you to doubt his innocence. Your friend obviously is going to care about your perception and will do everything in his power to convince you of his innocence. If not, he runs the risk of being arrested and possibly indicted for murder. If it goes to trial and he is found guilty, he will most likely be sentenced to either life in prison or the death penalty. I would say that he would have a vested interest in not only declaring his innocence, but also defending his innocence.

This is an extreme example of how deceived we can be by the schemes of the enemy. The deceptive emanation from your visual image is tainted just enough to cause you to doubt and question his innocence. I repeat: the enemy wants to engage us in his play of deception in order for those around us to doubt and separate from us.

In the temptation of Christ, we read in Matthew 4:9 that Satan used his play of deception on Christ by saying, "All these things I will give You if You will fall down and worship me." You might ask, "Why is this play deception?" Satan was basing it on a truth: Adam forfeited dominion over the earth, so from Satan's perspective, it was his to give.

However, Jesus already owned everything, thus the deceptive lie within his statement. We showed in John 1:1 that He and God are one. Jesus was right there at the beginning of all creation. Satan used this in an attempt to trick Jesus into bowing to his authority, "worship me." It was Satan's intention to get Jesus to doubt the truth and turn away from God, in essence trying to get Jesus to negate His purpose of providing eternal salvation to all.

Deception can be very subtle and to the general public may not even look like deception at all. How many times in your life has this play been run on you? Paul spoke about the deceptiveness of Satan. In other words, don't trade your destiny for sin, because sin is very deceptive.

> But I fear, lest somehow, as the serpent deceived Eve by his craftiness, so your minds may be corrupted from the simplicity that is in Christ. (2 Corinthians 11:3)

> Beware, brethren, lest there be in any of you an evil heart of unbelief in departing from the living God; but exhort one another daily, while it is called "Today," lest any of you be hardened through the deceitfulness of sin. For we have become partakers of Christ if we hold the beginning of our confidence steadfast to the end. (Hebrews 3:12-14)

Let us return to the Garden of Eden, to the first place where we have factual written evidence of Satan using his primary weapons. Imagine for a moment it is all a game, and the game is being played in an arena called Eden. This arena was climate controlled and the field manicured better than any you have ever seen. It was a perfect and ideal setting. Surely not the type of place where you would envision some evil force to be playing. Of course, it is even more difficult when you are ignorant that evil even exists. However, we know today based on our own experience that there were two teams competing that day: good and evil.

On good's team there was Adam and Eve, and on evil's team there was the serpent. Earlier in this book, we read the account in Genesis 3 where the serpent sets up his offense, ready to run his plays. He runs his first play on Eve by getting her to engage in conversation by asking a question that later will cause her to doubt God's command and entice her to give into temptation. "Has God indeed said, 'You shall not eat of every tree of the garden'?" Eve innocently responds, "We may eat the fruit of the trees of the garden; but of the fruit of the tree which is in the midst of the garden, God has said, 'You shall not eat it, nor shall you touch it, lest you die.'"

The serpent knew that Eve had received instruction from Adam. Thus, his play proves effective when she misquotes God's command, "but of the tree of the knowledge of good and evil you shall not eat, for in the day that you eat of it you shall surely die." So the serpent proceeds to run his plays.

First he uses deception, "You will not surely die." Secondly he accusses God of withholding knowledge, the ultimate accusation, "For God knows that in the day you eat of it your eyes will be opened, and you will be like God, knowing good and evil." Now he has Eve's full attention, and we find that her curiosity had been aroused, "So when the woman saw that the tree was good for food, that it was pleasant to the eyes, and a tree desirable to make one wise." Satan's plays have broken through her line of defense. Now it was fourth down and Eve has an opportunity to hold the line, but what does she do? She gives into temptation and by doing so violates Adam's directive of God's command. "She took of its fruit and ate. She also gave to her husband with her, and he ate."

As a result, here you and I are thousands of years later still facing the same plays. Satan's plays haven't changed, and our defense, like Adam and Eve's, hasn't changed much either. What is the ultimate reality of sin? It exposes us to its evil by getting us to question what we know in our heart to be true, ultimately separating us from that truth. Which is the very foundation of our relationship with God. Sin opened Adam and Eve's eyes to a completely new spiritual dimension and thus brought about separation from God.

> Then the eyes of both of them were opened, and they knew that they were naked; and they sewed fig leaves together and made themselves coverings. And they heard the sound of the LORD God walking in the garden in the cool of the day, and Adam and his wife hid themselves from the presence of the LORD God among the trees of the garden. (Genesis 3:7-8)

The best defense is always a good offense. We need to study God's Word so we will be able to speak it at the appropriate time. Thus, guard against engaging the enemy in his game or defending our actions in hopes that others won't see us through Satan's lies. He has been running these plays since the beginning of time. The only defense we have is in our response. We can only respond correctly if we hold fast to our belief in the living God through His living Word. If we allow our sin nature to react, he will gain a lot of yardage on us. But if we will stand strong—we stop Satan dead in his evil tracks!

The Armor of God

In the game of football, in order to protect a player's body from the attacks of the opposing team, one dons a uniform. The uniform is specifically designed to protect every area of the player's physical body.

In the spiritual game of life, it would make sense to don the armor of God as we prepare our defense in order to spiritually protect every aspect of our being. God's armor is strong and protects us against the many options Satan runs from his three main plays. By putting on the whole armor of God, we gain an understanding and a peace that makes us less vulnerable to the enemy: the principalities, powers, rulers of the darkness, and the spiritual hosts of wickedness.

> Finally, my brethren, be strong in the Lord and in the power of His might. Put on the whole armor of God that you may be able to stand against the wiles of the devil. For we do not wrestle against flesh and blood, but against principalities, against powers, against the rulers of the darkness of this age, against spiritual hosts of wickedness in the heavenly places. Therefore take up the whole armor of God, that you may be able to withstand in the evil day, and having done all, to stand. (Ephesians 6:10-13)

In football, the shoulder pads protect the upper torso. The helmet protects the head. Hip, thigh, and knee pads protect the lower areas. Shoes with cleats provide traction on the field. Our spiritual armor is much the same, the difference being that this armor protects us spiritually from the pounding the enemy will inflict in the game of life. Once the armor is in place, we are called to stand in confidence that the Lord is with us and will protect us.

> Stand therefore, having girded your waist with truth, having put on the breastplate of righteousness, and having shod your feet with the preparation of the gospel of peace; above all,

> taking the shield of faith with which you will be able to quench all the fiery darts of the wicked one. And take the helmet of salvation, and the sword of the Spirit, which is the word of God. (Ephesians 6:14-17)

First, we gird our waist with the truth. Meaning that we must speak the truth at all times. Second we are called to put on the breastplate of righteousness. Meaning we are to cover our hearts from the influences of the world that intend to take us out of a right standing with God. Third, we shod our feet with the preparation of the gospel of peace. Meaning that we consciously acknowledge God's peace as we walk along the paths of life. Fourth, we grasp the shield of faith that enables us to ward off all the attacks the enemy throws at us. Fifth, we put on the helmet of salvation with full assurance of our eternal destiny. Sixth, we take up the sword of the Spirit, which is the Word of God. By taking the sword of God, the Word, we are able to keep our perspective, as we stand fully-equipped for the battle.

However, there are two very important aspects to understand about wearing the spiritual armor of God: we must pray always and remain watchful with perseverance.

> Praying always with all prayer and supplication in the Spirit,
> being watchful to this end with all perseverance
> and supplication for all the saints. (Ephesians 6:18)

When you grasp this biblical concept, the difference is this: when the attacks come, they only lead you deeper into more of a righteous relationship with the Father. Rather than run with the herd, we are called to do the opposite of what society teaches, push instead of pull.

We embrace our persecutions and see them as evidence of the Holy Spirit working within our heart. We grow in our Christian faith, knowing that we are moving in the right direction and are on the right path. In God's kingdom, you shouldn't be surprised to find that His ways are not your ways.

> For My thoughts are not your thoughts, Nor are your ways
> My ways, says the LORD. (Isaiah 55:8)

Look back on your life and see if you can identify how the enemy has attacked you with his three primary plays/weapons. See how, in doing so, he has kept you either from the knowledge of your purpose or has kept you from executing your God-given purpose. As you look back, God will begin to show you how you have been used in the lives of those around you. You will get a glimmer of how He has been using you all along in spite of your sinful nature. He has used you according to your purpose, whether you knew what it was or not. Satan actually defeats himself when he tries to attack us.

I remember a time when the Lord showed me pointedly how the enemy was trying to negate my purpose by attacking me with his weapons. I received a letter from a very embittered person. His intention was to draw me into a fight by belittling my character, accusing me of being a failure, and then offering a deceptive defense of his own actions, as if I had a limited memory of the actual events and circumstances. When I finished reading the letter, the Lord revealed to me that it contained all three of the enemy's primary attacks: temptation, accusation, and deception.

Being covered with the armor of God, I was protected from these attacks. When I was tempted to defend my honor, I didn't respond. In essence, I held up my shield of faith and warded off the attacks by not engaging. Instead, I evaluated every aspect of what had been stated to make sure that I could stand before God and offer a defense if necessary. After all, God knew the truth and my heart. Ultimately, He is the only one to whom I would have to offer up a defense. In essence, I strapped on the breastplate of righteousness and protected my heart from being tainted with the enemy's lies.

Furthermore, since God is for me and not against me, there was no reason for me to respond to Satan's attack. I had my feet shod with the Lord's peace and my loins girded with His truth. In so doing, kept my spiritual helmet in place, my salvation secure with the Lord. I lifted not the sword of engagement, but the sword of understanding that comes from God's Word. I gained revelation that it was the enemy (S.I.N.) attacking through a confessed brother in Christ, another one of God's children.

The enemy attacks us through other people, sometimes through our own family, friends, and even the church. He attacks through our circumstances and life's struggles. We have a natural inherent tendency to defend ourselves and thus engage the enemy. Just as we learned in the self-defense example, our natural response and our learned response are not always the same. In this case, the Lord wanted me to lay down my weapon of defense. He wanted me to trust Him. In fact, He wanted me to immediately forgive this person.

But, why would I want to do that? These words stung at my inner core. Who was this person to offend me? Didn't I have a right to defend my honor? Did the Lord really want me to turn the other cheek?

When someone attacks you with any or all of these three weapons, what is really happening? S.I.N. is lingering at your doorstep, and its desire is for you. His intention is to lure you into his trap, the trap of engagement. He does not care about resolving the issues in your life. He only cares about keeping you stirred up, stirred to the point where you start to doubt yourself. He wants you to embrace the lies meant to separate you from other christians.

> You are of your father the devil, and the desires of your father you want to do. He was a murderer from the beginning, and does not stand in the truth, because there is no truth in him. When he speaks a lie, he speaks from his own resources, for he is a liar and the father of it. (John 8:44)

There is an old question, "Why do we hurt the ones we love?" Of course, in the letter I received, if you asked the person who wrote the letter, "Don't you love him?" Your answer would probably be a resounding, "No!" However, Jesus Christ instructs us that love will cover a multitude of sins. He told us to lay down our offense, go to our brother, and make amends. He does not qualify his counsel by saying if you are the offended or the offender then wait for an apology.

Jesus wants us to know that either way, our struggle is not with one another. Our struggle is with a spiritual entity that has one purpose, and one purpose only, and that is to take us with him into eternal damnation. He attacks our core in an attempt to destroy us foundationally—to destroy our faith so that we will give up all hope.

However, by keeping our spiritual armor firmly in place, we avoid our natural urge to engage. Instead we are called to invite the Lord into the situation and allow Him to fight the battle for us.

> You will not need to fight in this battle. Position yourselves, stand still and see the salvation of the LORD, who is with you, O Judah and Jerusalem! Do not fear or be dismayed; tomorrow go out against them, for the LORD is with you.
> (2 Chronicles 20:17)

When we grasp this spiritual reality and place it over us, as the armor in Ephesians 6, there is a power in the unseen that none of us can quantify in the physical. If the enemy attacks us through anything or anybody, they run the risk of facing the Lord's vengeance. Do you not know it is a fearful thing to fall into the hands of the living God?

> Beloved, do not avenge yourselves, but rather give place to wrath; for it is written, "Vengeance is Mine, I will repay," says the Lord. (Romans 12:19)

> It is a fearful thing to fall into the hands of the living God. (Hebrews 10:31)

Playing life—isn't that what we are supposed to do? God desires that you know the purpose for which He created you. However, the sin within your heart (which was birthed as a result of man's fall), knows you were created with a godly purpose and wants to do everything in its power to keep it from you. Satan will try to attack you on several fronts to keep you from fulfilling that purpose or coming to the revelation of the God-ordained purpose which He placed in your heart.

Are you willing to stop and reevaluate your life? Are you running with the herd? Where is the herd leading you? Are you following God's will and direction for your life? Are you interpreting scripture and unknowingly justifying a sinful nature? Are you pulling away when you should be pushing in? Are you under the attack of temptation, accusation or deception? Have you put on your spiritual armor today?

Isn't it about time we got in the game with the proper perspective, that we take a stand in the spiritual battle and grasp the revelation that God is on our side? Isn't it time we don't defend against or engage an enemy who has no intention of resolution and does not care about right or wrong?

> Now see that I, even I, am He, And there is no God besides Me; I kill and I make alive; I wound and I heal; Nor is there any who can deliver from My hand. (Deuteronomy 32:39)

Chapter VI

Climactic Deliverance

Remember the TV series *Star Trek?* One of the things that fascinated me about the series was the transporter rooms that converted an object or character to energy, sent them to a particular destination, and then reconstituted their energy back into matter. Many of us can still remember Captain Kirk saying, "Beam me up, Scotty." Supernaturally Kirk would be transported to another planet, time zone or whatever was written into the script for that particular episode.

Did this ability to be transported get your attention? Did it stir your curiosity? Wouldn't we all like to have the ability to be transported? Wouldn't you love to be able to remove yourself from negative situations, deliver yourself from pain and suffering, free yourself from the sin that surrounds you and, in doing so, instantly transform your life?

We all have a curious nature and if honest, would love to entertain that kind of supernatural power. Earlier in the book, we explored the events in the garden by looking at Adam and Eve. We learned that Eve was created from Adam, and their curious natures allowed the enemy to deceive them both into thinking that they could instantly have something more—they could be like God.

Today, our curious natures are still leading us astray. You have probably heard the expression, "Curiosity killed the cat." Just like Adam and Eve, our curious natures have us seeking similar experiences, ones that would propel us beyond our current circumstances and deliver us from our afflictions. S.I.N. has been there since the beginning to tap into our God-given curious nature. Desiring for us to have a distorted view of true spiritual deliverance in order to keep us in bondage to our sin.

We have unavoidably become products of the generations that have lived before us. We have developed into a society that seeks quick fixes and has bought into the law of entitlement. We want it now. We think we deserve it now. Rather than discipline ourselves to work hard and work smart, we have come to expect certain luxuries.

If we don't have those luxuries, society leaves us with the feeling that somehow we are not as good or that we have failed. At times, we too judge other people by thinking somehow they are not as good or somehow they have failed because they don't have the toys we have. That way of thinking is based on S.I.N.'s deceptive lie.

Even though there is an element of comfort stemming from our material possessions, when we lose our spiritual perspective—all that seems good is really leading us down a destructive path toward death.

Deliverance is available to us all, but it is not a quick fix to our problems. Instead, we must build strong foundations in life. In order for deliverance to be effective long-term, it takes time and discipline on our part.

My purpose here is to show you the reality of how easily Satan has influenced our society. How he has led us into thinking we can be instantly delivered from our burdens without any discipline on our part. God on the other hand wants us to experience *Climactic Deliverance*; deliverance from sin for all eternity.

Quick Fix

Examine your life and ask yourself, "What kind of deliverance am I seeking in life? Do I want something that is long-term that will lead to deliverance for all eternity, or do I want something that is a quick fix that will last only until I die?" Satan's desire is to distort the concept of climactic deliverance by creating a smoke screen so we can't see the true reality behind the concept of deliverance.

Does your state have a lottery? I live in Texas. When the lottery began, we were told the proceeds would go to our education system. Yes, millions would be funneled to our schools, offsetting our limited state budget and directly affecting our children in a positive way. Of course, over time people started asking, "What are they really doing with the proceeds of the lottery?" One must wonder why they had to ask that question. Shouldn't it have been obvious by the change seen in the school system?

To my knowledge, not one of our politicians to date has dared to answer that question. Why? Because there wasn't any magic being performed in or on our schools. In fact, they passed a law called "Robin Hood" which required wealthy school districts to support poorer school districts. Very interesting and very suspect, don't you think?

In essence, they had created a smoke screen, luring us into participating in the lottery. Have you ever bought a lottery ticket? Oh come on, one lottery ticket? If not, I applaud you. Many people buy lottery tickets because they desire to be delivered from their financial burdens or to experience a windfall, hoping to make their life easier.

Out of ignorance, many of us desire a quick fix in life and, without realizing it, are buying into S.I.N.'s deceptive lie. It echoes, "You deserve to be better off in life and after all the proceeds are going to help our schools." It doesn't matter what your social status is, because the curious nature in all men says, "I want more, I need more, and I deserve more."

Yes, we play right into S.I.N.'s hand when we start thinking thoughts like, "If I had more money, I could live a better life, and be happier. I could take care of my family without any worry. I could take care of my kids without any concern. I could send my kids to college with everything they need. I could prepare for retirement and live anywhere I wanted. I could buy that second home I always wanted. I could have this toy or that toy."

Most of us have heard the old saying, "Money won't make you happy, but it sure will let you live more comfortably while being miserable." The sad reality is many people spend much of their disposable income chasing dreams, hoping to win that elusive jackpot in life. They play the lottery, play the option market, gamble and entertain multi-level marketing schemes, or other games of chance.

Trust me, the odds are not in your favor! Just take some time to study the people who have won some of those elusive jackpots. Listen to their stories and you might be a little surprised at what you find out about the effect on their lives. In essence, we unknowingly have bought into the deceptive societal lie that says, "Money will make life better, easier and bring peace, joy, and happiness." In reality, it can and will bring destruction when gained hastily—when money is just given to us without being earned. Without the shedding of our blood, sweat and tears, it just doesn't have the same ownership appeal as it does when we have earned it.

> An inheritance gained hastily at the beginning Will not be blessed at the end. (Proverbs 20:21)

We squander away our hard earned living buying a ticket that holds a remote chance of winning a fortune. Many justify their purchase, thinking, "If I don't buy a ticket, how can I win? After all, someone is going to win." Even some Christians say, "If I don't buy a ticket, how can the Lord bless me as the winner?"

Does that mean that everyone that wins something or receives a gift necessarily squanders it or brings destruction upon himself or herself? No, because some of us are responsible and already have the proper spiritual perspective in life. But don't be deceived. There is always a story or testimony that the enemy will inject with the intention to contradict scripture, so we begin to doubt and remain in bondage. The lottery is just one tool the enemy has been able to use by appealing to our inherent curious natures in order to manipulate us into a quick-fix mentality.

The next time you pull up to an intersection in your city, look around. What do you see? You see cars worth thousands of dollars being driven by every age group. Drive through most neighborhoods in your city and what do you see? Homes are being torn down to make room for bigger homes. I would say bigger and better, but that is not always the case. Many of those homes being rebuilt don't have the architectural quality or uniqueness of the original homes.

You might be thinking, "There are many areas that need to be revitalized and updated." To which I would respond, that is a true, valid, and a very responsible thought. Of course, there needs to be progress, progress that is based on a long-range plan to improve the community; a plan that is well thought out and where funding has been secured. This sort of progress is prudent.

However, we have slowly been enticed by our selfish desires into thinking we need bigger and better places to live, bigger and better cars to drive, and that somehow we deserve a better lifestyle. Without paying much of a price to get it. The temptation of fortune has always been enticing and the arguments used to sell us are the same. We have allowed this way of thinking to dominate and cloud our sensibility.

Let me give an example of how good people that are successful and well-meaning can be deceived. I knew a young man who was dating a girl in high school who had wonderful parents. They had started a business in their garage and built it into a multi-million dollar venture. When the girl turned 16, her daddy bought her a brand-new BMW SUV, but she wasn't content with it and voiced her displeasure to him. How did the father respond? He simply traded it in for a brand new BMW coupe. After all, they could afford it.

I cite this example to show how easily we have become deceived into thinking bigger is better. How we are fueling the engine called laziness and complacency, which drives our desire toward quick fixes for the problems of life. Fortunately, at the time, I was able to use this example as an opportunity to share a principle with the young man. I asked him, "If you were to marry her, how would you be able to compete with daddy's affection for her heart?" I told him that out of ignorance, this well-meaning father was spoiling his little girl.

I ask you reading this, how many fathers out there, if they had the wherewithal, would not do the same? Our little girls are precious, are they not? Aren't they all princesses and deserve to be taken care of? Most definitely. I will be first to stand in line and defend that argument. This should be every father's intention toward his daughter. Men everywhere should take up their rightful place in the family and learn to treat their daughters with love and respect. But this doesn't mean that we lavish our daughters with expensive gifts and subliminally give the impression that this is a normal way of life.

This father was a good man, but ignorant to the fact that he was setting his daughter up for unrealistic expectations in life. She will most likely grow up comparing her husband to her daddy, and most likely she will expect him to match—if not exceed—her daddy's giving ability. If her husband fails in doing so, will she have the same respect for him as she does her daddy?

Satan was at work in this father's heart, and he didn't even know it. Are you beginning to see how we can be deceived in even the most well-meaning of situations? S.I.N. will always distort our good intentions when we are ignorant to its schemes. One can only hope that this father educated his daughter, preparing her for that fateful day he has to let her go, and entrust her care to another man. Hopefully, he taught her that enduring tough times with her husband, standing by his side at all costs, would help to build a foundation. The type of foundation that later in life will sustain their marriage and bond them closer together.

I spoke to another father that was visibly shaken and angry with his in-laws. Why? They had bought his son a Chevy Tahoe without his consent. They justified their decision by saying they had the money, and he had a need. Out of ignorance, they thought, "What is the harm? Shouldn't we all long to give our children a better life?" Of course, but not at the expense of educating them on the evils associated with our issues being solved by the desired climactic quick-fixes. When we lavish gifts on our children without the proper education, we can't always be sure what the ultimate outcome will be.

To the daughter, we must communicate that the father will always be there for her and will always be there to take care of her. But this father is God, not her daddy. Therefore, in marriage she will look to God for the ultimate supply and will encourage her husband in his efforts to be a conduit for their supply.

When girls are not instructed properly in the love of the father, they most often grow up spending their adult years trying to find a replacement for their father. Unfortunately they do so in their relationships with the opposite sex. Girls long for a loving father and when they have experienced that love, they grow up with a sense of belonging and wholeness.

To the young man, we need to teach that you gain ownership when you put some of your sweat, blood, and tears into the acquisition of a material possession. Young men who have been properly instructed and grow up knowing the value of hard work will experience a sense of accomplishment and self respect.

Aren't most of our young adults today responsible? Aren't they helping around the house, going to school to better themselves, participating in extracurricular activities to build solid resumes, and holding side jobs to help pay the family expenses?

Of course, most of you will be thinking, "Are there really kids like that in our society?" Let's face the facts: this is the exception, not the rule. Overall, there hasn't been a generation on the planet that could claim to be that responsible. For generations, children have been curious by nature and, given the chance, they would much prefer the climax of having what they want now instead of working hard and seeing the value of earning it later.

Our kids today are no different. In fact, they expect their parents to write the check as if to say, "You have an obligation as my parent to support me, so give it to me now!"

Surely, you have heard of or read in scripture about the prodigal son. The full story is found belowin Luke 15:11-31, where we find that the son squanders his inheritance and ends up homeless and hungry. He remembers that his father's servants are better off, so he makes the decision to return. But no longer being worthy to be called a son, repents and pleads with his father to take him back and count him as a servant. Of course, the father sees him from afar, runs to him, bestows his forgiveness, clothes him with a robe, ring and sandals, and kills the fatted calf to celebrate his return.

> Then He said: "A certain man had two sons. And the younger of them said to his father, 'Father, give me the portion of goods that falls to me.' So he divided to them his livelihood. And not

many days after, the younger son gathered all together, journeyed to a far country, and there wasted his possessions with prodigal living." (Luke 15:11-13)

Prodigal Defined - Given to extravagant expenditure; expending money or other things without necessity; recklessly or viciously profuse; lavish; wasteful; not frugal or economical. (8)

The youngest son desired a quick fix for a dull and uneventful lifestyle. He knew his father was wealthy and obviously had been told that one day, half of everything his dad owned would be his. There was a stirring in the young man's heart and a curiosity longing to be satisfied. He wanted his inheritance now. He was going to get it one day anyway and who knew when that would be. His father could have lived to a ripe old age, and then what? Life might pass him by, and he would have missed the adventure of a lifetime. In his eyes, it seemed wise to take it now. After all, he could handle it. And obviously, he knew what he was doing, so why should anyone question or counsel him?

In fact, we don't read that the father argued, pleaded or even tried to stop him. It seems he freely conceded, by dividing his inheritance and sending him on his way. The father, being a wealthy man, had probably educated his son. So it makes sense that the son had acquired knowledge of this far away land, and as a result of that knowledge, was enticed by the seeming pleasures offered therein. In his limited worldview, it made perfect sense to take his inheritance early, risk the protection and covering of his family, and set out to experience the excitement of a foreign land—satisfying his sense of adventure. Our enemy, S.I.N., will always tempt us into thinking we are missing out; that there is something better, more exciting, awaiting us.

Sometimes in S.I.N.'s deceptive magnetism, we are drawn away from the spiritual protection and covering that our families provide. In the case of the prodigal son, he was not only drawn away from his father's house, he also squandered his inheritance.

We might read this story and think, "How could he have been so stupid? If I had that inheritance, just think of what I could do with it!" Let's face it, we all long for something more, and if we had the opportunity to receive a large inheritance, we might very well find ourselves closely associated with the prodigal son. Many of us would be content not to toil our lives away earning a living and seemingly wasting precious time that could be spent exploring foreign lands. Given the choice, we might too say, "Give me mine now."

The story doesn't relate the dialogue between the father and son, but one could assume the son was prepared to argue and justify his thinking, just in case his father objected. Some of those arguments and justifications might be the same ones we use today to deceive ourselves into thinking we should have ours now.

How many of us have longed for that item or vacation that is really too expensive for our budget? Have you ever used any of the following lines to justify spending money on something you knew in your heart was really going to satisfy a lustful desire?

> "I deserve it. After all, I've been working hard."
> "I might miss this great opportunity."
> "Life is passing me by, everyone else is doing it."
> "It would be fun, and I haven't had much fun lately."

These could very well be some of the arguments the son was prepared to give his father, if necessary. Yes, like the prodigal son, we have bought into the lie that having stuff (or whatever the enticement) will somehow make life better, more joyous or more fulfilling. This is a quick-fix mentality that can easily draw us into a similar quandary, especially when we have limited life experiences.

I remember getting a phone call from a young man telling me he was receiving a large bonus from his new company. He went on to tell me how he was going to ask them to give it to him in cash so he could avoid paying taxes on the money. In his vast experience and knowledge of life, he had come to the intelligent conclusion that by doing so he would be better off. It made perfect sense in the natural, but he gave no thought to the legal and spiritual ramifications had he followed through with his plan.

Immediately upon hearing his plan my heart ached, but I was able to instruct him why this would be a poor decision. I not only told him that it was illegal, I also warned him about the perception he would be communicating to his employer, that he was willing to cheat to get what he wanted. He hadn't thought about it in those terms, because his intention wasn't to do something illegal or immoral.

He was a good and fine young man, but like the prodigal son, he was deceived into thinking that everything would be all right and that he knew what he was doing. How could one be so deceived? Because he didn't have the experiential knowledge to back up his head knowledge! He was about to jump off the same cliff many young men before him had already jumped off.

I might also add that few return from that cliff without bruises and breaks, some are even paralyzed for the rest of their life. The bonus that was meant to be a blessing would be received in sin and, in effect, be cursed. Had he followed through with his plan, no matter what he did with that money, the Lord could not bless it. Fortunately, he listened to me and learned a valuable life lesson. As a result, his life today continues to be blessed.

> Treasures of wickedness profit nothing,
> But righteousness delivers from death. (Proverbs 10:2)

We learned in the previous chapter that Satan wants all of us to jump off that same cliff and squander our spiritual inheritance. He has one goal and one goal only, and that is to take as many people to hell to live eternally separated from God as he possibly can. If he can distort our thinking by integrating himself deeply into our society in such a way that we buy into his schemes, using his lies to justify our actions, then he doesn't care about right or wrong. He will have already accomplished his purpose. We play right into his hand and will eventually self-destruct and forfeit our inheritance. In essence, we will have become like the prodigal son and already would be dead.

> ..."For this my son was dead and is alive again; he was lost and
> is found." And they began to be merry. (Luke 15:24)

Today, many kids would rather sit in front of a flat-screen television playing video games than go outside. Much less explore opportunities that will help them grow and possibly put some money in their pocket. Instead, they are buying into the liberal lie of entitlement, which states: "Life is not fair, everyone should be equal, everyone is entitled to and deserves the finer things that life has to offer."

Life has become a series of events where we have limited attention spans and, as a whole, have become impatient. There is nothing wrong with having the finer things life has to offer. If we are willing to work hard, exercise our faith and have patience to see that hard work come to fruition. But, we are on verge of breeding a whole generation that finds their reality wrapped up in this liberal lie of entitlement.

Earlier generations have unknowingly perpetuated the lie by being deceived into thinking that because their parents are successful, they too are successful and their children deserve to be successful. The problem with this way of thinking is that it is void of the truth; someone down the ancestral line worked hard for that success. The successive generations want the same, but they don't want to work as hard for it.

Many in my age group had parents that served in World War II. They didn't know if they were going to live or die. Then the Korean War hit and some of those same men that fought in World War II had to go back to Korea. Many of these people for years had not known what was going to happen; they had grown up in the Great Depression only to emerge and see their love ones sent off to war. Thus, upon return from those wars, they were quick to populate and rebuild our nation. Simply put, my generation emerged because men came home from the war and made up for lost time in the bedroom. In so doing, they birthed what we call the *Baby Boom* generation.

During the war, our factories invented new technologies, and better and faster methods of production. We took those technologies, utilized them in other areas of production, and our country thrived. After the war, older men spoke into younger men's lives, took them under their wings, and took them into business, mentoring and training them. They worked hard in order to put our country back on firm footing. As a result, the country prospered. Industry prospered. Technology prospered. And the economy on the whole prospered.

More and more material objects were added to our inventory. People's taste buds became heightened and increased, and hope was restored. When the dust finally settled, men and women had a different outlook on life and made the decision to live it to the fullest.

The enemy, S.I.N., however, watched patiently during this time and slowly planted seeds of deception that led to a mindset that said, "I never want my kids to suffer the way I did, I want my children to have the best."

I still remember my brothers and myself hounding my father, on a weekly basis, to buy a color television because we wanted to watch Walt Disney in Technicolor. Most of us can still remember the stars bursting and flash of color at the beginning of the show. I look back now, a mere 40 years later, and think just how incredibly backwoods we were compared to today's society. It is amazing how far we have come in such a short period of time.

All the while, the enemy was watching and devising ways to utilize this boom period to exercise his destructive plan through the culture in which we live. As a result, some of our prevailing thoughts have become: "After all we have been through, we deserve the best. I've got to have the best technology if I want my life to improve, after all technology will save me time. I've need that new car. We have got to keep up with the Joneses. They have nothing on us."

Of course, there is an element of truth in these thoughts. Because as we have learned, the enemy always mixes a little truth into his lies. The truth is technology does make life easier, but it also makes life faster. We don't slow down enough to enjoy the journey of life.

During the rebuilding period after WWII and beyond not much thought was given that the emerging *Baby Boom* generation, up until Vietnam, would not experience any major catastrophes that would test their resolve and prepare them for a life of hard knocks.

In fact, when our country became embroiled in Vietnam, that *Baby Boom* generation rebelled against the societal engines that were running the world. They asked such questions as, "Who are they to impose their political agendas on the masses? Who are they to thrust us into war? Who are they to tell us how to live our lives?" There was an obvious element of truth to their questioning, but one must not forget the evil force that perpetuated the atrocities in Vietnam that our government proposed to eradicate. That evil force wore a veneer called communism.

Regardless, a generation awoke and did so with placards, sit-ins, and other rebellious behavior. Statements were made in the clothing they wore and their hairstyles. Somehow, they lost respect for the generation that had gone before them, the generation that rebuilt the country and many parts of the world after WWII and the Korean War.

S.I.N. all the while was sitting on society's door step, ready to fuel the confusion and usher in the destructive forces in order to divide our nation. Drug use became rampant, sexual intercourse outside marriage became the standard, and the veil of justification everyone hid behind was peace and love.

Do you remember John Lennon and Yoko Ono's famous internationally televised interview from their bedroom? They became the spokespeople for the movement influencing our beliefs. The media flashed pictures around the world of a billboard they rented that stated "Give Peace a Chance." In one of John's songs, he relayed that he didn't believe in Jesus or anything for that matter, but only believed in himself.

Hey, don't get me wrong, I'm all for giving peace a chance, and I still feel John was one of the most gifted artists the world has ever known. In fact, I have always asserted that his best music was ahead of him. It is so sad that to my knowledge he never acknowledged Jesus as His Lord and Savior or the fact that his talent was a gift from God. Satan used John, Yoko, and their message as pawns to confuse a nation and a world with the sole intention of fueling division and distorting our values as defined by God's Word.

Many of you reading this remember those times and in some way yearn to return to those times. When no one was held accountable, where there seemed to be a freedom to do anything you wanted, and where there was not a care as to what the future might hold.

I ask you, "What came out of that generation?" Could it be that the liberal mindset we are dealing with today in our society was birthed during this era and is being perpetuated by the generation of people that lived during that era? The liberal mindset that says, "Take from the wealthy and give to the poor. After all, everyone deserves to live a comfortable and luxurious life. We know what is best for you."

So what have these intellectual giants done? They have perpetuated the lie of entitlement. They have been deceived by S.I.N. into thinking that the same governing authority that deceived them by telling them the Vietnam War was not political can better manage their healthcare, educate their children, and care for them in their old age. Oh my, can you imagine ignorantly buying into that kind of deception?

So what are the truths and what are the lies contained in this liberal way of thinking? The truth is all men are created equal and should have the right to prosper. The lie is all men deserve to prosper without having to work for it.

The expectation perpetuated is that anyone who has achieved success or inherited success should fund everyone else's prosperity. Many people are well-meaning and actually believe this way of thinking should be our reality. Are you starting to see how the lies are mixed in with the apparent truths, and that even the most well-meaning individuals can and have been deceived?

S.I.N. has perpetuated these lies for generations. The only difference, of course, is in the way they have been presented based on the political and economic climates at the time. Satan is a spiritual being and has always used current times to spin his tale of deception and destruction.

One only has to look at the USSR to see how a whole nation crumbled as a result of a liberal and deceptive governing system. Millions of people struggled, lived in poverty and were denied the very benefits that the system proposed to offer. Everyone was on the same level all right, except the governmental authority. The governing authority thought it was exempt from the very standards they were holding everyone else accountable to and that somehow they were justified to live in luxury while everyone else suffered. Isn't it interesting that all the while they attempted to convince the public it was for their own good? The ruling authority had became Satan's puppets, deceived into thinking they were better than the masses.

How long will you put up with the enemy's lies? As Christians, we are expected to go to church on Sunday, say our prayers, and read our Bible. We are to ask God for those things we are lacking and to provide for our financial needs. We ask Him to heal our sicknesses and diseases. We ask him to provide for and protect our children. But how many of us really alter our behavior so God can answer those prayers? How many of us really press into the Word of God and pray for Him to reveal the truth contained therein?

How many of us really serve with love—not out of a selfish obedience—every day dying to self and doing things for other people that will make the world a better place? How many of us check ours motives at the door, and ask God to let us see with His eyes, hear with His ears and act in such a way that would make Him proud of our actions?

Instead, are we desiring a quick fix that says, "God should be 'Johnny on the Spot,' after all, I deserve to be happy?" Are we silently thinking that anytime we have issues, problems, pains and/or needs, God should show up? Do we expect that when we do good things to others and live our lives correctly, God should bless us and block anything and everything from harming us?

So what is my point? The point is this—life is hard and it takes discipline to walk with God. Sure, there are supernatural moves of the Lord, and God answers prayer supernaturally at times, because he is a supernatural God. However, He usually answers prayer through the natural course of our lives. There are no long-term magical cures.

> Do not pray for easy lives;
> pray to be stronger people.
> Do not pray for tasks equal to your powers;
> pray for powers equal to your tasks.
> Then the doing of your work shall be no miracle,
> but you yourself shall be a miracle.
> Every day you shall wonder at yourself,
> at the richness of life which has come to you by the grace of God.
> Phillips Brooks (1835-1893)

If your expectation and standard in life is that you should be successful because those who have gone before you were successful, then the enemy has already set you up for spiritual failure. You have fallen right into S.I.N.'s hands and headed down a path of eternal destruction.

Recently, I heard a pastor make a profound statement to the youth who were graduating from college, "You are getting ready to embark on life's journey, a journey to find your personal success. You are going to climb the proverbial ladder of success. May I suggest that you make sure when it is all said and done, that your ladder is leaning up against the right building: God's Kingdom!" We all need to check and see which building our ladders are leaning up against.

So what does society scream at us? "If you could just do this or do that; if you go here or could go there; if you could be like so-and-so; if you could win the prize; just think how much easier life would be or better yet how much happier life would be?" Well, maybe so, but for how long?

> Do not love the world or the things in the world. If anyone loves the world, the love of the Father is not in him. For all that is in the world—the lust of the flesh, the lust of the eyes, and the pride of life—is not of the Father but is of the world. And the world is passing away, and the lust of it; but he who does the will of God abides forever. (1 John 2:15-17)

See, a quick fix is something that only lasts a very short time. Our true desire is to find a long-term answer that will deliver us. But because of the sinful nature of our hearts, we entertain material possessions, relationships, and climactic events to medicate the pain we so long to be free of.

Many men and women have climbed mountains in their lifetime. They have felt the exhilaration associated with reaching the summit, standing on that conquered mountain, and peering out at the incredible landscape surrounding them. However, when they come down from the mountain they must return to the valley, and the only way to regain that feeling is to go back up the mountain.

I once was invited to drive a stock car several laps around the track at Texas Motor Speedway, and I reached speeds of up to 140 miles per hour. Man, what a rush that was. Talk about a climax. I experienced the thrill of shifting the gears, holding a shaking steering wheel through the turns, and the exhilaration of gunning it down the straightaway. I stepped out of that car, on top of the world, thinking, "Mario Andretti you got nothing on me." Of course, some of you younger people would be thinking, "Danica Patrick or Kyle Busch you got nothing on me."

CLIMACTIC DELIVERANCE

I felt great, but once I was out of that car, it occurred to me that the only way I was going to get that feeling back was to get back in that car and do it again. I could go on and on using examples of sports, especially the extreme sports, which have become so popular. Why? Because we all long for that thrill. We long for the ultimate climax. If truthful, most of us want to be great and want to have it all right this second. In fact, you too can experience that rush, if you are willing to pay for it. So I ask, what is your mountain or sports car of choice?

The reality is this: anything that is going to have sustaining impact on your life will take time to acquire and will involve a process over time. I didn't step into that race car and automatically become one of the world's best drivers. In fact, anyone reading this that knows me will be thinking, "No amount of time would get him there." But in order to improve long-term—to have lasting deliverance—one must perfect the skill over time. It takes years to become one of the best drivers.

It is no different in other areas of life. We must endure God's process, knowing that change takes time, and to be perfect in any area takes hard work. See, when someone tells you that you can be *delivered*, they are stating a true biblical fact. However, when they do so by telling you that the deliverance comes without any pain or effort on your part, they are perpetuating the lie the serpent used to deceive Eve in the garden.

In life, these climactic experiences will sometimes bring you temporary deliverance from your past; however, they are usually just short-term fixes for your more deeply rooted issues.

Let's say you were able to use one of these experiences to totally eradicate some root issue in your heart. This still would not thwart the enemy, because he will always do a workaround. Remember the movie *Jurassic Park*? There was a scene early in the movie when the main characters were on a plane headed to the park and Jeff Goldblum, playing the character Dr. Ian Malcolm, (a fictional mathematician and self-professed "chaotician"), claims that Chaos Theory teaches that "Life cannot be controlled...Life finds a way."

Of course, so-called chaoticians would have us believe that God is not in control, but rather the universe found a way to evolve all on its own. Don't ever underestimate the enemy's grip on our lives. Remember that he is working from the inside of us, out of the sinful seed planted in our hearts the day we were formed.

Deliverance can be a scary thing if not kept in the proper perspective. Think about it for a moment and let that resonate in your mind. How many deliverance seminars are available today? They mainly appeal to Christians, right? Why? Because as Christians we have been taught, rightfully so, that it is the Lord's desire to deliver us from the power of darkness.

> Giving thanks to the Father who has qualified us to be partakers of the inheritance of the saints in the light. He has *delivered us from the power of darkness* and conveyed us into the kingdom of the Son of His love, in whom we have redemption through His blood, the forgiveness of sins. (Colossians 1:12-14)

But somehow, we have bought into a lie that says, "Once you have been delivered, you are free from your addiction, problem, and/or issue." Let me pose a simple example to make the point clear. Say you are allergic to shellfish, you attended a deliverance seminar where someone prays for you to be delivered from this affliction, and you sense in your heart that you are no longer bound by this allergic reaction. How are you going to know you are truly delivered? The only way to know is to eat some shellfish and see if you have an allergic reaction.

Well, is that what you are going to tell a drug addict that has been delivered, an alcoholic that has been delivered, a sex addict that has been delivered or an abusive husband that has been delivered? Of course not! You are going to tell them to cease the behavior. Of course, we should also encourage them to join a good Bible-believing church, surround themselves with solid accountability, and seek God on a daily basis by reading and studying His Word. It will take effort on their part to sustain the deliverance.

Unfortunately, our desires can become distorted because of the climactic nature of our hearts. We have a tendency to think, "I deserve to be delivered." And so we expect to be delivered, but we don't necessarily embrace that we have a responsibility to change our behavior in order to stay delivered. We are called to be fellow workers with God. In other words, we need to take responsibility for our behavior in order for Him to enact the change in our hearts.

> For we are God's fellow workers; you are God's field, you are God's building. (1 Corinthians 3:9)

> We then, as workers together with Him also plead with you not to receive the grace of God in vain. (2 Corinthians 6:1)

When we embrace the liberal way of thinking that deliverance is automatic and without any effort on our part, deception easily creeps in. We begin to buy the lie that anyone can go to a seminar and God is automatically going to deliver them from whatever ails them. It seems to make spiritual sense for God to immediately remove all impediments of our character and all the deep-seated roots that have caused manifestations to occur in our life. Those that have caused so much destruction—some of which we are still paying consequences for.

Let me be clear, I am not against deliverance ministry by any means, and I believe it is an important aspect of Christian ministry. We all need deliverance from the enemy. It is true that some of these seminars bring immediate healing, or release from the strongholds the enemy has placed on an individual's life.

However, what I am conveying in this writing is that a deliverance which is really just a quick-fix—one where you don't have to put any rubber on the road so to speak; one that you really don't have to mix any discipline with; one that you don't have to exercise any Lordship in; is not a deliverance at all. In fact, it might be a temporary state that S.I.N. has allowed to deceive you into thinking that God has brought you out of bondage.

Then what does the enemy do? He lies in wait for the opportune time where he can pounce and reintroduce his devastation on you. Then you begin to doubt all that you thought you had been delivered from. When that one issue that was so overwhelming, the issue that you thought you had been delivered from, rears its ugly head—the enemy wants to confuse you into thinking that it is still deeply seated in your heart. When it rears its ugly head, S.I.N. wants to use it to destroy your faith and belief in God's Word.

He is "a roaring lion, seeking whom he may devour." We have to be careful of the sin, which so easily ensnares us. It is all around us and appeals to the sin that is already planted in our hearts; the seed of sin that caused all the roots to take hold in the first place.

The biblical question about this inevitable reality of life is, what are you going to do when the enemy pounces and tries to devour your soul? What are you going to do when the issues of life rear their ugly heads once again?

> Be sober, be vigilant; because your adversary the devil walks about like a *roaring lion, seeking whom he may devour.*
> (1 Peter 5:8)

True Deliverance

I want you to know that true climactic deliverance is available to us all. Now you must be thinking, "This guy is loony. He has been making this big deal out of deliverance, telling us that we have this climactic nature and because we have come to expect everything in life, it is wrong to want instant deliverance without working for it. Then he turns around and tells us we can receive a climactic deliverance." Well, if you were one of those thinking this, you would be right. The Lord wants us to understand a simple truth: when we ask Him into our heart and put our trust in Him as our Lord and our Savior, we are delivered at that very moment. At that instant, you have experienced *Climactic Deliverance!*

However, this deliverance takes work on our part. Yes, true deliverance happens the day you die spiritually and become *born again*. However, like any newborn baby, you will need to crawl before you walk.

> There was a man of the Pharisees named Nicodemus, a ruler of the Jews. This man came to Jesus by night and said to Him, "Rabbi, we know that You are a teacher come from God; for no one can do these signs that You do unless God is with him." Jesus answered and said to him, "Most assuredly, I say to you, unless one is *born again*, he cannot see the kingdom of God." (John 3:1-3)

> Pharisee - a member of a Jewish sect that flourished during the 1st century BC and 1st century AD and that differed from the Sadducees chiefly in its strict observance of religious ceremonies and practices, adherence to oral laws and traditions, and belief in an afterlife and the coming of a Messiah. (27)

> Sanhedrin - the highest council of the ancient jews, consisting of 72 members, and exercising authority from about the 2nd century BC. (27)

Nicodemus was a well-respected religious scholar of the day, a Pharisee and member of the Sanhedrin. He obviously came at night so none of his peers would ridicule him for meeting with Jesus. He told Jesus that he believed Jesus was a teacher sent from God because of the miraculous signs Jesus was performing. However, Jesus interrupted him by saying, "Unless one is born again, he cannot see the kingdom of God." Jesus was speaking from a spiritual perspective because, like Nicodemus, everyone knows you can't be physically born a second time.

Obviously perplexed, Nicodemus decides to instruct Jesus by posing the question anyway: "How can a man be born when he is old? Can he enter a second time into his mother's womb and be born?" Here was one of the greatest scholars of the day, but he could not grasp the simple but profound Spiritual Law that Jesus was sharing with him. Jesus didn't get frustrated with Nicodemus, but explained it to him in hopes the he would understand the spiritual importance of being "born of the spirit."

> Nicodemus said to Him, "How can a man be born when he is old? Can he enter a second time into his mother's womb and be born?" Jesus answered, "Most assuredly, I say to you, unless one is born of water and the Spirit, he cannot enter the kingdom of God. That which is born of the flesh is flesh, and that which is born of the Spirit is spirit. Do not marvel that I said to you, 'You must be born again.' The wind blows where it wishes, and you hear the sound of it, but cannot tell where it comes from and where it goes. So is everyone who is born of the Spirit." (John 3:4-8)

Unfortunately, for Nicodemus, he could not bring himself to understand this seemingly strange example he was hearing from Jesus. He might have even felt Jesus was playing with him, as evidenced by his next question,

> Nicodemus answered and said to Him, "How can these things be?" (John 3:9)

> Jesus pointedly responded with His own question, Are you the teacher of Israel, and do not know these things? (John 3:10)

The scriptures don't say how Nicodemus felt, but it would be safe to say that he left feeling pretty confused and quite possibly even questioning the authenticity of Jesus' ministry. The unfortunate truth is that he didn't realize that at that very moment the Kingdom of God was within his grasp. Jesus was speaking to him of an unseen Kingdom, one that is built on faith. Christ was drawing Nicodemus to the Kingdom, and he couldn't let go of his earthly reasoning to grasp the eternal truth Jesus was showing him.

How sad for Nicodemus. How often do we do the same thing? The Lord is always knocking at the door to our hearts in hope that we will accept His revelation of truth. He is still patiently awaiting our invitation for Him to come and dine with us.

Are we really that much different from Nicodemus? Maybe some of us can relate to him. How often have we walked away from the Word of God, thinking it makes no sense at all, or thinking that maybe it's for someone else? Every time we fail to claim God's promises, we have become like Nicodemus. Every time we are moved by our circumstances and refuse the truth, we miss an opportunity to see the Kingdom of Heaven. We too, like Nicodemus, sometimes come to the Lord hiding from the world in order to ask our questions. Questions such as, but not limited to these alone:

- What does it mean to be born again?
- Are You real?
- Who are You really?
- Is there really a physical heaven and hell?
- Don't You understand my circumstance?
- Where were you when I needed You?
- Don't You care?
- Why won't You answer my prayer?
- Surely if You loved me, my circumstances would be different?
- Why all the war and devastation around the world?
- Why do You allow innocent people to suffer?

God's answer is going to be the same every time: "Turn to My Word and you will find the real truth." Like Nicodemus, He speaks to us according to the Spirit, for His Kingdom is always near, and always within our grasp.

> Now when He was asked by the Pharisees when the kingdom of God would come, He answered them and said, "The kingdom of God does not come with observation; nor will they say, 'See here!' or 'See there! For indeed, the kingdom of God is within you." (Luke 17:20-21)

Some versions of scripture say, "God is in your midst." In other words, our Creator is everywhere and thus always near to us. Patiently waiting in anticipation for us to acknowledge His presence and invite Him into our hearts. Are we willing to claim this truth? Do we truly want to walk in victory over S.I.N., or do we want to keep on searching for a quick-fix to the issues in life?

I challenge that many in church today claiming to be christians don't know what it means to be spiritually *Born Again*. How many times have we stood in church reciting some liturgy, anxious for the service to end? How many times have we criticized the pastor's message? How many times in church have we turned and looked the other direction when we see a brother or sister approach that we don't want to speak to? How many times have we raised our hands in church or prayed aloud, but as soon as someone unfamiliar comes close, lower our hands and are careful not to pray too loud? I am sure everyone who has ever attended church is guilty of some form of offense.

At the beginning of this book, I challenged you with a question: "If you died and went to Heaven and the Lord just happened to be standing at the gate the very moment of your arrival and asked, 'Son/Daughter why should I let you in?' What would your answer be?"

Many will answer this question knowing they do not have a leg to stand on. With heads hung low and eyes toward the ground, they will quietly say, "I don't know. I don't think I deserve to go to heaven." This would be a true answer, because based on our sinful nature, none of us really deserve to go to heaven.

Then there are others, including many *professed christians*, who will stand tall and boldly announce, "Well, I am a good person. I have led a good life." Though this might be a true statement because many of us do lead good and fruitful lives, being good is not the answer to God's question. We read in Luke that Jesus Christ tells a ruler that no one, including Himself, is good, only God.

> Now a certain ruler asked Him, saying, "Good Teacher, what shall I do to inherit eternal life?" So Jesus said to him, "Why do you call Me good? *No one is good but One, that is, God.*" (Luke 18:18-19)

Some people might question if Christ really lived. Others say He lived, but was just a good prophet, a good teacher or just a good man. In the world we live in today, if someone claims to be somebody, only later to be discovered a counterfeit, aren't we disappointed? In fact, if that person held public office we would impeach them. If they led a company, the members of the board would fire them. Or if they called themselves our friend, we would distance ourselves from them.

So doesn't it seem a little odd that most other religions acknowledge Christ's existence but qualify it by saying he was a good man or a good prophet? The Bible even warns us that many will proclaim their own goodness. So if Jesus did not include himself as being good, how could we possibly believe that we could gain access into God's kingdom by being good?

> Most men will proclaim each his own goodness, But who can find a faithful man? (Proverbs 20:6)

What would your answer be? What would you say to the Father of the Universe? Would you like the biblical answer to that question? Evantell Ministries in Dallas, Texas founded by Dr. Larry Moyer, has a wonderful answer to the question. It is called the bad news/good news * presentation of the gospel. It starts with, "May I ask you a question? Has anyone ever taken a Bible and shown you how you can know for sure that you're going to heaven?" If your answer is no, then I would like to ask, "May I?" With your permission, I would like to share the following:

BAD NEWS
1. We are all sinners.

> for all have sinned and fall short of the glory of God, (Romans 3:23)

Let's assume someone asked you to throw a rock and hit an airliner at 20,000 feet. No matter how strong your arm, you would fall short of the mark. Because of our sin, we have all missed the mark. We all have fallen short of the glory of God.

2. The penalty for sin is death.

> For the wages of sin *is* death, but the gift of God *is* eternal life in Christ Jesus our Lord. (Romans 6:23)

Imagine you have worked long and hard all week. When you go to pick up your pay check wouldn't you expect to be fairly compensated for your labor?

---

* Bad News/Good News - Copyright © 2012 EvanTell, Inc. All rights reserved. (28)

In the previous verse we learn that there is a wage or consequence for our sinful nature. That wage is death and robs us of God's gift of eternal life. Fortunately, God stepped down from Heaven and dwelt among us.

GOOD NEWS
1. Christ died for you.

> But God demonstrates His own love toward us, in that while we were still sinners, Christ died for us. (Romans 5:8)

There was a man sentenced to die for the crime he committed. However, right before the judge read the decision a man burst through the doors of the courtroom and called out, "Wait your honor, I will take his punishment, I will pay with my life, for this man's crime." Do you think the man who committed the crime was relieved? Of course! He was freed to live out his life while his substitute was set to die. In essence that is what Christ has done for you and me. While sin was slowly causing our death, He became our substitute and died for us, sacrificing himself for our sin.

2. You can be saved through faith.

> For by grace you have been saved through faith, and that not of yourselves; *it is* the gift of God, not of works, lest anyone should boast. (Ephesians 2: 8,9)

Think about walking into your office and sitting in the chair behind your desk. Do you first pick up the chair to see if it will hold your weight? If you are like most of us, your answer will be no. Of course not, we expect or trust the chair will support us. Unkowingly, when we sit down, we have exercised faith. We have a gift from God that will also support us and we don't receive it from our labor. We put our trust in him through faith for our salvation.

Now that I have shared the bad news/good news I want to ask if there is anything that is keeping you from trusting in Christ as your Savior right now?

You might be thinking at this very moment, "But how do I really do that and know that the Lord will hear and believe me?" All you need to do is get right with the Lord in your heart and leave the rest up to Him. He is the only one who truly knows your heart.

> I, the LORD, search the heart, I test the mind, Even to give every man according to his ways, According to the fruit of his doings. (Jeremiah 17:10)

Would you like to tell God you are trusting Jesus Christ as your Savior? The following is a suggested prayer between you and the Lord that will mark the beginning of your walk with Christ here on earth. Why not take a step of faith and experience God's saving grace? Or if you have already made a profession of faith, be open to a deeper revelational experience with the Lord?

> Jesus, I believe that you suffered persecution, gave your life by dying on the cross and by your blood that was shed, you covered all of my sin. So today, I invite you to enter my heart and ask you to forgive my sin, past, present and future. I believe that God raised you from the dead on the third day and that you are living and reigning in heaven for all eternity. From this day forward, I announce you as the Lord of my life and I commit to live for you as the Lord of my life. All this I pray in your name, Jesus Christ. AMEN.

Assurance of Everlasting Life

> "Most assuredly, I say to you, he who hears My word and believes in Him who sent Me has everlasting life, and shall not come into judgment, but has passed from death into life. (John 5:24)

> That if you confess with your mouth the Lord Jesus and believe in your heart that God has raised Him from the dead, you will be saved. For with the heart one believes unto righteousness, and with the mouth confession is made unto salvation. (Romans 10:9-10)

We are instructed to hear God's word, believe in God, and trust Jesus Christ as our personal Lord and Savior. We confess it openly with our mouth and invite the Holy Spirit into our heart, believing that God raised Christ from the dead on the third day. We put our trust in Christ alone for our salvation.

It is not the prayer that brings salvation, but the belief in your heart. You won't hear any bells and whistles go off. You probably won't experience a supernatural move of God, but you will feel a sense of peace.

I am not going to tell you that you will suddenly be free from all of life's burdens. I'm not going to tell you that all your problems will dissipate and fortune and fame will be yours to claim. What I am going to tell you is that you will be *Climactically Delivered* for all eternity, because the Holy Spirit will enter in, and enact a change in your heart.

The Lord will make a deposit in your heart of His eternal salvation, a deposit no one and nothing is able to steal. It will bring about your rebirth in the spiritual realm and alter your eternal course.

> As far as the east is from the west, So far has He removed our transgressions from us. (Psalm 103:12)

Your decision will allow the Lord to enter your heart and search out the seed of S.I.N. planted when you were still in your mother's womb. The Holy Spirit will uncover and expose the lies attached to that seed, which will begin the painful process of purification, which is necessary to free you from the enemy's grip!

> But God has revealed them to us through His Spirit. For the Spirit searches all things, yes, the deep things of God. For what man knows the things of a man except the spirit of the man which is in him? Even so no one knows the things of God except the Spirit of God. Now we have received, not the spirit of the world, but the Spirit who is from God, that we might know the things that have been freely given to us by God. (1 Corinthians 2:10-12)

> The refining pot is for silver and the furnace for gold, But the LORD tests the hearts. (Proverbs 17:3)

Think about your body for a moment. If you need to lose weight, do you just close your eyes and will the weight away? Do you go to a seminar and have someone deliver you from the excess weight? The obvious answer we all know to be true is no. However, sometimes it takes us closing our eyes and asking for help, or going to a seminar and receiving revelation that change needs to take place.

We need to receive revelation that the power to change is available to us. But, the stern reality is, if we don't monitor what we eat and exercise, we will not lose the weight! There is a response that we must give and an action we must take. There will be pain and self-sacrifice involved. Over time, as the weight begins to be shed, we feel good about ourselves. We also become more confident and are less inclined to be insecure with ourselves.

Anything that is worth having, is worth working for. When we do our part, we have ownership in whatever it is that we are trying to achieve. We all know in the physical realm that to have ownership of a material possession simply means we hold the deed and no one can take it away from us. Guess what? When we have ownership of the Holy Spirit living in our hearts, we are given a spiritual deed that no one can take from us. This is true deliverance and it is climactic, not because you went to a seminar or someone laid hands on you. No, it is climactic in nature because it instantaneously grants you *everlasting life*.

Next, I would encourage you to be baptized in the same manner John the Baptist baptized Jesus in the Jordan. When Jesus shared with Nicodemus in John 3, "Most assuredly, I say to you, unless one is *born again*, he cannot see the kingdom of God." Jesus was using an analogy of the birthing process. We know that when a newborn baby emerges from the birth canal it is a new creation. However, it has been forming in the womb for nine months and preparing for the day it is ready for the outside world.

Our new birth is similar. The only difference is, we have been in our culture's womb for years, developing bad habits and a sinful nature. As we emerge from the waters of baptism, we are new creations just like the baby. From that day forward, it will be a purification process that lasts a lifetime and will not end until you draw your last breath.

Jesus Christ, being fully God yet fully human, went to that cross (or as we learn here, that tree) and freely offered His blood as a sacrifice for your sins, so that you could live for righteousness. There was no deceit found in Him; the fruit of His righteousness is your tree of life.

> The fruit of the righteous is a tree of life, (Proverbs 11:30a)

> For to this you were called, because Christ also suffered for us, leaving us an example, that you should follow His steps: "Who committed no sin, Nor was deceit found in His mouth"; who, when He was reviled, did not revile in return; when He suffered, He did not threaten, but committed Himself to Him who judges righteously; who Himself bore our sins in His own

> body on the tree, that we, having died to sins, might live for righteousness—by whose stripes you were healed. For you were like sheep going astray, but have now returned to the Shepherd and Overseer of your souls. (1 Peter 2:21-25)

Can you really imagine the weight of the sin Christ took on? Close your eyes and imagine nails being driven into your hands and feet. The cross lifted into the air, gravitational pull tugging at your limbs, your skin ripping, and your bones aching. Yes, with your eyes still closed, imagine his pain and feel the weight of everyone's sin, past, present, and future. All the sin He bore on that cross. Now open your eyes to His eternal gain. He took upon himself all of YOUR sin. He rose from the dead. He served notice on Satan that it was finished. His light illuminated the darkness, allowing each one of us to shed Satan's seed of S.I.N. in our hearts forever.

Thus, based upon your belief in His death and resurrection and His Holy Spirit flowing through you, your light will pour out on those around you, to the glory of God. You may not feel like your lamp is lighting the world. But, when the God of the Universe, by His spirit, comes into your heart, you can't help but light up the world.

> You are the light of the world. A city that is set on a hill cannot be hidden. Nor do they light a lamp and put it under a basket, but on a lamp stand, and it gives light to all who are in the house. Let your light so shine before men, that they may see your good works and glorify your Father in heaven. (Matthew 5:14-16)

When we embrace the Bible, the Holy Scriptures, as our point of reference, this literature testifies who Christ was and who Christ is. When we study about this man we see His goodness. We see that He was a prophet. We see He was a visionary. We see that he built a mighty ministry. We see that He truly was the "Son of God."

> Then they all said, "Are You then the Son of God?" So He said to them, "You rightly say that I am." (Luke 22:70)

So I ask you, "On what basis do we believe anything else?" What literature as authentic as the Bible do we have that disputes what the word says?" Show me authentic literature that disproves God's declaration that Jesus was His Son and disputes they were one being. God sent Jesus, His

Son, to suffer, to be persecuted, and to ultimately die for your sin...my sin...everyone's sin...the sin of everyone living at that time and everyone that was to come after.

FOUR KEYS TO THE KINGDOM

If you said that prayer for the first time or made the decision to say the prayer in order to renew your commitment to the Lord, I want to suggest some crucial keys. Keys to help you unlock your mind and soul in order to receive ongoing spiritual revelation from the Lord.

1. Share the Good News

I want to encourage you to share the Good News with someone else who claims to be a christian. You might be asking, "How do I quantify if they are truly a christian?" Well, ask them God's question about why He should let them into heaven and test their response.

> Beloved, do not believe every spirit, but test the spirits, whether they are of God; because many false prophets have gone out into the world. By this you know the Spirit of God: Every spirit that confesses that Jesus Christ has come in the flesh is of God, and every spirit that does not confess that Jesus Christ has come in the flesh is not of God. And this is the spirit of the Antichrist, which you have heard was coming, and is now already in the world. (1 John 4:1-3)

Satan will not be pleased at your decision and will attempt to distort the truth of the gospel in order to get you to doubt the transforming power of the Holy Spirit. By confessing to another, you break the hold that sin has on you and will gain strength for your journey. Invite them to pray for you, ask them for guidance and hear their testimony so that you can be encouraged to stay the course.

2. Read the Word

I want to encourage you to dust off your Bible or go out and buy a Bible. The New King James or the New International Version will be fine. Start with the book of John, which is full of Christ's own teaching during His earthly ministry. His words contained on those pages are living, powerful, and will guard you from S.I.N. and protect you from yourself.

Imagine for a moment that sitting in front of you is a glass full of water tainted with dirt and a pitcher full of pure water. Now, pick up the pure water and start pouring it into the tainted water. What happens? As you continue pouring the pure water into the tainted water, eventually the tainted water overflows until all the impurities are removed. That tainted water is our sin, and the pure water is the Word of God. The more pure water of the Word we pour into our tainted vessels, the purer our hearts become.

> Your word I have hidden in my heart, That I might not sin against You. (Psalm 119:11)

Thus, we are protected from the enemy within, renewed with God's spirit that is pure and unadulterated. We are making a deposit into our soul that is everlasting, and though we will never be fully purified until the day of our second death—little by little—we are renewed to newness of life in Christ Jesus. It also makes sense that if we deposit the Word in our heart, when it comes time to share our testimony of salvation with others, His Word will come forth out of our purified heart.

3. Join a Spirit filled Bible-Based Church
I want to encourage you to find and join a reliable, Spirit filled church, where the Word is preached. I'm not talking about religion. I'm talking about a church that is real, where the Lord's presence is felt through the power of the Holy Spirit, where His grace abounds, and the fruit of righteousness is evident.

Here again you might be asking, "How do I know if the church is for real?" Well, ask the pastor, priest or minister God's question and test his response. Do they openly acknowlege the power of the Holy Spirit? Is their fruit being produced? Do you sense His grace? Does that fruit line up with the Word of God? Is that fruit righteous, is it a tree of life, are they winning souls, and are those souls being transformed into Christ's image?

> Not forsaking the assembling of ourselves together, as is the manner of some, but exhorting one another, and so much the more as you see the Day approaching. (Hebrews 10:25)

When a woman becomes pregnant and her abdomen starts to grow, it is obvious that at some point she is going to give birth to a child. During the pregnancy, the child is going to develop within her womb until the day when it comes time for the baby to come into the world. That baby is, in essence, her fruit, and it is righteous in the sense that it is a child of God. When the baby emerges from the birth canal, it is a tree of life. But because of the sin of the mother and the father, that baby's heart is tainted and will need to be nurtured and instructed in righteousness. Unfortunately, the baby has no choice as to the house or environment in which it will grow up. There is no denying or escaping this reality. We know it is true, because every one of us has experienced this event.

Unlike that baby, when you are born again in the Lord, you are no longer tainted and have a choice as to which house you get to live in and a choice of who your spiritual father will be. Visit several houses and listen to several fathers, but listen to God. Let Him lead you to the house and to the father where you will be nurtured by the truth of the gospel and where you will experience mature growth as you develop into the child God desires you to become. Once you find a good church, you can then inquire about the process of baptism.

> Please Note: I am not suggesting you change churches. Especially if you are currently a member of a healthy church that believes the bible is the final authority and where the Holy Spirit is openly embraced. On the contrary, I want to encourage you to embrace their teaching and to feed others with the eternal truths being taught.

4. Spend Time Daily with God

I want to encourage you to spend time with God every morning and every evening. If He is going to be first in your life and you are going to live for Him, doesn't it make sense that you should start your day and end your day with Him? This should be a priority in your walk with Christ.

Why? Because in order to hear His voice and be led by His Spirit, you need to quiet yourself and learn what His voice sounds like. You need to spend time with Him in the morning to obtain direction and covering for the day's events. You also need to spend time with Him at night to shed the weight of the day and ask protection for a good night's sleep.

Remember the old water wells? There was a spigot with a handle sitting atop a platform of wood that covered a deep well. You could pump that handle all you wanted, but no water would emerge until you first primed the pump with some water. Once primed, as you pumped that handle, the water would flow freely, and you could fill buckets from that spigot. When we awake in the morning, we are not always ready to embrace spending time with the Lord. We sit there, and no matter how hard we try, nothing seems to flow. We need to prime our spiritual pump with the very substance we expect to come out of our time with the Lord.

I suggest you put on a good worship CD, spend some time in silence, speak to Him through prayer, and finally, open His word and let His life pour into you. For many, a worship CD will help the Word to flow. For others it might be sitting quietly in the dark. For still others it might help to first read the Word.

Another way to prime your spiritual pump is to read a daily devotional. One that I personally use is *My Utmost For His Highest* by Oswald Chambers. This devotional was not actually written by Chambers, but by his wife after his death.

> Gertrude Hobbs was a former court stenographer and could take dictation at 250 words per minute. Gertrude married Oswald in 1910, and she traveled with him during his ministry. They had a vision to begin a Bible college, so she started taking copious notes of his sermons in order to at least be able to offer correspondence courses. She later transcribed her notes and sent them out to her friends until finally putting them into a pamphlet, which later became the book that still communicates Oswald's messages from God. (29)

Now, you have four keys to unlocking the Kingdom of God in your life. Open your heart and ask Him to show you: what needs to change; what needs to be altered; what behaviors need to be dropped; and what behaviors need to be accentuated. Talk to Him as you would your best friend. Remember every day is a new day and a new opportunity to trust Him, believe in him, and walk with Him.

If you placed your trust in Jesus Christ for your eternal salvation you have been,
Climactically Delivered
For all eternity

CHAPTER SEVEN

STAIRWAY TO HEAVEN

Our journey in life is like a stairway. We come out of the womb and whether we like it or not, we start climbing life's stairway. The aging process has begun. Life moves slowly at first, but the older we get it seems the years pass faster and faster. We climb the stairway of life we become stronger, more intelligent, and more mature. We also hope to progress in our careers, relationships, and life in general.

Stairway to Heaven was a song popularized by Led Zeppelin in 1970 about claiming what you want without giving anything in return.

> There's a lady who's sure all that glitters is gold
> And she's buying a stairway to heaven
> And when she gets there she knows if the stores are closed
> With a word she can get what she came for
> Yes there are two paths you can go by
> but in the long run
> There's still time to change the road you're on (30)

One day, I felt God put in my heart that He too has a *Stairway to Heaven*—one that is real, where giving flows both ways and the stores are always open. We don't go there to get what we came for, but to dwell with Him for all eternity, because we are sons and daughters of the *Lord Almighty* and have an inheritance in His Kingdom.

> I will be a Father to you, And you shall be My sons and daughters, Says the LORD Almighty. (2 Corinthians 6:18)

> Blessed be the God and Father of our Lord Jesus Christ, who according to His abundant mercy has begotten us again to a living hope through the resurrection of Jesus Christ from the dead, to an inheritance incorruptible and undefiled and that does not fade away, reserved in heaven for you (1 Peter 1:3-4)

In life there are choices and like the lyrics of the song, "There are two paths you can go by," but in God's kingdom only one leads to His house. What stairway in life are you on?

> The way of life winds upward for the wise, That he may turn away from hell below. (Proverbs 15:24)

Do you remember going to the mall as a child and riding the escalators? Did you ever try to go the opposite direction on the escalators? I still remember how much fun it was to run up the down escalator; it was exhilarating to reach the top having conquered the mechanical stairs.

One day as I was praying, I felt the Lord speak to my heart, "The next time you are at a mall, I want you to ride the escalator, only this time, I want you to try running down the up escalator." I sat thinking and could not recollect ever running down an up escalator. Have you ever tried running down an up escalator?

I decided to take the Lord up on this challenge. The next time I went to the mall I found the bank of escalators and stepped on the one going up. About halfway up, I turned around, and started walking. That's when the little voice in my head said, "I told you to run." Being obedient I started running until I began to lose my equilibrium. So I stopped and turned back around. Immediately I heard the voice , "That is how much of your life with Me has been, you have been on my stairway leading to Heaven, but most of the time you have been turned around going the wrong direction."

The Lord was giving me a visual of what my life and walk with Him had been like; my spiritual journey was a lot like riding that escalator. Once I made a heartfelt decision to place my trust in Him alone for salvation, I climbed aboard His *Stairway to Heaven*. I was well aware of where His stairway was leading, but honestly, most of the time, I was turned around going the opposite direction. Sometimes I was running away from God.

Steps on the Stairway

Acknowledgement, Acceptance, & Trust
There can be no acceptance of God's love without first acknowledging that God exists and learning who God is. Only through placing our trust in Christ alone for our salvation can we have a born-again experience.

Conversion & Brokenness
The conversion process usually begins with some catalytic moment or event causing us to discover that our lives are heading in the wrong direction or spiraling out of control. We make a decided and determined effort to change, and through brokenness, we come to realize we are powerless to effect change in our life. We give into God's guidance and submit to His Lordship.

Restoration & Repentance
S.I.N. will attempt to draw us back into its clutches by reminding us of our past behaviors and circumstances. However, as we continue to turn away, ignoring S.I.N.'s advances, we continue to be restored in the image of Christ.

Purification & Eternal Salvation
Purification is the ongoing process of refinement until the day we draw our last breath and realize the eternal salvation promised by Christ.

Ministry
The great commission is a call for all Christians to joyfully carry God's message to the world through discipleship and teaching.

In order to get a better feel of how to climb God's stairway, we will look at each step in detail. But first, let's look at the life of one of the most influential Christians who ever walked the earth. His name is the Apostle Paul. He was originally Saul of Tarsus, a Pharisee, on a mission from the church to eradicate the so-called *Jesus freaks* of his day. Paul was persecuting the church, however, he was about to have his world rocked on the way to Damascus.

> Then Saul, still breathing threats and murder against the disciples of the Lord, went to the high priest and asked letters from him to the synagogues of Damascus, so that if he found

any who were of the Way, whether men or women, he might bring them bound to Jerusalem. (Acts 9:1-2)

Paul gives his personal testimony of his conversion experience in Acts. He writes how he was broken by Jesus Christ, as he addresses the Jews in Jerusalem. By his own admission, Paul had already taken the first step by fully accepting and acknowledging who God was. In fact, he had been raised his whole life to be in the ministry. However, he didn't know what it meant to place his trust in Christ.

We know that Paul was a scholar in his day, a devout follower of God. Like most Jews at the time, Paul did not believe that Jesus Christ was sent from God to save a lost world. Instead, Paul's purpose in life was to eradicate any Jew who worshiped contrary to the law given by Moses, having them bound in chains and punished.

> Brethren and fathers, hear my defense before you now. And when they heard that he spoke to them in the Hebrew language, they kept all the more silent. Then he said: "I am indeed a Jew, born in Tarsus of Cilicia, but brought up in this city at the feet of Gamaliel, taught according to the strictness of our fathers' law, and was zealous toward God as you all are today. I persecuted this Way to the death, binding and delivering into prisons both men and women, as also the high priest bears me witness, and all the council of the elders, from whom I also received letters to the brethren, and went to Damascus to bring in chains even those who were there to Jerusalem to be punished." (Acts 22:1-5)

The Lord was about to get Paul's attention on this trip. Paul relates his cataclysmic encounter with Jesus while traveling to Damascus to carry out his orders from the high priests. Paul didn't just see some apparition on the highway that day. He encountered Jesus Christ in the fullness of His glory, a light so bright that Paul was left blind and had to be led into Damascus. Yes, this great and powerful Pharisee was reduced to a stumbling, blind man being led like a child with no idea what his future held. Sounds like many of us today, wouldn't you agree? Paul was about to take his second step on God's stairway, a step of conversion and brokenness. In doing so realized that his life, education and ministry were not in accordance with God's will. In fact, his life up to this point had been used as a diversionary tactic by Satan to derail him from his true purpose.

> Now it happened, as I journeyed and came near Damascus at about noon, suddenly a great light from heaven shone around me. And I fell to the ground and heard a voice saying to me, "Saul, Saul, why are you persecuting Me?" So I answered, "Who are You, Lord?" And He said to me, "I am Jesus of Nazareth, whom you are persecuting." (Acts 22:6-8)

Paul was then instructed by Jesus to continue on his journey to Damascus, but for an entirely different purpose than what he had previously intended. Paul had been broken on that road, his life turned upside down. As he continued the journey he was now experiencing conversion and was no longer in control of his destiny. He had received a revelation that not only saved his soul from hell, but also was about to turn him into the biggest cheerleader for Christ who ever lived.

> And those who were with me indeed saw the light and were afraid, but they did not hear the voice of Him who spoke to me. So I said, "What shall I do, Lord?" And the Lord said to me, "Arise and go into Damascus, and there you will be told all things which are appointed for you to do." And since I could not see for the glory of that light, being led by the hand of those who were with me, I came into Damascus.
> (Acts 22:9-11)

Paul, the mighty Pharisee, who under authority of the high priest so boldly persecuted Christ's followers, fell to the ground, trembling, and astonished. What kind of power does this to a man of his stature? The power of Jesus by His Holy Spirit!

Paul had a choice. He could have ignored what happened and just gone about his way, pretending that it was a hoax or some freak of nature. Of course, Paul's eyes were wide open, but he couldn't see, so it might have been difficult to ignore. We learn earlier in Acts that Paul had been blinded by the light of Christ and on top of that, he must have lost all desire to sustain himself because he didn't eat or drink for three days.

> And he was three days without sight, and neither ate nor drank. (Acts 9:9)

When the Lord is ready to get your attention, you had better pay attention, because He is not moved by your ambitions or your circumstances. He is not threatened by your so called "letters" of authority, your diplomas or your bank accounts, much less your petty intellectual arguments about whether He was just a ordinary man, a prophet or a good teacher. When the God of the Universe is ready to get your attention, as we learned in the first chapter, you will be baptized with the Holy Spirit and with fire The Lord had Paul's attention.

The third step for Paul on the Lord's stairway came in the form of restoration and repentance. Upon his arrival in Damascus, he was led to the house of Ananias, a devout follower of the law who was well respected among the Jews.

Christ works through the natural as we see through Paul's experience. He told Paul to go into Damascus and wait until he is told what to do. Meanwhile, in Damascus, the Lord was also speaking to a man named Ananias in a vision. He told Ananias that "Saul of Tarsus" would be coming to visit in order to receive prayer and restoration of his sight.

> Now there was a certain disciple at Damascus named Ananias; and to him the Lord said in a vision, "Ananias." And he said, "Here I am, Lord." So the Lord said to him, "Arise and go to the street called Straight, and inquire at the house of Judas for one called Saul of Tarsus, for behold, he is praying. And in a vision he has seen a man named Ananias coming in and putting his hand on him, so that he might receive his sight."
> (Acts 9:10-12)

Ananias was not very pleased by this prospect and questioned God's reasoning, offering up factual evidence of Saul's persecution of the saints. Ananias must have been thinking, "What are you talking about God? You want me to do what?"

> Then Ananias answered, "Lord, I have heard from many about this man, how much harm he has done to Your saints in Jerusalem. And here he has authority from the chief priests to bind all who call on Your name." But the Lord said to him, "Go, for he is a chosen vessel of Mine to bear My name before Gentiles, kings, and the children of Israel. For I will show him how many things he must suffer for My name's sake."
> (Acts 9:13-16)

In the verse below we learn Ananias was obedient to the Lord. He immediately entered the house and laid hands on Saul so that he could regain his sight and be filled with the Holy Spirit. Paul was restored at that very second. "There fell from his eyes something like scales."

We also know based on Paul's own admission that when Ananias restored his sight, he also informed him of a new purpose: "You will be His witness to all men." Ananias had led him into repentance, which was the turning away from his previous life toward the purpose God had in store for him. We now know Paul faithfully and dutifully followed Jesus for the rest of his life.

> And Ananias went his way and entered the house; and laying his hands on him he said, "Brother Saul, the Lord Jesus, who appeared to you on the road as you came, has sent me that you may receive your sight and be filled with the Holy Spirit." Immediately there fell from his eyes something like scales, and he received his sight at once; and he arose and was baptized. (Acts 9:17-18)

> Then a certain Ananias, a devout man according to the law, having a good testimony with all the Jews who dwelt there, came to me; and he stood and said to me, "Brother Saul, receive your sight." And at that same hour I looked up at him. Then he said, "The God of our fathers has chosen you that you should know His will, and see the Just One, and hear the voice of His mouth. For you will be His witness to all men of what you have seen and heard." (Acts 22:12-15)

The fourth step in Paul's journey was purification, the cleansing of his sinful nature, and the realization that his eternal salvation was secure.

Ananias didn't waste any time. After restoring Paul, he tells him to "Arise and be baptized," which signified the washing away of his old sinful nature. Paul, now "in a trance," receives another visitation from the Lord instructing him to flee the city, away from death. The Lord was directing him away from a life of death toward a new life leading to eternal salvation.

> And now why are you waiting? Arise and be baptized, and wash away your sins, calling on the name of the Lord. Now it happened, when I returned to Jerusalem and was praying in the temple, that I was in a trance and saw Him saying to me,

> "Make haste and get out of Jerusalem quickly, for they will not receive your testimony concerning Me." (Acts 22:16-18)

Later we learn in the first chapter of Galatians that it was three years after Paul's conversion that he returned to Jerusalem and spent 15 days with Peter. However, Paul goes on to tell us in the second chapter of Galatians that it was 14 years later that he returned and his real ministry took off.

> Then after three years I went up to Jerusalem to see Peter, and remained with him fifteen days. (Galatians 1:18)

> Then fourteen years after I went up again to Jerusalem with Barnabas, and took Titus with me also. And I went up by revelation, and communicated unto them that gospel which I preach among the Gentiles, but privately to them which were of reputation, lest by any means I should run, or had run, in vain. (Galatians 2:1-2)

No one really knows what happened to Paul during this period, but I challenge you to think that it was a period of ongoing refinement—purification, if you will—preparing Paul for the years ahead. As a result of that purification process, Paul's influence on christian thinking was unparalleled at the time and still is today.

The fifth step for Paul was a call to ministry; a step that, unknown to him at the time, would end up having an impact on mankind for years to come.

Through Ananias, the Lord was commissioning Paul and sending him to the Gentile world in order to preach the gospel and share the truth of His eternal salvation. His life would never to be the same from that day forward. Of course, in Paul's extreme wisdom, he decides to instruct the Lord that this is probably not a very good idea.

> So I said, "Lord, they know that in every synagogue I imprisoned and beat those who believe on You. And when the blood of Your martyr Stephen was shed, I also was standing by consenting to his death, and guarding the clothes of those who were killing him."
> (Acts 22:19-20)

The Gentiles, I might remind you, at the time were considered archaically pagan and heathenish by the Jews. God sending Paul to the Gentiles, in a Jew's way of thinking, would be like sending your dog to the wolves.

Are we not like Paul? The Lord speaks to us daily, warning us of impending danger. And all we can do is remind Him of the obvious. "You want me to do what? Don't you know there are pitfalls along that path?" Maybe we don't use those exact words or the same argument as Paul, but we say it in our actions as we turn and go in the opposite direction. However, the Lord is not moved by our petty arguments. And judging by His response to Paul, He was obviously not moved by Paul's either.

> Then He said to me, "Depart, for I will send you far from here to the Gentiles." (Acts 22:21)

Jesus repeated a similar charge to his disciples in Matthew 28:19, when He said, "Go therefore and make disciples of all the nations, baptizing them in the name of the Father and of the Son and of the Holy Spirit." The disciples, like Paul, were not very well liked during their time, but were faithful to heed the call. Once we start scaling the steps on God's stairway to heaven, He will call us into ministry, whether we like it or not.

STEP I - Acknowledgement, Acceptance, & Trust

There can be no acceptance of God's love without first acknowledging that God exists and learning who God is. Only through placing our trust in Christ alone for our salvation can we have a born-again experience.

Thus, the first step we must make in order to climb the stairway of heaven is to acknowledge that God is real, and accept the fact He loves us. And then we are to place our trust in Him alone for salvation by inviting Him into our hearts by the power of His Holy Spirit.

Jesus paved the way by His sacrifice. In doing so, He told His disciples that He would go to prepare a place for them. Without this first step, we are lost in our sin and deceived.

Many people are living comfortably in their surroundings of choice. Some live in small homes with very little and others in big homes with many possessions. The common denominator in our society—regardless of our surroundings or the size of our toys—is that most of us are putting up a front, pretending to be happy.

My thoughts drift back to the day I sensed the Lord's urging in my inner man. It was clear that I, like most christians, was practicing the same behaviors in life, expecting different results. It was Albert Einstein who said, "Insanity is doing the same thing over and over again and expecting different results."

Oh, I was attending church every Sunday, even serving faithfully as a Chalice Bearer ordained by the Episcopal Bishop and was president of our men's group. But I wasn't fully aware of what it meant to walk with the Lord in my heart. Like many I was regularly attending church and practicing certain behaviors, but not expecting to bear the consequences associated with those behaviors. Some reading this will be able to relate.

Of course, there are many in our society who rarely—if ever—attend church and still others who are *holiday christians*, meaning they only attend church at Christmas and Easter. Simply stated, without the knowledge of God's truth found in His Word we are lost.

Consequently, once we gain knowledge of the Word and embrace God's truth our behavior will change for the better. For this reason, each of us should be asking, "God am I on your stairway to heaven?"

> I know your works, that you are neither cold nor hot. I could wish you were cold or hot. So then, because you are lukewarm, and neither cold nor hot, I will vomit you out of My mouth. Because you say, "I am rich, have become wealthy, and have need of nothing"—and do not know that you are wretched, miserable, poor, blind, and naked. (Revelation 3:15-17)

Whether we want to admit it or not, if we don't abide by His Word, but continue to indulge in sinful behavior, we will be keeping God at arm's length. Sinful behavior includes moral ineptitude, unethical behavior, pride, arrogance, lust, lying, cheating, cussing, idolatry, fornication, substance abuse, sexual abuse, pornography and others. If we are going to be completely honest with God, we are all guilty! No one is exempt from sin. In fact, just fill in the blank with the sin of your choice.

> For if we sin willfully after we have received the knowledge of the truth, there no longer remains a sacrifice for sins, but a certain fearful expectation of judgment, and fiery indignation which will devour the adversaries. Anyone who has rejected Moses' law dies without mercy on the testimony of two or three witnesses. Of how much worse punishment, do you

suppose, will he be thought worthy who has trampled the Son of God underfoot, counted the blood of the covenant by which he was sanctified a common thing, and insulted the Spirit of grace? (Hebrews 10:26-29)

Sin, once conceived, has a toehold in our life and manifests in various ways. It will have its way with you and in most cases with those around you.

> He who walks with wise men will be wise, But the companion of fools will be destroyed. (Proverbs 13:20)

The question then becomes, "Are we willing to acknowledge our sin or not?" If we choose not to acknowledge our sin, then we are separated from God. If we are separated from God, then we cannot be free of the pain of that separation. Oh sure, some of you reading this might be thinking, "I'm not in pain. In fact, my life is pretty good." To those of you who think you are not in pain, I ask, "How are you medicating your pain?" To which you might respond, "What do you mean? I'm not in pain. I am happy. After all I have a good job, a big house, several cars and a loving husband/wife?" Are you sure? How do you know that you aren't using those possessions to medicate your spiritual pain—your separation from God?

It is one thing to acknowledge God exists, but another to accept His "way, truth and life." The fact that no one goes to the Father except through Jesus Christ.

> Jesus said to him, "I am the way, the truth, and the life. No one comes to the Father except through Me." (John 14:6)

The scripture is clear we must place our trust in His sacrifice in order to have salvation. We come to the Father who no longer sees our sin. No longer are we condemned by the law given to Moses. No longer do we fear eternal damnation. Instead our names are written in the "Lamb's Book of Life."

> But there shall by no means enter it anything that defiles, or causes an abomination or a lie, but only those who are written in the Lamb's Book of Life. (Revelation 21:27)

Revelation is given by the Holy Spirit. After our conception or rebirth has taken place, we begin to understand who Jesus really is and what His love for us really means. Like any child, we are reared in a society of a different choosing. It is only through a revelatory experience that we can have a new understanding of our surroundings.

In the stock market, we learn that the price of a stock will fluctuate between a floor and a ceiling. In order to hedge our investments, we must understand this concept. We watch the price of a stock over time, charting its upward and downward movements. When the trends appear we know it is either time to buy or sell that stock. Our intention is to limit our downside risk and maximize our upward potential. Unfortunately, with God, the only way to limit your downside risk is to truly trust Him in your heart.

God knows the true nature of your heart, so no one can make a false decision to place their trust in Jesus in hopes of hedging his or her spiritual bets. God cannot be deceived and God will not withhold His love. Once you make a heartfelt decision to trust in Jesus Christ, you have stepped on the Lord's up escalator (stairway) and are on your way to heaven. Unlike the mall escalators, God's escalator never breaks down and never stops running. No one can snatch us out of the Father's hand.

> My Father, who has given them to Me, is greater than all; and no one is able to snatch them out of My Father's hand. I and My Father are one. (John 10:29-30)

STEP II - Conversion & Brokenness

The conversion process usually begins with some catalytic moment or event, causing us to discover that our lives are heading in the wrong direction or spiraling out of control. As a result, we make a decided and determined effort to change. Through brokenness, we come to realize we are powerless to effect change in our life and give into God's guidance, submitting to His Lordship.

When we first truly trust Christ as Lord and Savior we feel exhilarated, a peaceful feeling comes over us and we want to tell everyone about our decision. But an interesting thing happens when we encounter the second step: areas of our life become exposed; certain behaviors are revealed; and the process of conviction sets in. At first, it feels condemning because we don't realize that God is responding to our call. However, in time, as we experience brokenness, we come to realize there is a newfound freedom in Christ that brings lasting peace. We come to an understanding that our life has eternal meaning.

Try to reflect back to a time in your life when you cried out for help, maybe asking the Lord to come to your rescue. Can you remember His response to your call? Some may not remember ever crying out to the Lord, but nevertheless, most everyone has cried out at one time or another in some form or fashion—possibly to some higher power. God is always listening and it could very well be in those moments that our spiritual journey starts to take root. Revelation sets in, and God slowly begins revealing our shortcomings, and exposing what needs to happen in order for them to be removed.

For some, it takes years before they truly grasp revelation of God's presence in their life. The weeds may have grown up, choking the memory that they once cried out to God. It is not until after they are broken that God brings it back to their memory. There are others who have walked away, but clearly remember times when they cried out.

God is patient, longing to reveal that He has been by your side all along, even in the midst of your rejection and rebellion. There will be some who are so infected by their upbringing and circumstances that the revelation of God's love will have to hit them over the head with a hammer. We learned earlier in the chapter that Paul experienced this on the road to Damascus and, like Paul, anyone who has ever experienced the Lord's hammer can relate.

Of course, there will be some of you who have lived a nearly sin free life. These are the rare cases, but you will have struggles. God must break you down as well in order to change your societal/inherent thinking, so that you may mature in your christian walk. No one is exempt. We are all born into sin. Therefore, we all must experience conversion and brokenness if we wish to scale God's stairway.

> Therefore, just as through one man sin entered the world, and death through sin, and thus death spread to all men, because all sinned. (Romans 5:12)

Throughout the conversion process, we begin to own up to our past behavior and the consequences associated with that behavior. We learn that God has been at work long before we acknowledged Him trying to get our attention. Yet out of loving respect for each of us, He has waited until the day we made that heartfelt decision and asked Him to remove our shortcomings.

If you are indeed on His stairway to heaven, you will sense conviction in the areas of your heart where you are not lined up with His will. If you don't deal with those areas, eventually you will experience the pain of separation. Unfortunately, we aren't always ready to embrace that conviction. We might fight the conversion process and make a decision to rebel. It is at those times we have turned around and are walking down God's stairs. We might even be thinking that life would be easier if God would just leave us alone.

Fortunately, God's stairway is always going up, and once we step on it, there is no getting off. He will bring conviction out of His love for us. He will never be content to sit back and let your sin remain long-term. Yes, regardless of your shortcomings and regardless of the direction you are heading, you are always going up, because He will "never leave you or forsake you."

> Let your conduct be without covetousness; be content with such things as you have. For He Himself has said, "I will never leave you nor forsake you." (Hebrews 13:5)

He will always bring you around to the right way of thinking. Yes, it might take years. But make no mistake about it, God will not be denied.

If you have children, think about this for a moment. Say your male child grabed a knife from the block in the kitchen, what do you do? Do you just sit idly by, waiting for him to cut himself to pieces? No, you educate him on the dangers of sharp objects. But let's assume that you were too late and the child had already cut himself. Do you just scold him and walk out of the room, disgusted by his ignorance? Of course not! You don't abandon him, but nurse his wound, and once again educate him on the dangers of sharp objects. It might take awhile, but in time he will learn not to play with knives. Your long-term goal is that this lesson would burn deeply into his heart and protect him in future situations.

God's goal is the same for us. Sin is like that sharp object. If we don't learn to avoid it, it will cause us pain because no one escapes the effect that pain will eventually have on the heart. It is an absolute impossibility. If you don't feel the pain then you need to re-evaluate your commitment to the Lord by asking, "Is Christ really the Lord of my life?" This is not a question I need to ask you and it is not a question for others to ask you. It is a question between you and the Lord because it is up to you and the Lord to "work out your salvation."

> Therefore, my beloved, as you have always obeyed, not as in my presence only, but now much more in my absence, *work out your own salvation* with fear and trembling. (Philippians 2:12)

Luke gives us an account of how Jesus attempted to bring conviction in the hearts of the Pharisees. Pharisees were supposed to be the most intelligent and godly men among the people. But as Jesus spoke the truth, what should have brought conviction actually brought condemnation. Out of their prideful ignorance, they purported not to acknowledge any evidence that Jesus was the Son of God.

> Now the Pharisees, who were lovers of money, also heard all these things, and they derided Him. And He said to them, "You are those who justify yourselves before men, but God knows your hearts. For what is highly esteemed among men is an abomination in the sight of God. (Luke 16:14-15)

> But there were also false prophets among the people, just as there will be false teachers among you. They will secretly introduce destructive heresies, even denying the sovereign Lord who bought them—bringing swift destruction on themselves. Many will follow their depraved conduct and will bring the way of truth into disrepute. In their greed these teachers will exploit you with fabricated stories. Their condemnation has long been hanging over them, and their destruction has not been sleeping. (2 Peter 2: 2-3)

Like the Pharisees, sometimes when our behavior is not lined up with God's Word, we too will start to feel condemned. It is extremely important to understand the difference between conviction and condemnation. The spiritual pain of conviction is different from the physical pain of condemnation. Conviction appeals to our inner man and our sense of right and wrong. Condemnation will try to entrap you based on your past or present actions, causing you to doubt that your sin was ever forgiven.

> There is therefore now no condemnation to those who are in Christ Jesus, who do not walk according to the flesh, but according to the Spirit. (Romans 8:1)

> And when He has come, He will convict the world of sin, and of righteousness, and of judgment: (John 16:8)

Oftentimes, we might not even understand where the conviction is coming from or why we feel convicted, but somewhere down deep inside, we know our behavior is skewed. Most often, until the Lord brings conviction, we aren't even aware of certain sins. But once we make the decision to invite the Holy Spirit into our hearts, the Lord begins our conversion. Even if we continue to make the wrong decisions, the Lord will be patient and will not give up. He will eventually break us of all sinful behavior.

Some of us will suffer more brokenness than others due to the addictive choices that have been extracted from our societal upbringing prior to that point in time. It is not until we stop and surrender that we begin to appreciate being on His stairway to heaven. Then we can embrace what He is teaching: God loves us and desires for our sinful hearts to be exposed in order to set us free from S.I.N.'s grasp.

When we own that revelation and allow those behaviors to be eradicated, something begins to happen. We start longing for Him. His Word comes to life within us as we begin to read with a new understanding. It is now that we actually start walking up His stairway; some might even begin to run.

My own conversion phase started early on when I was a young boy attending church with my parents. We attended the Methodist Church every Sunday, and I can remember being excited about going through sixth grade confirmation. Unfortunately, about this time, there was a transition in my father's life, and our family started only attending church sporadically and on holidays. I no longer looked forward to sixth-grade confirmation and consequently don't remember ever attending Sunday school again.

A few years later in high school, my friends and I had been invited to a Young Life meeting. The only reason we attended was out of the desire to meet some new girls. At the end of the meeting, they handed out these little pamphlets that explained man's sinful nature and how that sin had separated us from God. It went on to say that God sent his only begotten Son to live among us, only to have His family and friends reject Him and ultimately execute Him on a cross. Finally, it showed that He bore the burden of all our sin on that cross, but that God raised Him from death. As a result, we could have a personal relationship with Him through the power of the Holy Spirit of God. If we would only put our trust in Jesus Christ, we would have eternal life. At the end of the story, there was a short prayer you could recite to trust and invite Jesus Christ into your heart.

Evidently, I had some fear of the Lord, because I remember fearfully thinking, "This could very well be true, so I better say the prayer." I felt that if He was real, then He must have created everything, and I sure didn't want to be on the outside looking in. What I didn't know at the time was that fear came from the Lord and fear was a good thing. Why? Because as we learned earlier in chapter five, the word tells us,

> The fear of the Lord is the beginning of knowledge, But fools despise wisdom and instruction. (Proverbs 1:7)

Somehow, I felt that if I didn't recite the prayer, He would abandon me like so many others had in my life. I had pain inside, but I had enough medication in the form of drugs and alcohol that kept me from fully dealing with the pain. That night, a conversion took place in my heart that was just the beginning of my journey on His stairway to heaven.

Let me relate another testimony about a good friend who experienced conversion later in life, which might help you better understand how the Lord works. He was a prominent executive, revered by the professional community. He had risen up through the ranks until, at the height of his career, he was responsible for thousands of employees. Outside, he had all the appearances of a man who had made it. He had two homes, numerous cars, several boats, multiple hunting leases, and went on several vacations per year, oftentimes to exotic places. He would take business associates, some married, on trips where they would indulge in sinful pleasures.

At home, his wife turned to drinking, eventually becoming an alcoholic, and his kids came to resent him. Throughout the business community, rumors began circulating about his extreme bursts of anger and his management style. The style that had emerged said, "Do as I say not as I do, and if you don't do what I say you will have me to deal with." If anyone crossed him, he would cut his or her legs out from under them. If anyone confronted him about his behavior, he would get in their face and intimidate them until they just gave up. His journey through life wasn't pretty, and he was corrupting many lives.

Suddenly, in a burst of outrage, he left his wife and family, failing to acknowledge that he was the problem. Instead, he blamed everyone else. Friends ceased calling and business associates cut a wide path around him, avoiding confrontation. The business he was managing started having problems and there was little he could do to fix them. He became isolated and alone, and his mind began racing. No amount of medication could eradicate the pain he was feeling. By his own admission, as he looked back over his life and career, he saw dead bodies lying along the road where he had traveled. He began to feel the guilt of his actions and condemnation set in, until he felt like it would be best for himself and everyone if he took his life. He contemplated suicide and began to think of ways to end his life in such a way that his family would be taken care of financially.

Then one night, sitting alone in an apartment, the pain became too much to bear. He dropped to his knees and cried out, "God I can't take it anymore! Please help me, take the pain, and forgive me for ruining the lives of so many, especially my family! Take my pain, help me, Lord! I don't want to live like this anymore! I need you Jesus, please Lord come into my heart."

The next day, he felt as if a 100-pound weight had been lifted off his shoulders. He began attending a local church, where it turned out he knew several members. Of course, initially they kept a good distance from him, but he showed up in their small groups and started crying out for help. A few men got around him, started praying for him, and agreed to meet with him on a regular basis. At work, people started warming back up to him and suddenly many of the problems started to dissipate and became less of a burden to deal with.

For the first time in his life, he started to see people as human beings, not as slaves. He started to have compassion for them and began to realize the affect his behavior had on them. How his behavior had affected their ability to perform.

Do these testimonies sound familiar to you? Can you see any of the patterns outlined above in your life? If you still feel trapped by your shortcomings, embrace Him, cry out to Him and ask Him to begin the conversion process in your heart. God longs to reveal your sin through conviction in order to free you. But it is up to you to take action, asking Him to remove it. You don't have to wait until you are completely broken and destitute.

Understand that society has provided various ways for you to medicate your pain, such as drugs and alcohol, but let's not leave out the love of money, material possessions, work, food or sexual relationships. Maybe it is time to cease medicating.

> But know this, that in the last days perilous times will come: For men will be lovers of themselves, lovers of money, boasters, proud, blasphemers, disobedient to parents, unthankful, unholy, unloving, unforgiving, slanderers, without self-control, brutal, despisers of good, traitors, headstrong, haughty, lovers of pleasure rather than lovers of God, having a

> form of godliness but denying its power. And from such people turn away! For of this sort are those who creep into households and make captives of gullible women loaded down with sins, led away by various lusts, always learning and never able to come to the knowledge of the truth. (2 Timothy 3:1-7)

We have already shown that all of these medications are a form of societal addiction. They will either pull you into the pit of hell, which leads to eternal separation from God or cause the pain of conviction to come into your heart so that you will ask God to remove your shortcomings.

Freedom comes through the revelation that Jesus Christ died on the cross for your sin and by the process of brokenness and conversion, you climb the stairs to eternal life. Wouldn't you agree that this freedom is just a little bit important? After all, eternity is an awful long time!

> **Eternity:** 1. infinite time; duration without beginning or end. 2. eternal existence, esp. as contrasted with mortal life: the eternity of God. 3. Theology. the timeless state into which the soul passes at a person's death. 4. an endless or seemingly endless period of time: We had to wait an eternity for the check to arrive. (27)

The choice is yours: acknowledge you are powerless over S.I.N. and embrace God's conviction or hide, ignore the pain, and suffer condemnation. We need to wake up and quit denying that the real choice we are talking about is *eternal life or eternal death*.

> "He who believes in Him is not condemned; but he who does not believe is condemned already, because he has not believed in the name of the only begotten Son of God. And this is the condemnation, that the light has come into the world, and men loved darkness rather than light, because their deeds were evil. (John 3:18-19)

STEP III - Repentance & Restoration

S.I.N. will attempt to draw us back into its clutches by reminding us of our past behaviors and circumstances. However, as we continue to turn away, ignoring S.I.N.'s advances, we continue to be restored in the image of Christ. We must remain alert, because the enemy will try to steal God's deposit from our heart. Jesus forewarns us in Matthew when he spoke to the people in a parable about the sower. He gives us a visual of how an invisible enemy works to steal the truth of His Word.

> Then He spoke many things to them in parables, saying: "Behold, a sower went out to sow. And as he sowed, some seed fell by the wayside; and the birds came and devoured them. Some fell on stony places, where they did not have much earth; and they immediately sprang up because they had no depth of earth. But when the sun was up they were scorched, and because they had no root they withered away. And some fell among thorns, and the thorns sprang up and choked them. But others fell on good ground and yielded a crop: some a hundredfold, some sixty, some thirty. He who has ears to hear, let him hear!" And the disciples came and said to Him, "Why do You speak to them in parables?" (Matthew 13:3-10)

Afterwards, Jesus met with his disciples, but they too were confused and asked why He spoke in parables. Jesus went on to explain to them what the parable meant. Some hear the Word without revelation and immediately it is snatched away. Others hear the Word and gain an elated feeling, but having limited faith, when tribulation or persecutions arise, they stumble. Some hear the Word with revelation, but the cares of the world and the deceitfulness of riches steal its meaning and the fruit to be gained by it. However, as our hearts are molded and the seed of sin is eradicated, the Word will take root, because we receive it on fertile ground with understanding—as evidenced by our walk and the fruit produced by our deeds.

> Therefore hear the parable of the sower: When anyone hears the word of the kingdom, and does not understand it, then the wicked one comes and snatches away what was sown in his heart. This is he who received seed by the wayside. But he who received the seed on stony places, this is he who hears the word and immediately receives it with joy; yet he has no root in himself, but endures only for a while. For when tribulation or persecution arises because of the word, immediately he stumbles. Now he who received seed among the thorns is he who hears the word, and the cares of this world and the deceitfulness of riches choke the word, and he becomes

> unfruitful. But he who received seed on the good ground is he who hears the word and understands it, who indeed bears fruit and produces: some a hundredfold, some sixty, some thirty. (Matthew 13:18-23)

The key is to remain in God's Word through faith, so that the seed of truth will prevail in our hearts. That seed germinates in the good ground of our heart, and as it grows, it brings godly sorrow through conviction and calls us to repentance. As we turn away from our sinful behavior toward God's goodness, eternal fruit is produced.

It is an incorruptible seed that abides forever through the Word of God, and the eternal fruit that is produced by that seed is our salvation or immortality.

> Having been born again, not of corruptible seed but incorruptible, through the word of God which lives and abides forever (1 Peter 1:23)

> Incorruptible - aphthartos; undecaying: not corruptible, immortal. (31)

You remember Peter, don't you? Peter was the disciple Jesus told in Matthew 16:18 that he would build His church on: "And I also say to you that you are Peter, and on this rock I will build My church, and the gates of Hades shall not prevail against it." Of course, this is the same Peter who denied Christ three times and forsook Him at His greatest hour. Aren't we a lot like Peter, in the sense that we turn away when we are faced with difficult circumstances and feel abandoned by the Lord? It is at these times that we might even doubt Christ's sovereign power.

Have you ever prayed so hard for something, only to be left holding your head in your hands thinking that your prayer has fallen on deaf ears? Or have you ever thought, "Maybe I have believed a lie. After all, if Christ is real, why would He allow me to be beaten down by my enemy?" Don't you think Peter was thinking these same thoughts? After all, he had walked faithfully with Christ for three years only to arrive in the garden of Gethsemane to witness Jesus' arrest.

> When Jesus had spoken these words, He went out with His disciples over the Brook Kidron, where there was a garden, which He and His disciples entered. And Judas, who betrayed

> Him, also knew the place; for Jesus often met there with His disciples. Then Judas, having received a detachment of troops, and officers from the chief priests and Pharisees, came there with lanterns, torches, and weapons. (John 18:1-3)

Peter was perplexed, to say the least, and was probably thinking, "This can't happen to my savior who has come to assume the throne and rule His earthly kingdom!" So Peter, full of vigor, immediately draws his sword, ready to do battle. Suddenly, Peter's expectations came crashing down around him as Christ rebukes him, telling him to sheath his sword.

> Then Simon Peter, having a sword, drew it and struck the high priest's servant, and cut off his right ear. The servant's name was Malchus. So Jesus said to Peter, "Put your sword into the sheath. Shall I not drink the cup which My Father has given Me?" (John 18:10-11)

In what would be Christ's finest hour, his faithful and loving servant Peter denied ever knowing him. Yes, we are just like Peter in the sense that every time we sin, we are denying Christ. We learn in the book of John that Christ longs to restore His saints, and He restores Peter.

> This is now the third time Jesus showed Himself to His disciples after He was raised from the dead. So when they had eaten breakfast, Jesus said to Simon Peter, "Simon, son of Jonah, do you love Me more than these?" He said to Him, "Yes, Lord; You know that I love You." He said to him, "Feed My lambs." He said to him again a second time, "Simon, son of Jonah, do you love Me?" He said to Him, "Yes, Lord; You know that I love You." He said to him, "Tend My sheep." He said to him the third time, "Simon, son of Jonah, do you love Me?" Peter was grieved because He said to him the third time, "Do you love Me?" And he said to Him, "Lord, You know all things; You know that I love You." Jesus said to him, "Feed My sheep. Most assuredly, I say to you, when you were younger, you girded yourself and walked where you wished; but when you are old, you will stretch out your hands, and another will gird you and carry you where you do not wish." This He spoke, signifying by what death he would glorify

God. And when He had spoken this, He said to him, "Follow Me." (John 21:14-19)

Isn't it interesting that just as Peter denied Christ three times, Christ restores Peter three times? Each time, telling Peter to feed and tend His flock. Christ restores Peter in such a way that Peter becomes the rock that Jesus had earlier prophesied to him about. It is only by our sinful admission that we experience the same godly sorrow Peter felt that leads us to repentance. Repentance because of godly sorrow allows us to break down our sense of pride and turn from the exposed sin toward God's saving grace.

It was always Christ's intention to drink from the cup His Father had given Him by suffering death. And it was always God's intention to bring restoration through Christ's resurrection for all mankind. God loves us as sons and daughters.

STEP IV - Purification & Eternal Salvation

Purification is the ongoing process of refinement until the day we draw our last breath and realize the eternal salvation promised by Christ. No matter how fast we try to run on God's stairway, we don't reach heaven any sooner. Once we accept Christ's love by acknowledging His death and resurrection, our stairway to heaven becomes more of a guided escalator with God controlling the speed of the belt. Over time, we become more aware of the root issues that caused our sinful behavior. Even though we have been delivered from that sin, there is residual buildup that needs to be stripped. Thus, the process of purification continues.

I recently visited Home Depot to pick up materials to refurbish a deck. The first step was to wash the old wood cleaning off any mold or mildew. The second step was to use stripper to remove the buildup of the old finish in order to restore the wood to its original condition. The final step was to put on a fresh coat of stain to achieve the desired look.

Our spiritual purification process is much the same way. The Lord cleanses us of our sin, strips down our hearts through the process of conviction, and then continually restores us until one day we will assume new bodies made in His image. His ultimate goal should be our ultimate goal—to be like Christ.

When we are confronted with the various areas in our lives that need to be stripped, we should be obedient, submissive and steadfast in our response. Jesus was.

> And for their sakes I sanctify Myself, that they also may be sanctified by the truth. (John 17:19)

Why do you think Jesus told his disciples that in order to enter the Kingdom, we must become like little children? Could it be because children are so full of faith? Jesus wants us to trust, not to doubt or question, but accept Him by faith. Jesus desired to take His disciples deeper, where a completely new world would open to them.

> Assuredly, I say to you, whoever does not receive the kingdom of God as a little child will by no means enter it. (Mark 10:15)

All they had to do is grasp the elementary but profound truth of how God molded us to learn. I challenge you to look more deeply into what Jesus was trying to show them. Jesus understood how God created us. He also understood clearly how we become tainted by S.I.N. as we grow up influenced by our surroundings.

As babies, we soak in all the sights and sounds and begin to explore our surroundings. Then it is on to early childhood, where we are weaned and taught to stand on our own and to walk.

Next we continue to grow and learn throughout our adolescent years. Oftentimes, negative seeds are planted that one day will have to be extracted in order for us to live a productive life. As we mature during adolescence, we are expected to conform and obey, but more often than not we rebel and the personalities that have been there all along become more distinct.

As we move into young adulthood, we are encouraged to search, gain knowledge and expand our understanding of the world in which we live. Over the years, every generation ultimately challenges the system in one form or another, searching for answers.

Then it is on to adulthood, where we are supposed to make as much money as possible so we can realize our dreams. During this process, we start taking on the cares of the world.

The next phase is the senior years when we are supposed to relax, travel and experience all of life's pleasures. It is usually during this time we begin to understand what it's like to be a child again. In fact, children are even more attracted to us. I remember seeing a cartoon of a little boy talking with his grandfather. The boy's father enters the room and the grandfather says to his grandson, "Uh-oh, the enemy."

Inevitably, over time, our loved ones will begin to fall ill and eventually die. One would hope that before death comes that we would reach the truth—that all of our earthly striving was in vain. Why? We can't take anything with us. Upon this revelation, the spiritual realities in life become more apparent. For one, we have an eternal inheritance in the kingdom of God.

Children initially take everything at face value, trusting unconditionally, and they are moldable. Our Lord longs to have communion with us, if we would only lay down our intellectual pride and our agendas. By becoming his spiritual children and by His loving grace, we too will grow in knowledge, wisdom, and understanding.

> But grow in the grace and knowledge of our Lord and Savior Jesus Christ. To Him be the glory both now and forever. Amen. (2 Peter 3:18)

The Kingdom of God can only be realized through faith. It is at our fingertips. It is ours for the taking.

Do you remember being water baptized and the cleansing power of that event that washed away all your mold and mildew, your sinfulness? Let me pause here to say if you haven't been water baptized by this time, why delay? Why not take advantage of all God has to offer by realizing a spiritual rebirth and allowing him to clean off your mold and mildew? Then from that day on, ask the Lord to strip away the darkness lurking in your heart, ask Him to slowly change you from the inside out and form you into His image in preparation for the day you will pass from this life to a life after death.

The Lord purifies us by rebuilding our lives in such a way that, over time, we take on more and more of His character, being conformed to the image of Christ. The purification process lasts a lifetime as we continue climbing His stairs!

> For whom He foreknew, He also predestined to be conformed to the image of His Son, that He might be the firstborn among many brethren. (Romans 8:29)

STEP V - Ministry

Earlier, we read this scripture in the gospel of Matthew. It is known as *The Great Commission*.

> And Jesus came and spoke to them, saying, "All authority has been given to Me in heaven and on earth. Go therefore and make disciples of all the nations, baptizing them in the name of the Father and of the Son and of the Holy Spirit, teaching them to observe all things that I have commanded you; and lo, I am with you always, even to the end of the age." Amen. (Matthew 28:18-21)

First, we must go into our daily lives living out the principle He has taught us through the purification process. In doing so, we all become ministers or representatives of Christ's love. We are called to make disciples. Jesus then commands us to baptize "Them in the name of the Father and of the Son and of the Holy Spirit." This means we are to joyfully share the truth of His gospel by letting them know there is no other message that will wash them of their sins. They can only be washed by the blood of the Lamb and renewed by a revelatory understanding of the Trinity. Next, He instructs us to be teachers of His Word, following the example He set forth in His own ministry, while here on earth. We must read His Word daily and study it vigorously, imbedding it deep in our hearts so we as faithful servants can then impart that knowledge to faithful people.

The apostle Paul understood this concept better than anyone did when he was instructing Timothy.

> And the things that you have heard from me among many witnesses, commit these to faithful men who will be able to teach others also. (2 Timothy 2:2)

Finally, yet most importantly, He wants us to know that we are not alone on our journey to share His love with others. He is always with us, because when He departed after dying on the cross and rising again to be with God in Heaven, He imparted His unseen power that is unsurpassed here on earth. It is a spiritual power that, once embraced, understood, and exercised, allows us to move the spiritual mountains surrounding us—the mountains of S.I.N. The enemy has surrounded us with these mountains, attempting to discourage and disappoint us so we will lose hope and turn away from the truth of the gospel.

In 2001, I was asked to lead a group from my church, in conjunction with an international ministry team, to a country in the Caribbean. This call from the Lord would result in one of the most meaningful events of my life up to that point.

Upon entering the country and searching out the church we were to be aligned with during our stay, I found that they had not been prepared to receive us. In fact, they weren't too excited when we showed, up because another ministry team had just returned to the U.S. after spending time with them. We were told this team had so many internal struggles that they actually hindered the work of the ministry this church was called to carry out. When we arrived, you can imagine their first reaction. By their own admission they were thinking, "Who are these people? They come from the U.S. thinking they are going to tell us what to do, only to shower us with gifts and then return to their cushy existence."

Fortunately, we had a different agenda. Instead of telling them what we wanted to do, we asked them what they wanted us to do. We came to listen, to serve and to come under the authority of their pastor. We awaited instructions as to how we could best come alongside them and assist in propelling their ministry. We did what we were told. As a result, in that one week, more than 200 people trusted in Jesus Christ as their Lord and Savior and a satellite church was birthed that, to my knowledge, is still in existence today.

When the Lord sends us out, He doesn't usually send us with an agenda. His desire is to lead us in accordance with His will. When we lay down our agendas, cares, burdens and intellectualism, He is able to use us in ways that we could never imagine. We learn from Romans that it is a blessing to serve the Lord.

> For "whoever calls on the name of the LORD shall be saved." How then shall they call on Him in whom they have not believed? And how shall they believe in Him of whom they have not heard? And how shall they hear without a preacher? And how shall they preach unless they are sent? As it is written: "How beautiful are the feet of those who preach the gospel of peace, Who bring glad tidings of good things!" (Romans 10:13-15)

Remember when the Lord washed His disciple's feet? Don't you think He was glad that they had beautiful feet? Their feet were beautiful because they had been serving Him. But, what if they had chosen not to serve the Lord, would He have still been as excited to wash their ugly feet? All joking aside, there is an incredible feeling—an intimacy that comes from serving the Lord.

There is one prayer that I encourage you to say upon arising each morning. It is a simple yet effective prayer, one that will keep your life from ever becoming spiritually boring. "Father, use me as an instrument of Your will." There will not be one day that goes by as you reflect back over the day's events that God did not take you up on your request. He longs to use us as His representatives in order to have an impact on generations for His kingdom purposes.

The Father of creation has molded you into His glorious image for one purpose and one purpose only, to serve Him. Isn't it amazing that He desires to work in the natural through wretched sinners like you and me? Along the way on the Lord's stairway to heaven, He plucks you out of the world, washes you clean, refurbishes you and puts His protective armor on you, then places you back in the world. He sanctifies you with the truth.

> They are not of the world, just as I am not of the world.
> Sanctify them by Your truth. Your word is truth. As You sent
> Me into the world, I also have sent them into the world.
> (John 17:16-18)

Everyone born to this earthly existence has a God-given purpose to fulfill. Unfortunately, because of the effects of S.I.N., most go through life as if on a treadmill heading nowhere. For many of us, there might have been a time where we genuinely expected to achieve great things during the course of our lives. Of course, our desire was to be recognized for that achievement.

For those who of you who have not achieved greatness I ask, "When did that desire burn out?" When did you become content just being on life's treadmill, knowing the belt just rotates around and around, not really propelling you anywhere in particular? When did you become content just dreaming about achieving greatness?

Once you have accepted the Lord's Spirit into your heart, nothing is impossible. Why not ask Him to reveal the purpose He put in your heart while you were still in your mother's womb?

> And He Himself gave some to be apostles, some prophets, some evangelists, and some pastors and teachers, for the equipping of the saints for the work of ministry, for the edifying of the body of Christ, (Ephesians 4:11-12)

The fact is Jesus gave us these gifts so we could equip His Saints for the work of ministry. Who are His Saints? You and me! Folks, this isn't rocket science.

Thank God for the teachers we have been blessed with during our lifetimes. How else could we learn to read and write unless there were teachers dedicated to that cause? How else could we grow in knowledge of the different subjects that ultimately would prepare us for our vocational pursuits?

> Till we all come to the unity of the faith and of the knowledge of the Son of God, to a perfect man, to the measure of the stature of the fullness of Christ; that we should no longer be children, tossed to and fro and carried about with every wind of doctrine, by the trickery of men, in the cunning craftiness of deceitful plotting, (Ephesians 4:13-14)

Jesus doesn't want us to be tossed to and fro by every doctrine of man. The church today has become like a substitute God. We hold the church up on a pedestal as if the church were our savior. We expect pastors, priests and ministers to pray to God for us, to intercede on our behalf. We hold them in awe, as if by their decision to enter the ministry or their knowledge of the scriptures, they somehow have a more direct line of communication to God. We give them enormous power over our lives. And if they are not true representatives of God, then folks, we have put ourselves at risk.

It is up to us to read and study God's Word so we will know in our heart if their ministries are true. Remember the Pharisees? They too were held in awe during their day, obviously more learned in the Holy Scriptures than the majority of people in the church. What did this Jesus do? He read the mail of their hearts and rebuked their evil intent.

> Brood of vipers! How can you, being evil, speak good things?
> For out of the abundance of the heart the mouth speaks.
> (Matthew 12:34)

We don't need anyone to intercede on our behalf with God. He will speak directly into our heart and lead us according to our gift set.

Now, don't get me wrong, the church and our ministers are to be revered and respected. They are agents of a Most High God, and each has their own unique calling. Theirs is a unique calling, a calling to equip the saints of God, to do the work of ministry and be an extension of the church's mission. We need our church and ministers to aid us in identifying our true calling and confirm that what we are hearing is in fact from the Lord. We then need their assistance in the development of that calling in order to be sent out to instruct others.

It is my hope that each of you will discover your calling before entering into a life of service. We have a divine God that created you with a specific eternal purpose for the day that He calls you into service.

Everyone has a chosen vocation in life, and to be effective in that chosen vocation, one must also master his/her trade. Think about it. Do accountants, doctors, nurses, architects, electricians, plumbers and ministers usually study their vocation in advance in preparation for the day they are called into service? Of course, and the vocational list is endless.

> For as the body is one and has many members, but all the members of that one body, being many, are one body, so also is Christ. But now God has set the members, each one of them, in the body just as He pleased. (1 Corinthians 12:12,18)

> Every good gift and every perfect gift is from above, and comes down from the Father of lights, with whom there is no variation or shadow of turning. (James 1:17)

Thus, it makes sense that to derive joy out of your chosen profession, it would be important to know if it is the vocation for which God created you. I challenge that God's purpose and your vocational purpose are linked. If you find joy in your chosen profession, it is because something you are doing is lining up with your God-ordained purpose. Everyone has a part to play in God's kingdom here on earth, as well as eternally in heaven.

We are called to speak to one another in love and encourage each other in our giftings, so that we may all grow up or mature in Christ.

We can relate this to our own bodies in the sense that each part functions separately, yet is part of the whole, no individual part being more important than the sum of all the parts.

> But now indeed there are many members, yet one body. And the eye cannot say to the hand, "I have no need of you"; nor again the head to the feet, "I have no need of you."
> (1 Corinthians 12:20-21)

Don't be discouraged if you feel like you don't know what part you are to play in His kingdom. Be content that if you are reborn then you are on His stairway — you have been called into His glorious light. For if you could see into the spiritual realm, faith would not be required.

Being reborn in a spiritual sense is obviously different from being born in the physical sense, one being visible, and the other being invisible. If we blow into our hand, we can feel our breath, but unless it is a cold day, we can't see our breath. It is difficult to describe that which we cannot see, but yet we know it to be real, because we can feel it. When the Holy Spirit shows up in our lives, we can't see it, but we can feel it. Therefore, we enter the kingdom of God by faith.

> Now faith is the substance of things hoped for, the evidence of things not seen. For by it the elders obtained a good testimony. By faith we understand that the worlds were framed by the word of God, so that the things which are seen were not made of things which are visible. (Hebrews 11:1-3)

We all need the Lord to reveal our positions in His body, the Church. We all need the Lord to confirm our callings and our ministries. So we hold fast in faith, knowing He is faithful, and trust that we are important cogs in God's gears of life.

Now that we have entered into a spiritual realm that is not visible to our eyes, we are no longer bound by our sin and death no longer has a hold on us. We are released to a new life; a life of purpose and meaning in Christ's Kingdom.

In closing, my challenge to you is this—why wait to climb God's stairway to heaven and enter into Heaven's spiritual realm? The Lord wants us to embrace the fact that once we step on His stairway, we step into the eternal realm. There will be no more tears, no more death, no more sorrow and no more crying. Don't wait until you die in the physical sense to find out these truths are real. Choose to reborn in Christ and know, "the former things have passed away!"

> And God will wipe away every tear from their eyes; there shall be no more death, nor sorrow, nor crying. There shall be no more pain, for the former things have passed away.
> (Revelation 21:4)

No matter how good you are or how much of a wretch you are, the possible destination is the same, heaven. When you trust in Christ alone as your Lord and Savior, you are headed to the spiritual heaven described through John's vision in the book of Revelation. You will be living in the eternal realm.

> And he carried me away in the Spirit to a great and high mountain, and showed me the great city, the holy Jerusalem, descending out of heaven from God, having the glory of God. Her light was like a most precious stone, like a jasper stone, clear as crystal. Also she had a great and high wall with twelve gates, and twelve angels at the gates, and names written on them, which are the names of the twelve tribes of the children of Israel: three gates on the east, three gates on the north, three gates on the south, and three gates on the west. Now the wall of the city had twelve foundations, and on them were the names of the twelve apostles of the Lamb. And he who talked with me had a gold reed to measure the city, its gates, and its wall. The city is laid out as a square; its length is as great as its breadth. And he measured the city with the reed: twelve thousand furlongs. Its length, breadth, and height are equal. Then he measured its wall: one hundred and forty-four cubits, according to the measure of a man, that is, of an angel. The construction of its wall was of jasper; and the city was pure gold, like clear glass. The foundations of the wall of the city were adorned with all kinds of precious stones: the first foundation was jasper, the second sapphire, the third chalcedony, the fourth emerald, the fifth sardonyx, the sixth sardius, the seventh chrysolite, the eighth beryl, the ninth topaz, the tenth chrysoprase, the eleventh jacinth, and the twelfth amethyst. The twelve gates were twelve pearls: each individual gate was of one pearl. And the street of the city was pure gold, like transparent glass. (Revelation 21:10-21)

We are all destined to spend eternity somewhere. Of course, no matter which stairway we are on, we still have to deal with life's struggles and hardships. Wouldn't it be nice to have the confidence that the day when you pass from this life to the next, you know where you will spend it? Christ told the thief on the cross next to Him which stairway He was on and where that stairway ended.

Then he said to Jesus, "Lord, remember me when You come into Your kingdom." And Jesus said to him, "Assuredly, I say to you, today you will be with Me in Paradise."
(Luke 23:42-43)

When we enter into the spiritual realm not visible to the eyes, we are no longer bound by sin. Death no longer has a hold on us. We are released to a new life, a life of purpose and meaning in Christ's kingdom.

God's stairway leads to a wonderful place void of pain and suffering, a place Jesus called "Paradise."

Chapter Eight

Practice Rounds

Tiger Woods stood on the number one tee box at Augusta National for the first time and must have been thinking that he had finally arrived.

Augusta is the pinnacle in golf, the coveted prize, the tournament that awards the winner what others have titled "golf immortality." Tiger had prepared himself to stand on that tee box in hopes of becoming one of golf's all-time greats and don the green jacket. Tiger Woods didn't just show up the day of the tournament and decide he was going to play in the Masters. No, he arrived days earlier and played the allotted practice rounds with his caddy, studying the course, analyzing every hole, and taking copious notes. They noted wind direction, the grain of the grass on the fairways and greens and where the water and sand hazards were. They studied every tree and determined the distances of each shot necessary to avoid being thwarted in their effort to accomplish their goal.

> Please Note: This book had not gone to print when the news broke about Tiger Wood's indiscretions and the enormous burden he placed on his family, friends, and fans. It was suggested I remove him from the book and use another great golfer, Jack Nicklaus in lieu of Tiger. So, I did just that until the Lord woke me up early on a Saturday morning with the conviction in my heart that I was throwing Tiger under the bus like so many others. God revealed a bigger picture to me—Tiger is plagued with the same enemy, S.I.N., as the rest of us.

The difference, his is center stage and visibly effects many more lives. He does have a responsibility to his family, friends and fans, but he is not a god. It is my prayer for the Wood's family that through this adversity Tiger and his family will come to the saving knowledge and grace of the Lord Jesus Christ and as a result Tiger will use the platform the Lord has given him to reach thousands with the gospel of Christ. For no one can deny that God bestowed an incredible talent on the young man. The enemy working through Tiger's sinful nature has seemingly taken him out of the game. Tiger knows better than most that it is how you finish the game that is most important. So the question for Tiger becomes, "How will you finish this game called life?" With this note in place, I will continue on.

Yes, preparation is the key. John Wooten, an all-time great basketball coach, once said, "Preparing to fail is not preparing at all."

Our life experiences are a series of practice rounds, and if we don't embrace them and utilize them along our journey, they become wasted. There are many golfers who claim the same right as Tiger, to stand on that tee box for a chance to compete for the prize and claim victory. But how bad they want it will be in direct proportion to how much effort they have put into their game before they ever step foot on that tee box.

Tiger's journey didn't start the day he arrived at the Masters or with the practice rounds before the tournament began. No, it all started when he was just knee high to his father and could barely swing a golf club. For the next 15-plus years he prepared for the day that he would compete for the green jacket and the right to say, "I came, and I conquered Augusta." He played many practice rounds and countless other tournaments in preparation for that day. Don't you know that Tiger had many setbacks on the journey to Augusta? Not every shot hit the mark, not every swing was executed to perfection. It took years of practice and perseverance to be able to hit the ball the way he does today.

Now let's be real, we all know that the best and most well-meaning preparation still doesn't ensure victory. Because not everyone has the same talent, not everyone will stand in the winner's circle at the Masters.

Just like Tiger and many other golfers, we are also in preparation for a final tournament. Prior to that final tournament, we are going to endure many practice rounds. Those practice rounds have a name. They are called life experiences. Our practice rounds become our testimonies along the way.

If we embrace them, not only will they propel us on our journey, but we will be able to use them as we speak into other people's lives. We use them to help propel others on their journey through life.

We all hope to reach our spiritual and our secular goals, whether it is in ministry, business, family or some other endeavor in the game of life. We begin our time of preparation the day we enter this world through childbirth, and the journey takes us on many strange and different paths. All in preparation for that final tournament where we compete for the prize. Oh the prize, a prize that no one really understands. A prize so wonderful that generations of people have competed for the right to it—the right to say I have reached the pinnacle and received the crown.

> Do you not know that those who run in a race all run, but one receives the prize? Run in such a way that you may obtain it. And everyone who competes for the prize is temperate in all things. Now they do it to obtain a perishable crown, but we for an imperishable crown. (1 Corinthians 9:24-25)

The difference in our preparation for the final and ultimate spiritual tournament is this: we all have a chance to win, and our reward is "an imperishable crown." That crown of righteousness is immortality, life eternal with God the Father, Son, and Holy Spirit. So I ask, "Why would our practice for the tournament of life be any different than the practice Tiger and the other professional golfers employ in their quest for the coveted green jacket?" The tournament of life is much bigger than the Masters.

Just like all the practice that takes place before competing at the Masters, our life experiences are the practice rounds that we must endure. Before we stand on the tee box—a tee box that is much grander than the first tee box at Augusta. Our tee box is on the edge of the universe and overlooks eternity. We stand ready to tee off with hope and anticipation of winning that immortal prize. Make no mistake about it, when that day comes, we will be praying that our lives have counted and that God himself will look at us on that fateful day and say, "Well done, good and faithful servant."

> His lord said to him, "Well done, good and faithful servant; you were faithful over a few things, I will make you ruler over many things. Enter into the joy of your lord."
> (Matthew 25:21)

I know for many reading this you might be thinking, "This is a little too theatrical for my taste. Let's be real, no one is going to stand at the edge of anything when we die." But I ask you, does it really matter what you think, because if what I say is true you won't have any choice but to stand. If what I say is true, stand you will, trembling before the Creator in hopes that your life has counted.

We have all heard the saying, "Don't shoot the messenger." Well, you can close this book right now and you won't hurt my feelings. But closing this book and ignoring the truth supported by the scripture contained herein will not alter your fate. We will all be held accountable for how we prepare for the tournament of life.

> For the time has come for judgment to begin at the house of God; and if it begins with us first, what will be the end of those who do not obey the gospel of God? (1 Peter 4:17)

How have your practice rounds been going? In the words of Dr. Phil, "How has that been working for you?" We have much more at stake than Tiger and the other golfers who long for the opportunity to wear a green jacket and receive a trophy. Have you really considered and grasped the importance of the tournament called life?

The incredible thing about this tourney is that we all get to compete. In life, we will play many practice rounds throughout the years in preparation to stand on that sacred tee box in order to vie for the coveted prize. We have our immortality at risk. But as we read in Matthew 7:14, "Because narrow is the gate and difficult is the way which leads to life, and there are few who find it," some will win, but some will lose.

BIBLICAL PRACTICE ROUNDS

The Lord has given us a set of instructions, a rule book if you will, that helps us compete for the prize. Compete in such a way that all who follow the rules and stay in the game will ultimately win the prize. We have been referencing this rule book throughout this writing. The rule book is the Bible, and we already determined that it is God's *Word*.

> He who does not love Me does not keep My words; and the *word* which you hear is not Mine but the Father's who sent Me. (John 14:24)

I want to take you to God's Word and share a story from the Bible about a man who endured through years of hardship and, as a result, altered the course of history. I could have chosen numerous stories in the Bible, but I want to use the life of Joseph to show that there are lessons in life made possible through the various practice rounds the Lord allows us to experience.

When we learn to embrace those practice rounds, we gain valuable insight and life becomes much more meaningful and fulfilling. We obtain the revelation that those experiences are paramount to the fulfillment of God's ordained purpose for us here on earth.

CASE STUDY: THE LIFE OF JOSEPH

Our case study is about the life of Joseph, and you can read the story in its entirety in the book of Genesis chapters 37 through 45. To set-up our study of Joseph, I will share the first part of the story out of Genesis 37 and then share scripture sporadically up through Genesis 45 in order to show how Joseph's life experiences were actually practice rounds preparing him to fulfill God's purpose for his life.

> This is the history of Jacob. Joseph, being seventeen years old, was feeding the flock with his brothers. And the lad was with the sons of Bilhah and the sons of Zilpah, his father's wives; and Joseph brought a bad report of them to his father. Now Israel loved Joseph more than all his children, because he was the son of his old age. Also he made him a tunic of many colors. But when his brothers saw that their father loved him more than all his brothers, they hated him and could not speak peaceably to him. (Genesis 37:2-4)

We learn that Joseph was dearly loved by his father, Jacob (Israel), but despised by his stepbrothers. Joseph was one of two sons Jacob had with Rachel, whom we learn through scripture was his favorite wife. Joseph was the second youngest among eleven brothers, and Benjamin was the youngest. Joseph has two dreams, which he shares with his family, and as a result, his brothers become incensed, and Jacob rebukes him. It is important to note here that though Jacob rebukes Joseph, he also "kept the matter in mind."

> Now Joseph had a dream, and he told it to his brothers; and they hated him even more. So he said to them, "Please hear

this dream which I have dreamed: There we were, binding sheaves in the field. Then behold, my sheaf arose and also stood upright; and indeed your sheaves stood all around and bowed down to my sheaf." And his brothers said to him, "Shall you indeed reign over us? Or shall you indeed have dominion over us?" So they hated him even more for his dreams and for his words. Then he dreamed still another dream and told it to his brothers, and said, "Look, I have dreamed another dream. And this time, the sun, the moon, and the eleven stars bowed down to me." So he told it to his father and his brothers; and his father rebuked him and said to him, "What is this dream that you have dreamed? Shall your mother and I and your brothers indeed come to bow down to the earth before you?" And his brothers envied him, but his father kept the matter in mind. (Genesis 37:5-11)

Joseph's brothers had about all they could take from this arrogant and prideful 17-year-old. They decided the best course of action would be to kill him and eliminate any threat he might have for their father's affection. However, when Reuben, one of the brothers, found out what they intended to do, he came to Joseph's rescue. Reuben tried to appeal to his brothers out of common sense. His plan was to trick them into putting Joseph in a pit so that he could return later, retrieve Joseph, and take him back home to his father.

But Reuben heard it, and he delivered him out of their hands, and said, "Let us not kill him." And Reuben said to them, "Shed no blood, but cast him into this pit which is in the wilderness, and do not lay a hand on him"—that he might deliver him out of their hands, and bring him back to his father. (Genesis 37: 21-22)

Unfortunately for Joseph, another brother, Judah, didn't care to go along with Reuben's plan and instead convinced the brothers to pull Joseph from the pit and sell him into slavery. Thus, they sold Joseph to Ishmaelites, who transported him to Egypt with the intention of selling him for a profit.

So Judah said to his brothers, "What profit is there if we kill our brother and conceal his blood? Come and let us sell him to the Ishmaelites, and let not our hand be upon him, for he is our brother and our flesh." And his brothers listened. (Genesis 37: 26-27)

Of course, when Reuben returned to the pit intending to rescue Joseph, he was nowhere to be found. Reuben tore his garment out of desperation, fearful of returning home to his father. The brothers, in their infinite wisdom, then came up with another devious plan, this time to deceive their father into thinking that Joseph has been killed. They dip Joseph's tunic in goat's blood, then send it to Jacob. Notice two things here. First, the brothers deceive Jacob by lying about finding the tunic and leave him to draw his own conclusion of what had happened and second, Reuben, who was so willing to rescue Joseph earlier, remained quiet. Of course, Jacob played into their hands, making it easy for them by stating, "A wild beast has devoured him."

> Then Reuben returned to the pit, and indeed Joseph was not in the pit; and he tore his clothes. And he returned to his brothers and said, "The lad is no more; and I, where shall I go?" So they took Joseph's tunic, killed a kid of the goats, and dipped the tunic in the blood. Then they sent the tunic of many colors, and they brought it to their father and said, "We have found this. Do you know whether it is your son's tunic or not?" And he recognized it and said, "It is my son's tunic. A wild beast has devoured him. Without doubt Joseph is torn to pieces." (Genesis 37: 29-33)

Further, in Genesis, we learn of Joseph's fate. The Ishmaelites had traveled to Egypt, and upon their arrival, sold Joseph to Potiphar, a captain of the guard in Pharaoh's army. However, because the Lord's hand was on Joseph, "he was a successful man." Interestingly enough, Potiphar, being pretty astute in his observance, intelligently put two and two together. "And his master saw that the LORD was with him and that the LORD made all he did to prosper in his hand." Potiphar had come to the conclusion, "If I put Joseph in charge of my affairs and the Lord's blessing is on him, I will be blessed through Joseph." One must assume that Joseph made known his faith by sharing it openly. Otherwise, how would Potiphar have known it was the Lord who was blessing Joseph? As a result, we learn that Potiphar gives Joseph ultimately authority over all his household and business affairs.

> Now Joseph had been taken down to Egypt. And Potiphar, an officer of Pharaoh, captain of the guard, an Egyptian, bought him from the Ishmaelites who had taken him down there. The LORD was with Joseph, and he was a successful man; and he was in the house of his master the Egyptian. And his master saw that the LORD was with him and that the LORD made all he did to prosper in his hand. So Joseph found favor in his sight, and served him. Then he made him overseer of his house, and all that he had he put under his authority. So it was, from the time that he had made him overseer of his house and all that he had, that the LORD blessed the Egyptian's house for Joseph's sake; and the blessing of the LORD was on all that he had in the house and in the field. Thus he left all that he had in Joseph's hand, and he did not know what he had except for the bread which he ate. Now Joseph was handsome in form and appearance. (Genesis 39:1-6)

Unfortunately for Joseph, being attractive was not to his advantage when he caught the eye of Potiphar's wife. She, being enamored with him, tries to lure him into bed by making an advance. Joseph not only remains loyal to his master by fleeing her advance, but he specifically tells her it would be a wicked thing to do and it would be a sin against God. She was obviously unmoved by Joseph's display of moral character. She immediately brought an accusation against Joseph and lied to her husband, saying that Joseph had been the one trying to take advantage of her. Potiphar, obviously upset, has Joseph thrown into prison.

> And it came to pass after these things that his master's wife cast longing eyes on Joseph, and she said, "Lie with me." But he refused and said to his master's wife, "Look, my master does not know what is with me in the house, and he has committed all that he has to my hand. There is no one greater in this house than I, nor has he kept back anything from me but you, because you are his wife. How then can I do this great wickedness, and sin against God?" So it was, as she spoke to Joseph day by day, that he did not heed her, to lie with her or to be with her. (Genesis 39:7-10)

> So it was, when his master heard the words which his wife spoke to him, saying, "Your servant did to me after this

> manner," that his anger was aroused. Then Joseph's master took him and put him into the prison, a place where the king's prisoners were confined. And he was there in the prison.
> (Genesis 39:19-20)

However, it seems wherever Joseph ends up, he is blessed. We learn that in prison, the Lord's Hand continued to be on him and after a period of time, he was put in charge of all the other prisoners.

> The keeper of the prison did not look into anything that was under Joseph's authority, because the LORD was with him; and whatever he did, the LORD made it prosper.
> (Genesis 39:23)

In prison, Joseph was tending to two of the King's men, a baker and a butler who, after offending the King, had been thrown in prison. Each of them awoke one morning distraught, and Joseph inquired why they were sad. They told Joseph that each of them had a dream but had no one to interpret them, so Joseph responded and interpreted their dreams.

> It came to pass after these things that the butler and the baker of the king of Egypt offended their lord, the king of Egypt. And Pharaoh was angry with his two officers, the chief butler and the chief baker. So he put them in custody in the house of the captain of the guard, in the prison, the place where Joseph was confined. And the captain of the guard charged Joseph with them, and he served them; so they were in custody for a while. Then the butler and the baker of the king of Egypt, who were confined in the prison, had a dream, both of them, each man's dream in one night and each man's dream with its own interpretation. And Joseph came in to them in the morning and looked at them, and saw that they were sad. So he asked Pharaoh's officers who were with him in the custody of his lord's house, saying, "Why do you look so sad today?" And they said to him, "We each have had a dream, and there is no interpreter of it." So Joseph said to them, "Do not interpretations belong to God? Tell them to me, please."
> (Genesis 40:1-8)

After interpreting the butler's dream, Joseph made a specific appeal, asking that he remember him when he went before Pharaoh. It is important to note that Joseph made the appeal to the butler by relating his heritage and defending his innocence, and of course, because he knew the butler would be the only one of the two alive to make the appeal before the King. As Joseph had predicted, the baker was beheaded and the butler was restored to his position. However, the butler, obviously a little shaken by the whole incident, does not keep the commitment he made to Joseph and forgets to tell Pharaoh about Joseph.

> Then the chief butler told his dream to Joseph, and said to him, "Behold, in my dream a vine was before me, and in the vine were three branches; it was as though it budded, its blossoms shot forth, and its clusters brought forth ripe grapes. Then Pharaoh's cup was in my hand; and I took the grapes and pressed them into Pharaoh's cup, and placed the cup in Pharaoh's hand." And Joseph said to him, "This is the interpretation of it: The three branches are three days. Now within three days Pharaoh will lift up your head and restore you to your place, and you will put Pharaoh's cup in his hand according to the former manner, when you were his butler. *But remember me when it is well with you, and please show kindness to me; make mention of me to Pharaoh, and get me out of this house. For indeed I was stolen away from the land of the Hebrews; and also I have done nothing here that they should put me into the dungeon.*" When the chief baker saw that the interpretation was good, he said to Joseph, "I also was in my dream, and there were three white baskets on my head. In the uppermost basket were all kinds of baked goods for Pharaoh, and the birds ate them out of the basket on my head." So Joseph answered and said, "This is the interpretation of it: The three baskets are three days. Within three days Pharaoh will lift off your head from you and hang you on a tree; and the birds will eat your flesh from you." Now it came to pass on the third day, which was Pharaoh's birthday, that he made a feast for all his servants; and he lifted up the head of the chief butler and of the chief baker among his servants. Then he restored the chief butler to his butlership again, and he placed the cup in Pharaoh's hand. But he hanged the chief

baker, as Joseph had interpreted to them. Yet the chief butler did not remember Joseph, but forgot him. (Genesis 40:9-23)

We learn it was another two years before Joseph was summoned to interpret another dream, however this interpretation would be for Pharaoh, the King of Egypt. Pharaoh had what he believed to be two separate dreams and called upon his "magicians" and all the wise men to interpret the dreams. To his dismay, none were able to tell him what they meant. Only then did the butler humble himself by admitting his fault and telling the King about a young Hebrew man he met in prison who correctly interpreted dreams for himself and the baker. Immediately Joseph was brought up out of prison, shaven, cleanly dressed, and set before the King. The King then proceeded to tell Joseph about his two dreams.

> Then Pharaoh said to Joseph: "Behold, in my dream I stood on the bank of the river. Suddenly seven cows came up out of the river, fine looking and fat; and they fed in the meadow. Then behold, seven other cows came up after them, poor and very ugly and gaunt, such ugliness as I have never seen in all the land of Egypt. And the gaunt and ugly cows ate up the first seven, the fat cows. When they had eaten them up, no one would have known that they had eaten them, for they were just as ugly as at the beginning. So I awoke. Also I saw in my dream, and suddenly seven heads came up on one stalk, full and good. Then behold, seven heads, withered, thin, and blighted by the east wind, sprang up after them. And the thin heads devoured the seven good heads. So I told this to the magicians, but there was no one who could explain it to me." (Genesis 41:17-24)

Joseph related to the King that his dreams were one in the same. There would be seven years of plenty followed by seven years of famine, and the famine would utterly deplete the land. Joseph went on to suggest that Pharaoh put someone in charge of managing his affairs and gather as much grain into his storehouses during the seven plentiful years as possible.

> Indeed seven years of great plenty will come throughout all the land of Egypt; but after them seven years of famine will arise, and all the plenty will be forgotten in the land of Egypt; and the famine will deplete the land. So the plenty will not be

> known in the land because of the famine following, for it will be very severe. And the dream was repeated to Pharaoh twice because the thing is established by God, and God will shortly bring it to pass. Now therefore, let Pharaoh select a discerning and wise man, and set him over the land of Egypt.
> (Genesis 41:29-33)

This is where the story gets interesting and is open to historical debate. Pharaoh turned to his servants, inquiring where they could possibly find anyone qualified to take on this task. We then learn that the King turned to Joseph and elevated him to the number two position in his kingdom.

Many find it odd that Pharaoh would give so much control to a non-Egyptian. Joseph had been introduced as a Hebrew, thus in the eyes of the Egyptians that would make him an Asiatic slave. The Asiatic people, with their lighter color skin, were looked down upon by the Egyptians during this period. However, it was not uncommon that some would be assigned as overseers of specific Egyptian affairs. Previous Pharaohs had determined that the brightest and wisest minds should manage certain aspects of government, regardless of whether or not they were Egyptian, because the nation would benefit.

Therefore, it was not necessarily a rare move, but a bold move all the same for the King to make Joseph the number two ruling entity in all of Egypt. He in essence bestowed upon Joseph a title that had been known in Egypt for dynasties, *Sealbearer of the King*. By giving him the signet ring and gold chain, the King had sanctioned Joseph to be the sole authority over Egypt's food supply and trade routes.

> Into the Fifth Dynasty, only the king's highest official, the Vizier, was the "Sealbearer of the King of Lower Egypt," authorized to supervise the movement of official parties or goods through Egypt. (32)

> Then Pharaoh said to Joseph, "Inasmuch as God has shown you all this, there is no one as discerning and wise as you. You shall be over my house, and all my people shall be ruled according to your word; only in regard to the throne will I be greater than you." And Pharaoh said to Joseph, "See, I have set you over all the land of Egypt." Then Pharaoh took his signet ring off his hand and put it on Joseph's hand; and he clothed

> him in garments of fine linen and put a gold chain around his neck. (Genesis 41:39- 42)

Joseph was 30 years old at this time, meaning he had endured thirteen years of hard practice in order to prepare him for this day. First, he gained favor in Potiphar's house by running his household and affairs. Then it was off to prison, where he took charge over all the prisoners. Now he was standing before the King of Egypt, clothed in garments of fine linens, with Pharaoh's signet ring on his hand. When the time came for him to tee up, he was fully prepared by the Lord.

One of the main things to remember in the game of life is most of the time we won't know where the Lord is leading us. We might join a cause or act on a vision, but it is usually not until the end as we are looking back on our lives that we see where God was working. All the time preparing us, and molding us for that day when He called us into service.

For Joseph, all the hardship he endured was for an incredible purpose: to save his family from destruction thus preserving the nation of Israel. The dream he had had many years before had been misinterpreted by his family. They had judged Joseph with their shallow intelligence, and as a result of their sin had tried to determine Joseph's fate. But God had another plan. We go on to learn that when the famine hit the land, Jacob and his clan were greatly afflicted.

> And he said, "Indeed I have heard that there is grain in Egypt; go down to that place and buy for us there, that we may live and not die." (Genesis 42:2)

Jacob learned that Egypt is selling grain, so he sent his sons to secure provisions for the family. Unfortunately for the brothers, they had no clue that the man they were going to be bargaining with was the brother they years earlier had intended to kill. When they arrived in Egypt they did not recognize Joseph, but Joseph knew them immediately. He spoke to them through an interpreter so they would assume he would not be able to understand their deliberations. Joseph then slyly accuses them of being spies, which results in their arrest and subsequent incarceration. On the third day, they attempt to defend themselves. They ignorantly reveal they have already lost one brother and have another brother at home with their father. We know that they were speaking of Joseph and Benjamin, but of course, the brothers didn't suspect the Egyptians would have any way of knowing this. Joseph was able to use their confession to his advantage.

> No, my lord, but your servants have come to buy food. We are all one man's sons; we are honest men; your servants are not spies. But he said to them, "No, but you have come to see the nakedness of the land." And they said, "Your servants are twelve brothers, the sons of one man in the land of Canaan; and in fact, the youngest is with our father today, and one is no more." (Genesis 42:10-13)

Joseph had planned for them to return to their father all along, but seized this opportunity to do so conditionally. In order to keep them honest, they must leave a brother behind in prison and promise to return with the youngest brother, Benjamin. Upon their return, they related their dilemma to Jacob, who became further distraught and rebuked them for losing another one of his sons, Simeon, and for disclosing the existence of Benjamin.

> You have bereaved me: Joseph is no more, Simeon is no more, and you want to take Benjamin. All these things are against me. (Genesis 42:36)

Jacob, fearful of losing Benjamin, forbids them to return to Egypt. However, over time the famine continued and became too much for them. Jacob has no choice but to send them back with more money to buy grain and, of course, with Benjamin, as requested. Once they arrived in Egypt, we learn that Joseph's steward received them openly and restored Simeon to their care.

Joseph, however, is not quite ready to let them off the hook. This time when he sends them away fully loaded, but instructs his steward to plant a silver cup on Benjamin. The plot thickens when Joseph sends his steward out to search them and upon finding the hidden cup, accuses the brothers of theft.

> And he commanded the steward of his house, saying, "Fill the men's sacks with food, as much as they can carry, and put each man's money in the mouth of his sack. ² Also put my cup, the silver cup, in the mouth of the sack of the youngest, and his grain money." So he did according to the word that Joseph had spoken. ³ As soon as the morning dawned, the men were sent away, they and their donkeys. ⁴ When they had gone out of the city, *and* were not *yet* far off, Joseph said to his steward, "Get

> up, follow the men; and when you overtake them, say to them, 'Why have you repaid evil for good? ⁵ *Is* not this *the one* from which my lord drinks, and with which he indeed practices divination? You have done evil in so doing.'" (Genesis 44: 1-5)

Benjamin, of course, is caught red-handed with the cup, which provided legal means for Joseph to retain the boy. The brothers wrought with fear come before Joseph and plead for mercy, knowing to return to their father without Benjamin would quite possibly cause his death. They attempt to appeal to Joseph's sense of goodness and family values in the hope that he would not arrest Benjamin. Joseph decides that he had let them suffer long enough. Not able to hold back any longer, he sends everyone out of the room so he could be alone with his brothers. A weeping Joseph makes himself known to them.

> Then Joseph said to his brothers, "I am Joseph; does my father still live?" But his brothers could not answer him, for they were dismayed in his presence. And Joseph said to his brothers, "Please come near to me." So they came near. Then he said: "I am Joseph your brother, whom you sold into Egypt."
> (Genesis 45:3-4)

One can only imagine what the brothers were thinking at this moment in time. I am sure they were mesmerized, to say the least. Their lives must have flashed before their eyes; guilt and condemnation had been their bitter drink for years. Now that the day of reckoning had finally arrived, surely God would enact His revenge for their sinful deeds? Surely, Joseph would have them all thrown into prison, shrouding them with shame—because they deserved to be punished. But what does Joseph tell them next?

> But now, do not therefore be grieved or angry with yourselves because you sold me here; for God sent me before you to preserve life. For these two years the famine has been in the land, and there are still five years in which there will be neither plowing nor harvesting. And God sent me before you to preserve a posterity for you in the earth, and to save your lives by a great deliverance. So now it was not you who sent me here, but God; and He has made me a father to Pharaoh, and lord of all his house, and a ruler throughout all the land of Egypt. (Genesis 45:5-8)

Joseph had played all the courses. He had spent hours upon hours preparing for this day. When the time came, instead of seeking revenge, he granted them mercy. He had come full circle and now knew decisively what the dreams had meant. His experience, his hardship, and his practice became his testimony. Rather than hold their anger against them, he instructed them in spiritual truth. God had schooled him in preparation for the day that he would deliver his father, his father's clan and subsequent generations from disaster.

We can't fully comprehend the Lord and all His ways. Our lives are His to do what he wants, and our part is to simply die to our own agendas by fully embracing what He is teaching us through life's circumstances. Oftentimes, He shows us or tells us through sources we are not comfortable with or circumstances beyond our control and our understanding.

In our story of Joseph, we learn that Joseph moved his father and all the family to live with him. Pharaoh blessed them with choice ground and disaster was averted. God, speaking directly to Jacob, told him not to fear, that He would make him a great nation and that Joseph would put his hand on his eyes. Jacob was also named Israel, a name God previously bestowed upon him in Genesis 32:28.

> So Israel took his journey with all that he had, and came to Beersheba, and offered sacrifices to the God of his father Isaac. Then God spoke to Israel in the visions of the night, and said, "Jacob, Jacob!" And he said, "Here I am." So He said, "I am God, the God of your father; do not fear to go down to Egypt, for I will make of you a great nation there. I will go down with you to Egypt, and I will also surely bring you up again; and Joseph will put his hand on your eyes." (Genesis 46:1-4)

Let's review what we have learned thus far from this story. Joseph, at the young age of 17 was the favorite son, destined, one could assume, to ascend life's ladder to fortune and fame. Instead, Joseph in his arrogance shared some dreams with his brothers, which set him in motion on a journey no one but God could have predicted. The following are just a few of the many lessons we can glean from the life of Joseph:

Action: Joseph at 17 acted arrogantly immature and as a result boasted about his dreams.

Consequence: Joseph, by angering his brothers, paid a dire consequence played out over several years, but in doing so also set in motion his ultimate fate.
Lesson: Had Joseph asked God to interpret his dreams and then sought confirmation from his father in private, the plan God was showing him might have played out in an entirely different way. His ultimate fate could quite possibly have been accomplished by other means.

Action: Joseph's brothers became jealous of their Father's love for their brother and treated him with contempt.
Consequence: Jealousy breeds contempt and since it is fear-based and the opposite of faith, the enemy can and will use it to cause us harm, sometimes long-term harm.
Lesson: Had his brothers ruled over their sin by dying to their selfish emotions, grasped hold of the fact that God loved them, and that His love is sufficient, they would not have been jealous of their father's love for Joseph. Instead they would have saved themselves the consequence of years of torment.

Action: Reuben compromised his values and by not standing his ground to do what he knew in his heart was right, paid the same price as his brothers.
Consequence: When we don't take a stand on what we know is right, but instead allow people who are not well-meaning to continue their wrongful acts, we run the risk of paying the consequences for their sins. In essence, we have become guilty by association.
Lesson: Had Reuben stopped his brothers by initially demanding that they return Joseph, he might have lost his life, but his dignity would have been intact. His brothers would have been hard-pressed to deceive their father into believing that two of his children had been devoured by a wild beast.

Action: Potiphar's wife became a vessel for Satan in his attempt to lure Joseph through temptation, accusation, and deception in order to thwart God's plan for his life.
Consequence: Potiphar's wife resorted to lies in an attempt to cover up her sin.
Lesson: Had Potiphar's wife known that she was being used by Satan as a vessel, she could have preserved her integrity by not lying to her husband. When we tell the truth we do not allow ourselves to be used as a vessel for sin. With the understanding of how the enemy uses other people's sin as instruments of destruction, we too can take a stand. Unfortunately, like

Joseph, we might have to pay a consequence, but fortunately, God sees all and will eventually bring good out of our situation.

Action: Joseph maintained his moral character and remained true to his God.
Consequence: Even though he is thrown into prison, the Lord's Hand remained upon him, and he prospered.
Lesson: No matter what circumstance we find ourselves in, if we remain faithful to the Lord, He will bless us. It is important to excel wherever the Lord places us.

Action: Joseph spoke boldly to the King as he interpreted the dreams.
Consequence: He was elevated to the number two man in all of Egypt.
Lesson: When we remain faithful and are true to our calling, when the time comes to speak and the pressure is on, we, like Joseph, have full assurance that God will show up and speak on our behalf. We are called to speak boldly to anyone, regardless of his or her perceived or actual status.

Action: Joseph's brothers felt the need to defend their position in hopes of avoiding further disaster for their family.
Consequence: The brothers were full of fear for the sinful act they committed against their brother many years before the famine.
Lesson: We are ignorant if we think just because we have fooled others that God is ultimately going to let us get away with our sinful acts. God sees all and lets no sinful act go unpunished. He enacts His wrath not because it is His nature to do so, but out of His love for us. When Joseph forgave his brothers, they experienced God's true nature, which is grace.

Action: Joseph had a revelation that everything he had experienced in life had been orchestrated by God to preserve life. He forgave his brothers and died to himself.
Consequence: He became humbly mature in the Lord, and, as a result, delivered his family from disaster and allowed God to birth a nation through his father Israel.
Lesson: When we forgive those that mean us harm, we are able to receive revelation of what the Lord is doing in and through our lives. This allows God to execute His plan and use us according to His will to have an eternal impact while we are here on earth.

Final Observation

God was using Joseph all along not just to deliver his people, but also to bless a nation. Joseph was sold into slavery, thrown into prison for his integrity and forgotten by his brothers, the very men he would eventually help. He had been seemingly forsaken by everyone he loved. However, through all the hardship, he endured the practice rounds of life, which ultimately prepared his heart for the *big event*. Joseph did not give up, and he did not give in.

God obviously knew something about Joseph that his family failed to grasp: his heart was good and his stamina was strong. Joseph's brothers gave no thought to the spiritual battle that would ensue for his life and the part they would play to carry out Satan or S.I.N.'s plan. The sin, which so easily ensnared them and clouded their ability to hear what the Lord was saying, caused them to act in such a way that they brought destruction upon themselves and those around them. The brothers thought they could silence Joseph by killing him.

Thus, through Joseph's life, we are reminded, once again, that God cannot and will not be denied. He was not denied in the garden, he was not denied on the cross, and he sure wasn't denied in the life of Joseph. God is not intimidated by Satan's attempts to thwart His plans. When God has a plan to accomplish something through us, no one and nothing will stand in His way. The calling on Joseph's life was irrevocable, and the calling on your life is irrevocable.

> For the gifts and the calling of God are irrevocable.
> (Romans 11:29)

It is my guess that Joseph is sitting pretty in heaven, looking down at you while you are reading this account of his life. Like Joseph experienced, life will deal us many blows, setting us back. However, without the proper biblical understanding, we might not see the blows as possible opportunities. Instead, we might see them as unfortunate occurrences that cause us great pain. Faith lacking, we might ask, "Why me?"

How many of us today grumble and complain when our lives seem difficult, not giving any thought to the fact that God might want to use us to change the world or to bless our nation? I challenge you to ask yourself, "What would I do if someone told me that God was going to use me to change the world? What would I do if I had a dream as profound and confounding as Joseph's?" What would your answers be? Would you take the time to seek Him and possibly ask Him for the true meaning of what He might be attempting to teach you? Would you be willing to lay your life down for the Lord?

On the other hand, maybe there has been a time in your life when you shared a dream or vision with loved ones, only to be misunderstood. Maybe they too took offense or casually cast the dream off as a scheme that would never amount to or mean anything.

Joseph must have felt very lonely and full of rejection at all that transpired at the hands of his family. But he endured through it all and his practice rounds proved effective, eventually leading to the salvation of many.

Unlike Joseph's family, we should embrace one another's dreams and visions in the hope that God wants to use us to change the world. We should tee up with one another and play a few practice rounds. The Lord knows our swings could use a little divine intervention.

The bible is full of stories about great people who endured through the practice rounds of life in order to be prepared for God's ordained purpose. Let's look at a few:

➢ Abraham, one of the greatest men who ever lived, spent a lifetime in preparation for the day God would give him a son and through him birth nations. "Look now toward heaven, and count the stars if you are able to number them." And He said to him, "So shall your descendants be." When God first called him, he was 75 years old. God told him to leave his comfortable surroundings and go to a land He would show him. Abraham had no idea of the journey he was about to embark upon. It would be another 25 years of hardship and practice before he would fully realize the prize God had promised. Abraham was 100 years old when he and his wife Sarah conceived Isaac.

➢ Jacob spent 14 long years laboring in the service of Laban to gain the hand of his daughter, Rachel. Jacob played numerous practice rounds, preparing him for the day he finally won his prize.

➢ Moses spent his childhood in Pharaoh's household, preparing for the day that he would lead his people out of Egypt. However, he sinned and spent 40 years in self-made exile before God called Him to lead His people. Moses then endured another 40 years of practice until God took him up on a mountain and showed him the land flowing with milk and honey.

➢ Joshua was 80 years old when Moses passed him the mantle and God ordained him to lead His people across the Jordan into the Promised Land. Along with Moses, Joshua endured those same 40 years of practice in preparation for the day God would call him home.

➢ John the Baptist practiced baptism after baptism, not knowing one day he would be called on to baptize Jesus Christ.

➢ Christ himself spent approximately 30 years on the practice field of life, preparing for the three and one half years that would shake heaven and earth and alter the course of eternity.

➢ The disciples spent approximately three years with Christ playing practice round after practice round, preparing to carry the gospel to an unbelieving and perishing world. All but John would be martyred unto death for their long and dutiful service.

➢ The Apostle Paul spent years thinking he had his swing down pat, until on the road to Damascus he learned God wanted him to learn a completely new swing. He then spent several years on the practice course of life before God sent him on his first missionary trip and propeled him in his ministry. As a result and because of Paul's dedicated service, he wrote much of the New Testament, which continues ministering to us today as we read God's Word.

I could have also included men like Noah who built the ark, David who slew Goliath, Job who suffered every affliction possible, or women like Ruth who rocked the world, and Mary who birthed the Christ child. They were all ordinary men and women who endured the practice rounds of life. As a result of their faith and enduring perseverance, they changed the world. Now as we look back upon their lives, we see that God used them in powerful ways.

Like these men and women, we are also experiencing life, in preparation, for what God wants to do in and through us. We will accomplish much more in our lifetime if we accept this fact and embrace those life experiences, fully expecting one day that we will be able to look back and see that our practice paid off. For that reason, I want us to look at some practice rounds we all encounter on our journey through life.

Relational Practice Rounds

The biggest decision you will make in your life is the decision to trust Jesus Christ for your salvation. The second biggest decision most of us will make is choosing the person we will marry and spend the rest of our days with here on earth.

Have you given consideration to the fact that all the relationships you have entered into are mere practice rounds in preparation for that one special relationship? Why not? If you did, wouldn't it make sense that you would be better prepared for that special relationship? By this, I don't mean you test the product physically and hone your intimacy skills. Nor do you assume that every relationship is going to be that one special relationship, only to be disappointed when it turns out not to be the one.

I am saying, be encouraged, because God wants the best for you, and He doesn't want you to settle for second best. Let's face it, we are all second best for many, and we are all the best for that one special person God has set aside for us. If a person doesn't want to be in a relationship with you, then they are second best. God has someone special for you and the best question to ask yourself is, "Am I willing to experience the practice rounds, patiently enduring, to receive the prize God has for me?"

Why not enjoy the journey and have some fun along the way? I am talking about clean, healthy fun, whereby you establish friendships in life. Why not try to be a blessing to those God puts in your path and set an example for your friends, family, and brothers and sisters in the Lord?

I had the privilege of spending several years meeting on a weekly basis with a young man. He called me one evening, saying he had an interest in one of the young women in our church. When he revealed who it was, I didn't hesitate in my response: "Not over my dead body!" I told him I was very aware of this young woman, that she was very discerning and intelligent and was whole in her walk with the Lord. I told him he was doing great, but still had issues to work through concerning past relationships and vocationally there were some challenges he was facing. I suggested that he remain friends with her but start observing her in a group setting, see how she handled herself with others. Then he could ask himself if there were any mannerisms that he wouldn't be able to live with long-term if she never changed, assuming the Lord even decided to put the two of them together.

To which he responded, "Oh that is good, that's what I will do." So he accepted my advice and we didn't discuss her for quite some time.

One day, I received a call from his sister-in-law asking if I had heard the news and instead of telling me, suggested I give him a call. I called him, obviously, fishing to see if he would openly discuss what had happened. To his credit, he told me there was a confession he needed to make. He had followed my advice to a degree, but when the young singles group at our church would go on an outing he was making a point to engage her in what seemed harmless conversation, but he was actually flirting, hoping she would respond. In his ignorance, he misperceived her kindness and spiritual strength for affection. So on her birthday he sent several dozen red roses and to his dismay, she responded by asking, "Are you flirting with me?" and then promptly returned the roses. I suggested that he humble himself, apologize, and then back off, respecting the fact that she was obviously not interested in a relationship.

Well, some seven or eight months later he gave me another specific call, asking for my advice. He told me a group from our church had planned a trip to Mexico to stand with a friend in prayer for his mother who had become ill and was in the hospital. The plan was to drive from Dallas to Laredo, leave their cars at a friend's house, and take a bus into the interior to Monterrey, Mexico. His dilemma: everyone had dropped out except two girls from our church. You guessed it, one of them was the young woman he had agreed to back away from. So I said, "Let me get this straight. You are going to let two of our spiritual sisters drive to Laredo, get on a bus by themselves and go to Monterrey? Why don't you get off the relationship kick and go with them, intending to be their bodyguard and protect them as a brother in Christ?" He responded by saying, "Oh, that is good. Yes, that's what I will do." He did just that and they traveled together and stood with their friend in prayer for his mother.

An interesting thing happened on that trip. The young woman saw the spiritual side of this young man, his strength of character, and steadfast faith in the Lord. Upon their return to Dallas, she called to tell him that she would be interested in going out with him. They began the process of Christian dating, meaning they went out, but did so in public places in order to not give into their intimate feelings. Then they naturally progressed to courtship where it was a foregone conclusion their destination was marriage. After a while, they became engaged and entered premarital counseling. They began making preparations for the ceremony, a ceremony where they would stand before God and exchange vows entering into an agreed spiritual covenantal relationship with the Lord.

I would also like to note that when they first started entertaining a relationship, he told her he didn't want to kiss until the altar. To which she replied, "Well, that is weird, but okay." Today they are happily married with two children and trust is not an issue in their relationship. Little did they know at the time that their dating process would be the practice rounds that God would use to solidify the foundation of their marriage and become the testimony they would share in order to help prepare other couples for marriage.

To all young and old alike, I say embrace the practice rounds of life, study God's Word, and fully prepare. So when the time comes for you to step into your calling, you will have a greater chance at success. God wants the best for you and for me, but if we allow our selfish natures to rule over us, we will cut our practice short and compromise what the Lord intends for us.

There is one woman for every man. There is one man for every women. And God knows who they are. Will we patiently endure our practice rounds until the Lord says it is time for the main event, or will we become frustrated in our solitude and take matters into our own hands?

There are thousands of websites on the internet that will encourage you to do just that. Meet your match. She is waiting for you. He is waiting for you. Why wait when you can have your cake and eat it too? After all, life is short, you deserve to be happy. Unfortunately, most of these websites don't tell you the pain and misery you will encounter when the relationship doesn't work out.

If you don't believe me, open your eyes and look around at all the division that has resulted from those lies. God can and will sometimes use these mediums, but the process of courtship is not negated. In our example above, because the young man came under accountability through discipleship, he experienced God's covering. As a result, he is no longer looking back through lonely eyes, wondering when he will meet his love. He is enjoying daily the woman God had intended for Him all along.

VOCATIONAL PRACTICE ROUNDS

When we make the decision to find employment in order to provide for our family, do we just wander about aimlessly? Hoping someone will discover our talent and put us to work. No, we have to prepare and for some, it takes months. They have to put a resume together, initiate the process by contacting companies and sending out those resumes. Then they must ask themselves tough questions in order to prepare for the interview process. Finally, they have to make a choice if and when they receive an offer.

For many, this is an emotional rollercoaster. Wouldn't it be smart once you get ready to interview to make a short list of companies in your related field and set as many appointments as possible in order to hone your interview skills? By this, I mean you should participate in several interview *practice rounds* with companies that are not at the top of your list. And if you receive an offer great, but if you don't, you won't be disappointed. This would give you an idea how your resume is perceived, help you to know what questions are going to be asked and assist you in honing your interview skills. It might possibly help you to be better prepared when you sit for the interview with a company for which you really have a desire to work.

Let's face it, you won't be able to overcome every obstacle put in your way any more than Tiger Woods himself could overcome every obstacle on the golf course, but because of your preparation you will be calmer, more confident and better prepared to provide appropriate responses to their interview questions. Questions such as:

- What are your talents?
- What happened when you were in fourth grade that impacted the course of your life?
- What has been your biggest failure in business?
- How did that failure impact your team?
- What did you learn from the failure?
- What is your life purpose and how are you fulfilling it?
- Give me an example where you were challenged by a coworker and how you dealt with the situation.

This is just a sampling of the types of questions one might encounter in the interview process. If you haven't spent time practicing your responses, you very well might walk away empty-handed.

Now, some of you might be asking, "What if, after all my preparation, I sit for an interview with the one company I desire to work for and they don't extend an offer?" To which I would answer, you embrace the fact that the Lord was protecting you from making a mistake and closed the door you never would have closed on your own. Remain encouraged and ask the Lord to provide the open door that He is guiding you towards. Yes, chalk it up to another practice round preparing you for the company and position that is the best for you at that particular juncture in your career.

> I know your works. See, I have set before you an open door, and no one can shut it; for you have a little strength, have kept My word, and have not denied My name. (Revelation 3:8)

We all have a tendency to cry out for God to help us, but the enemy can trap us when we attach prideful expectations to our prayers. If we truly trust that the Lord has our best interests at hand, we can pray specifically for what we think would be best or what we think we want. But, we are freed from disappointment if the answer to our prayer is no or looks different than we had hoped.

Using our earlier example of a golfer competing in the Masters, one might ask, "What if, after all that preparation, the golfer doesn't win the tournament?" The answer is simple. If the preparation is only to achieve the goal, not for the glory of the journey, he will never find enjoyment in life—whether he wins the prize or not. You set your sights on the prize, but you don't define the timing of that prize.

In life, we are like most of the golfers competing at the Masters. We have been playing the game for years, but have never won. Does not winning in the past keep those golfers from competing in the future? No, because one day they might accomplish their goal of standing in the winner's circle.

We must persevere, but die in our expectations and trust in the Lord's provision in every area of our life. We must come to an understanding that the tough times produce testimonies that we will share with others as we help them one day stand in the winner's circle.

Practice Rounds of Endurance

Paul reminded us that one of the most important aspects of our christian walk is to persevere through the ups and downs on this journey we call life. Proverbs instructs us that God's people perish without revelation (vision).

> Where there is no revelation, the people cast off restraint;
> But happy is he who keeps the law. (Proverbs 29:18)

Many of our life experiences won't seem like practice rounds preparing us to reach a specific goal or to achieve something better or more important in life. But if we remain steadfast in our faith and endure, as we look back, we can see that God knew all along the direction we needed to take to be successful.

My oldest son made a decision early in life that he wanted to earn the Eagle Scout designation from the Boy Scouts of America. He had a vision and a goal to strive for. His journey began in fifth grade, but wasn't complete until he was sophomore in high school.

Over the years, he had to attend weekly meetings, study various topics in order to earn the required number of merit badges, participate on campouts one weekend out of every month where he learned survival techniques. In addition to all the requirements, he had to overcome the peer pressure from friends and other kids his age. Let's face it. Shorts, knee socks, and neckerchiefs were not the accustomed dress for his age group. However, he persevered through the various levels of advancement: second class, first class, star, life, and finally, endured a grueling interview with former Eagle Scouts in order to present his compelling argument why he was qualified to receive such a distinguished honor.

It was six long years before he was able to stand on the stage and receive the ultimate and coveted distinction, Eagle Scout. The night he received this honor, he was joined on that stage by his football coach and all of his friends. They were there to support him and honor him for his achievement. No one was making fun of his uniform that night. He, like Abraham, had patiently endured and obtained the prize.

> For when God made a promise to Abraham, because He could swear by no one greater, He swore by Himself, saying, "Surely blessing I will bless you, and multiplying I will multiply you." And so, after he had patiently endured, he obtained the promise. (Hebrews 6:13-15)

Looking back, you could say my son endured many practice rounds on that six-year journey. I remember those weekend campouts as if they were yesterday. It didn't matter if it was hot, cold, raining or snowing, he and the other young men in his troop pitched their tents, chopped wood, built fire pits, cooked their own food and completed the projects assigned for that weekend. The journey was difficult and not always fun, but once it was completed and he stood on that stage, he felt a tremendous exhilaration.

The journey has had and will continue to have a lasting and positive effect on his life. Personally, I missed an incredible opportunity by not participating in scouts growing up. But I was fortunate enough to join my son on his journey, and I learned an interesting fact: men don't admit or talk about being a member of the Boy Scouts of America unless they persevered and received their Eagle Scout designation. To talk as a non-Eagle Scout would be an admission that they either quit or fell short of their goal.

In order for any of us to derive a benefit from our life experiences, we must stay the course and not give up until the day that we can say it is done. The Apostle Paul understood the importance of remaining focused as he played practice round after practice round until one day he looked up and said, "I have fought the fight, I have finished the race, I have kept the faith."

We too can have a vision or goal to shoot for and rest assured. If it is the Lord's will, all of our practice is preparation for that day when we are standing on the stage of life with prize in hand. Our testimony in life, like Paul's, becomes the lesson for others so they can endure through their own practice rounds.

> I have fought the good fight, I have finished the race, I have kept the faith. Finally, there is laid up for me the crown of righteousness, which the Lord, the righteous Judge, will give to me on that Day, and not to me only but also to all who have loved His appearing. (2 Timothy 4:7-8)

Unexpected Practice Rounds

It was pouring down rain on a highway in upstate New York when my youngest son became ill. He started throwing up had to go to the bathroom every few minutes. He couldn't stop and became hysterical, so his mother contacted our pediatrician in Dallas. She followed his instructions to take him to the nearest hospital, where she learned that his blood sugar was over 900.

To put it in perspective, a human's normal range is somewhere between 80 and 120. It was the summer after his fourth-grade year. He was on a vacation with his mother and brother on the way to see Nolan Ryan become inducted into the Baseball Hall of Fame. That trip would alter the course of his life. He learned the hard way what type 1 diabetes was, because the enemy gave it to him. Unfortunately, for Satan, he had already developed a reputation for being a hard worker with a tender heart, and developed strength of character that would prove instrumental in helping him deal with this devastating discovery and seeming setback in life.

That was a scary time in my son's life and resulted in many adjustments in his everyday routine. But now he runs four plus miles a day and is built like the rock of Gibraltar. Those previous practice rounds of life at an early age where he developed his strength of character, tender heart, and strong work ethic helped him to not only cope with the disease, but enabled him to be a role model and blessing to others afflicted with diabetes.

Not long after learning he had the disease, my son heard of another boy his age who had just been diagnosed. My son took it upon himself to call the young man and encourage him. He shared the fact that he too had diabetes and that everything would be okay.

I was coaching his little league team at the time, and as anyone knows who has coached at that age level, it is hard to find good players. At one of our practices, one of the players brought along a friend who had spent the previous night over at his house. Well, after seeing the boy throw I immediately asked if he would be interested in joining our team, to which he excitedly replied, "Yes." It turned out he had juvenile diabetes. It was the same boy my son had called to encourage.

My son's hardship had become a testimony, and he used it to comfort a friend. God had a plan, but at the time, we just thought this was another practice in preparation for our season. Little did we know that God was bringing two boys together in a special way. Needless to say, I was extremely proud of my son that day.

In life, we don't always know how many practice rounds we must play, nor do we always get to choose the course on which those rounds are played. The fortunate thing about having a personal relationship with Jesus Christ is this: He knows. And when we put our trust in Him, we can overcome any obstacle put in our path. We can endure through the good times and hard times knowing that our life experiences are continued preparation. Preparation for the day the Lord calls us into His service, introduces us to our potential husband or wife, helps us reach a vocational goal, or gives us the strength to endure a life-altering situation.

The Lord knows life is hard, and that we must face many adverse moments. He makes use of every situation to protect us, provide for us and, ultimately, prepare us for His eternal kingdom. Therefore, we can awake every day with an expectation that no matter what happens, by the end of the day we will be one step closer to Paradise. I shared these stories so that you too will stay encouraged to persevere on your own journey. Regardless, if you know where your journey is taking you, you can trust that God has a plan for your life, a plan that is meaningful and essential to His Kingdom.

Some of you might feel burdened by life's journey, beaten down and afflicted like Joseph or the others I have referenced. Don't give up. One day you too will be able to look back and rejoice, seeing that all the while God's Hand was directing your path.

> Trust in the LORD with all your heart, And lean not on your own understanding; In all your ways acknowledge Him, And He shall direct your paths. (Proverbs 3:5-6)

Persevere through your trials with hope, learning along the way to live godly lives. In spite of ourselves, when we make a conscious decision to follow the Lord, a process is already set in motion, ready to take us to a new level of play. God has already been working in our lives behind the scenes. His process of preparation becomes a reality. The journey from that point on isn't always a pleasant one, but a perfecting one.

God desires perfection for His children and will not be content until it is achieved. We play the practice rounds in life on God's course and with His rule book. Until the day we join with Him in Heaven, His Holy Spirit is right there coaching us, exposing our flaws, correcting our swing and instructing us. All according to the Father's will. Along the way we develop incredible testimonies that we can use to experientially speak into the lives of others.

Life is one big practice round glittered with many failures and near misses, but many victories. Like Tiger Wood's preparation for that first Masters, we shouldn't be content with anything less than perfection in preparation for our entry into God's eternal tournament. Prepare, practice, and persevere through life, and you too will lift the eternal cup in the air in front of the host of heaven and yell, *the victory is mine.*

Chapter Nine

God's Picture Puzzle

Have you ever worked on a large picture puzzle? The puzzle comes in a container, and on that container is a picture of the finished puzzle. The picture is the only instruction offered and becomes your road map acting as a guide toward the accomplishment of your goal.

You start with the end in mind, knowing that if you remain diligent to the task at hand and exercise patience, your puzzle will look as good as the picture on the container.

You begin by opening the plastic bag containing the pieces and carefully lay them on the workspace chosen for the project. It then becomes your quest to find the pieces that fit together. Thus the slow process begins of ordering all the pieces until the puzzle begins to take shape, which further propels your efforts. This gives you hope that you can actually accomplish the intended goal, a perfect image.

Now imagine you have been working for months on a large puzzle and are close to finishing it when you realize you are missing one piece. How would you feel? When finished, will the picture be complete? Will it appear the same as the picture on the container?

No, all your efforts will be ruined! Your goal cannot and will not be accomplished, and no matter how hard or how much you want it, all your efforts will seem futile and your time wasted. You will not be able to experience the true sense of joy that you would have otherwise felt if the puzzle were complete. Instead, it will be frustrating to have put forth all that effort only to sit back and gaze upon a puzzle with one piece missing.

Life is a lot like putting that puzzle together. We travel through life trying to find our place in hopes our piece will fit into the overall picture. We need to keep the end in mind when functioning within family. Whether that family is our personal, church, business or societal family, because without a clear picture, it is difficult to see how we fit in. Everyone is an important and valuable piece to the puzzle—the final picture, goal or outcome we desire to achieve.

I challenge you to think that God sees each one of as a valuable piece in His puzzle. If everyone has a God-given purpose for being on this planet, wouldn't it make sense that His ultimate goal is to construct His puzzle in such a way that every piece fits perfectly together?

One day, He will sit back and gaze on the final image, the image He preordained from the beginning of time—the image He had when He first created the universe, the heavens, the earth, and all mankind. God always begins with the end in mind.

The family is not one individual, but is made up of a group of individuals, where no member is more important than another. However, in every family there needs to be one head.

We saw how starting with Adam, men have abrogated their role in the family. Many women lacking a sense of security have assumed the role of headship in America's households. We wonder why there are so many divorces and there are so many kids growing up in split families. When men give up their headship in the family, the repercussions continue for generations. Women are doing what seems logical, but not what is biblical. So who do we blame, the men or the women? Blame leads to division and so the questions we should be asking are: "What role does God call us to play in the family? Why are there pieces missing in our family puzzles?"

The proper family order was established when God the Father impregnated Mary through the power of His Spirit. That child was born into his mother's loving care, where she was given charge to raise him to the best of her ability. God, for 30 years, instructed this son, Jesus Christ, and led him on the correct path toward His eternal destiny.

The example for family is found in God's Word, as we discussed at the beginning of this book. We looked at the creation and how God established a certain order to life. He created the Heavens and earth, and he created man then woman. Both were created in His image and were put on the earth to subdue it and multiply. They ruled over the animals, functioned together as a unit, procreated, and raised their children to the best of their ability. This was the first example of family.

But something happened as a result of their sin: Cain killed Abel. I am sure Eve suffered immensely, but the Bible doesn't tell us that. Adam had to grieve for his son, and you would think he would have taken corrective measures with his son. However, the Bible doesn't tell us that, either. The example the first family provided was not the model God intended. However, a natural family order did develop. The clan came into existence, and as man scattered out over the face of the earth, societies were formed. Often, those societies represented specific purposes in the way of vocation; some clans became herders, while others became farmers.

Those vocations became the family's primary purpose, but within each clan, the members had specific duties to carry out that helped the family as a whole function. They banded together and utilized the skill sets of each member. They protected each other and provided for one another's needs. There was a strong patriarch and a strong matriarch setting the example and training the other members of the clan. Traditions were passed down from generation to generation. They adapted to each other's style or combination of styles. Eventually, everyone conformed or the family had to deal with the individual or group not in conformance.

How well do we function in our own family? Do we stand tall for one another? Do we pray with our spouse, seeking God's wisdom and God's direction and covering over our children? The family is meant to be a safe place where we learn how to live righteously with peace and joy.

Spiritual family is no different; it is to be a place of safety, where we learn how to live by the word of God. We should be asking, "Why is there so much division within our natural families, our spiritual families and our societal families?"

> The elders who are among you I exhort, I who am a fellow elder and a witness of the sufferings of Christ, and also a partaker of the glory that will be revealed: Shepherd the flock of God which is among you, serving as overseers, not by compulsion but willingly, not for dishonest gain but eagerly; nor as being lords over those entrusted to you, but being examples to the flock; and when the Chief Shepherd appears, you will receive the crown of glory that does not fade away. Likewise you younger people, submit yourselves to your elders. Yes, all of you be submissive to one another, and be clothed with humility, for "God resists the proud, But gives grace to the humble." (1 Peter 5:1-5)

Throughout this book, we have identified and exposed the enemy of the family, S.I.N. (Satan/the devil) and established that he is out to steal, kill and destroy in an attempt to drag as many into hell with him as he possibly can.

> Therefore humble yourselves under the mighty hand of God, that He may exalt you in due time, casting all your care upon Him, for He cares for you. Be sober, be vigilant; because your adversary the devil walks about like a roaring lion, seeking whom he may devour. (1 Peter 5:6-8)

In my own family, we had a strong father and a strong mother. When I was growing up, my mother laid down the law and my father enforced that law. If we had acted up during the day, when my father returned home, we would be introduced to his belt.

However, later in my life, he became ill and my mother had to take on more of the enforcer role in the family. My father was present, but because of his illness, their roles became reversed over time.

For example, I remember as a young boy sitting up with my father late at night waiting for my brother, eight years my senior, to come home from a date. If he had not behaved properly, my father would deal with him but say, "Let's not tell your mother, no need to upset her." However, when I was older and started going out, it was my mother waiting up, ready to deal with my situation. She was the one telling me, "Don't tell your father, there is no reason to upset him."

Previously, we looked at Proverbs 1:8 where it tells us to obey the "Teaching of the Mother" and the "Instruction of the Father." Why do you think God put it in such a way? Could it be that there were distinct roles the mother and the father were to play in order to pass on the proper legacy, the proper blessing to the children? These roles are not exclusive of one another; the mother and the father are to work together. They are to provide a unified front. Children should not be able to play one parent against another. Parents must communicate or the enemy will be right there to take advantage of their ignorance.

Without the proper communication and biblical instruction, parents don't provide the proper example to their children and are running the risk that they will have problems later in life.

As a result of my father's illness, my brothers and I each grew up with a different perspective on family. My mother did a wonderful job and in no way shirked her responsibility as a parent. However, when my father became ill and wasn't able to biblically instruct the family, the family paid a spiritual price. On the other hand, earlier in their marriage, when my father took matters in his own hands and did not call my mother to his side, the family also paid a spiritual price. Even though my parents were very loving toward one another and enjoyed a long marriage, through illness the enemy had unknowingly attempted to disable them spiritually. The ultimate price the family paid was not a natural price, but a spiritual price.

As a result, each of their sons experienced divorce in their personal lives. We became victims of the enemy's scheme, the physical manifestation of spiritual depravity. The enemy tried to take advantage of the natural order in an attempt to steal our family's impact on society. Guess what? He failed, because everyone in our family believes Christ died for their sins and has trusted in Jesus as their Savior. Based on God's promise, we have eternal life with Him in Heaven. When all is said and done and we are resting in our graves, that will be all that matters. However, our spiritual legacy can and will live on in our children, so until that time, we don't want to rest on our laurels. We must grasp these truths and guard against the enemy's attacks.

There are many homeless kids, kids in gangs, kids from one-parent homes. Many are known as *latch-key kids*. They have keys to a home, but they come home to an empty house. We wonder why our society is corroding. These kids eventually grow up to be adults, and their past becomes the norm for them to pass on to their kids.

Jesus was approached in His earthly ministry and told that his mother and brothers were calling for him. We learn in Mark 3:33 how Jesus responded to the people by saying, "Who is My mother, or My brothers?" Jesus wasn't diminishing the role of his natural mother or his brothers, but rather making a point that we are all called to be brothers and sisters to one another.

We are to lift one another up in prayer and thanksgiving. We are to stand firm with one another holding each other up in support. We are meant to be in family, God's family, where we receive His instruction and covering from the pastoral leadership that He has ordained. We are to come alongside each other in fellowship on a regular basis. We are to enter into discipleship and hold one another accountable to a holy way of living. Men are to be fathers within the church and women are to be mothers within the church.

If a mother loses her husband, there should be plenty of father figures to provide biblical instruction. If a father loses his wife, there should be plenty of mother figures to assist in mothering. The church is meant to be a family, a safe haven, the one place where we can feel God's love through the nurturing body of each of its members.

Unfortunately, through the attack on the church, the enemy has been able to block the revelation of biblical truth to many. You have heard it said that the front door of the church is wide open, but so is the back door. Why would this be?

The Modern Church

There are a number of scenarios, but we will focus on three:

1. Churches are ill equipped to minister to all the needs of the body.

Many evangelical churches are led by a strong pastor who essentially and initially performs every function in the church. They fall into the category, "A jack of all trades and a master of none." As church membership increases, they become more and more controlling in order to keep their finger on the pulse. It is impossible for this church to flourish and grow, because the laity is not empowered to volunteer, suggest, and help mold the congregation.

The pastor can become burdened, stressed, and at times fall into a pattern of sin in his or her own life. This happens because they don't have a strong inner circle to encourage and empower them to keep their spiritual tanks full. The church may continue for an extended period of time, but it will never fully grow into its God-given potential.

2. The church doesn't feel like home or a safe place to let down one's guard.

Many mainstream churches fall under the authority of a much broader conical order and depending on the adopted practices, most often the body will either flourish or fade away. Many of these mainstream religious orders are splitting over gay rights issues and homosexual activity, abortion, ordination of women, and other random topical conflicts that Satan has orchestrated to divide God's church.

Our hearts have become hardened and God has given us over to our vices. Why? Because every one of these divisive issues is clearly addressed in God's Word, and human interpretation of God's Word has been twisted to justify whatever behavior the congregation desires to embrace.

3. The church preaches accountability, but lacks true spiritual accountability.

Still other churches start out with good intentions, but end up heading down the wrong path because they lack accountability. The leaders get caught up in a power trip and start taking advantage of the congregants. They ignorantly see the growth as a result of their own doing. They begin to think they are entitled to a more lavish lifestyle because they are somehow more blessed than the membership. They might be thinking, "After all, I'm putting in countless hours serving the community, the congregation, and the staff." Slowly, Satan is able to creep in, taint their minds, and turn them away from their first true love.

Some examples in the media are Jimmy Baker, Larry Lea, Robert Tilton, and we could name many others. Many of their followers use the excuse, "But look at all the lives they touched." Well, our answer to that can only be, "God will use us in spite of our evil intentions and the darkness present in the heart." He will put all the pieces of His puzzle into place even if we pull our piece of the puzzle out of His box.

> Now John answered and said, "Master, we saw someone casting out demons in Your name, and we forbade him because he does not follow with us." But Jesus said to him, "Do not forbid him, for he who is not against us is on our side." (Luke 9:49-50)

These ministries or spiritual families are dysfunctional and quite possibly could lead many astray. Their leaders will be held accountable unless they truly confess their sin and repent in their hearts before the Lord. The following scripture in Matthew, emphasizes the importance of following proper biblical doctrine.

> Not everyone who says to Me, "Lord, Lord," shall enter the kingdom of heaven, but he who does the will of My Father in heaven. Many will say to Me in that day, "Lord, Lord, have we not prophesied in Your name, cast out demons in Your name, and done many wonders in Your name?" And then I will declare to them, "I never knew you; depart from Me, you who practice lawlessness!" (Matthew 7:21-23)

Our religious congregations today are made up of people who come from dysfunctional family environments. Many have not been able to let their guard down at home or at work, so they come into the church and sit toward the back. They avoid attention or contact so no one can possibly know the pain they are in or the sin issues in their lives. Unfortunately, when they do confide their troubles, they are often judged or rebuked. As a result, many people are turned off by religion and church. The flesh and blood examples they see lead them to label christians as hypocrites. In other words, they come away with a distorted view of the church. Some isolate within the church while others, not wanting to change, exit out the back of the church and sadly, hardly anyone notices.

Of course, there are many reasons why people react this way. For one, they might hear a message that stirs up the guilt in their heart. But because they are in denial, they become offended at the person delivering the message and leave. Another reason might be that they feel challenged by the message, but are not ready to admit their shortcomings and turn from the behavior, so they leave. Others might be offended by the pastor's message or the pastor's counsel and will search for a home where the message or counsel doesn't cut as deep.

I am going to open a can of worms here. I am going to use one of the most controversial subjects in the church today as an example of how S.I.N. has brought division amongst God's spiritual family, and in so doing, keep many in bondage to his lies. The subject is tithing. Someone hears a message on tithing and thinks the preacher is out to get in their pocket. They might be hurting financially or possibly burdened by solicitors asking for money. So when they come into church and hear someone asking for their money, without revelation of the biblical concept of the tithe, they ignorantly assume the preacher is ill-intended.

Well, since we are all sinners and sinners are running our churches, one could realistically agree with their questioning. Truth be told, they are offended because they haven't grasped spiritual revelation, the biblical blessing and freedom from S.I.N. that God offers in return for the tithe.

After all, whether the offended person wants to believe it or not everything belongs to the Creator. We are encouraged through God's Word to give the tithe not to the church or to a preacher but to God, without condition. What we experience in return is release from the spiritual bondage that Satan or S.I.N. wants us to be in to our money and material idols.

> Will a man rob God? Yet you have robbed Me! But you say, "In what way have we robbed You?" In tithes and offerings. You are cursed with a curse, For you have robbed Me, Even this whole nation. Bring all the tithes into the storehouse, That there may be food in My house, And try Me now in this,

> Says the LORD of hosts, If I will not open for you the windows of heaven And pour out for you such blessing That there will not be room enough to receive it. And I will rebuke the devourer for your sakes, So that he will not destroy the fruit of your ground, Nor shall the vine fail to bear fruit for you in the field, Says the LORD of hosts; And all nations will call you blessed, For you will be a delightful land, Says the LORD of hosts. (Malachi 3:8-12)

S.I.N., working in the hearts of many reading this will have them saying to themselves, "That is Old Testament, and if you study the time it was delivered and the audience the author was addressing, it doesn't apply to us in New Testament times." To this, I offer the following, the balance we are to have when tithing is not to desire a monetary blessing, but a spiritual cleansing, and a release from the bondage of our sinful desires.

That being said, let us look at Jesus' opinion on tithing, because if we are honest, His counsel is much more reliable than our intellectual understanding of this principle. Jesus agreed the Pharisees should tithe, but not if they were going to deceptively extort those they were professing to lead. Jesus instructs them to continue tithing, but not to neglect justice, mercy and faith. One without the other leaves us out of balance in the spiritual realm.

> Woe to you, scribes and Pharisees, hypocrites! For you pay tithe of mint and anise and cummin, and have neglected the weightier matters of the law: justice and mercy and faith. These you ought to have done, *without leaving the others undone*. Blind guides, who strain out a gnat and swallow a camel! Woe to you, scribes and Pharisees, hypocrites! For you cleanse the outside of the cup and dish, but inside they are full of extortion and self-indulgence. (Matthew 23:23-25)

Bible scholars today will rightfully tell you that you are no longer under the curse stated in Malachi. They might say you are no longer obliged to pay out a tenth of your income. But if they are truly accountable to God, they will also tell you that the enemy wants to keep you in bondage to your material possessions and wealth.

> Now Jesus sat opposite the treasury and saw how the people put money into the treasury. And many who were rich put in

> much. Then one poor widow came and threw in two mites, which make a quadrans. So He called His disciples to Himself and said to them, "Assuredly, I say to you that this poor widow has put in more than all those who have given to the treasury; for they all put in out of their abundance, but she out of her poverty put in all that she had, her whole livelihood."
> (Mark 12:41-44)

The woman Jesus is referring to in Mark gave all she had to God, but I believe Jesus called His disciples because He wanted them to grasp the concept of total surrender. The woman put in all she had, "her whole livelihood."

The enemy easily ensnares our thinking when we hold onto anything in life that stands in the way of a right relationship with the Lord. If we aren't willing to give Him everything—our whole livelihood—then we are in bondage to whatever it is we are holding onto.

When it comes to tithing, why not cheerfully follow the recommendation of scripture and let your conscience be your guide by prayerfully considering what the Holy Spirit is showing you? For many, giving a tenth of their income is a mere penance, given out of guilt for a lifestyle they know is not in line with God's will.

> So let each one give as he purposes in his heart, not grudgingly or of necessity; for God loves a cheerful giver.
> (2 Corinthians 9:7)

George Washington, our nation's first president, once said, "Let your heart feel for the afflictions and distress of everyone, and let your hand give in proportion to your purse."

I think George got the picture, don't you? Doesn't sound like he was in bondage to the tithe or to some so-called *prosperity preacher*. No, he was free from the law, but understood the fulfillment of the law. He was instructing people to let the Holy Spirit convict their conscious minds. Hoping they would grasp the providential concept that if you are blessed, you are to be a blessing to others.

George Washington put his money where his mouth was. He gave one of the first endowments of its kind to what is now Washington and Lee University in Lexington, Virginia when he donated stock to the school. That gift continues to generate approximately $500,000 per year in income to the school.

> In 1796, George Washington saved the struggling Liberty Hall Academy when he gave the school its first major endowment—$20,000 worth of James River Canal stock. The trustees promptly changed the name of the school to Washington Academy as an expression of their gratitude. In a letter to the trustees, Washington responded, "To promote the Literature in this rising Empire, and to encourage the Arts, have ever been amongst the warmest wishes of my heart." The donation—one of the largest to any educational institution at that time—continues to contribute to the University's operating budget today. (33)

People's hearts have become hardened toward the biblical messages they are hearing instead of what God really wants them to grasp. Why else, when we hear a message that stirs up the dirt in our heart, do we have a tendency to back off and run away?

It is not until we embrace and get involved in spiritual family and come to an understanding there is healing in the functional church, that God's Word can penetrate and change our hearts. Instead, we will continue to transfer our guilt onto everyone around us, oftentimes talking negatively about our families, co-workers, politicians, people in church and other groups we have contact or exposure to…everyone but ourselves.

Blaise Pascal, a French physicist, mathematician and author who lived in the 1600s, once said, "There is a God-shaped vacuum in the heart of every man/woman which cannot be filled by any created thing, but only by God, the Creator." Determine your road map for success, evaluate it, and make sure it is in balance. Then make sure you have the right people around you to carry out your plan.

Finally, pour into others, helping to develop and mentor them so that you can create a lasting legacy of success. Yes, we are all an integral piece in God's eternal puzzle. His eternal puzzle will not be complete until our piece has been set in place.

Placing the Trinity Over Our Lives

In the very first chapter of this book, we defined the Godhead and His triune nature: Father, Son, and Holy Spirit. It is one thing to understand and even believe in the Trinity, but it is another thing entirely to place that Trinity over your life. The Trinity, as we have learned, is in perfect balance.

By placing it over our person, family, business, and the society in which we live, we can achieve spiritual balance and have the covering of Christ over our lives.

Imagine an equilateral triangle, three sides equal in distance. Imagine that our lives are contained within the lines of that triangle. With that said, in order to be successful in life, it would make sense that our triangles must remain in balance and have complete unity. Below is a visual to bring clarity to this concept. You can substitute other elements as well, because there will always be three core elements in any setting. God will always be at the helm and will flow in and through the other elements.

GOD • FATHER AND MOTHER • COMPANY

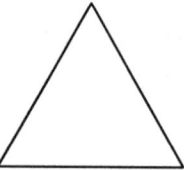

HOLY SPIRIT • FAMILY • CUSTOMERS   JESUS CHRIST • CHILDREN • EMPLOYEES

Let's explore what happens when the triangle gets out of balance by using a business scenario with three examples—each representative of one side of the triangle.

First, assume the company you are working for is intent on increasing its customer base by lowering the cost of its product. The decision is made to accomplish this by cutting employee salaries. This decision will frustrate employees, causing them increased stress, and eventually they will be disgruntled and seek employment elsewhere. The triangle is now out of balance and unfortunately, the smartest and more experienced employees will be the first to leave, creating a critical void. As you know, when people leave an organization, it costs a tremendous amount of money to recruit and train new employees, which jeopardizes the long-term survival of the company.

To make this point, let me share a personal story. My family owned restaurants when I was growing up. One thing my father always communicated was the importance of maintaining a balanced atmosphere in the workplace. He developed a bonus structure based on a 60/40 principle. The company financed the opening of their locations and took care of all capital expenditures throughout the life of the asset. Once the establishment was open, they split the profits with their management team and many were making six-figure incomes at a time when six-figure incomes were actually rare.

Years later, an offshoot of the original company became extremely successful. But eventually, the leadership forgot its roots and became more concerned with shareholder value than keeping the triangle balanced. Upper management decided they could save money by eliminating the bonus structure and putting all the managers on salary. The CEO at the time made the claim, "I can buy all the managers I want for one hundred thousand dollars." He was thinking they could put those savings back into the corporate coffers, finance a remodeling program, and increase shareholder profits. However, as a result of his decision, over 90 senior managers left the company. These managers had the longest tenure and were the most knowledgeable.

Two other major things happened. The first one was that all the younger managers who were working 60-plus hours a week for the carrot (lucrative bonus plan) started to ask, "If the carrot is gone, why am I busting my rear, working so hard?" They too vacated the company. The second one was that all these establishments were located in communities where the customers were extremely sensitive to change, so when this occurred, they got upset and showed their dissatisfaction by leaving. As a result of this decision—along with a failed remodeling initiative—the company that previously had been debt-free owed creditors over 80 million dollars. Wow, you think their triangle got a little out of balance? Everyone lost: the company, customers and employees.

For our next scenario, let's assume the company is having trouble keeping good people. So management decides to raise customer prices in order to increase the bonuses they are paying top executives. Eventually the customer will become frustrated, disgruntled, and quite possibly be forced to locate a similar product for less money. Rather costly given the amount of time, energy, and money it takes to develop a strong customer base, wouldn't you agree?

To make this point, let me share another example. A good friend of mine was appointed by a bankruptcy court to take over a failing restaurant chain. When he arrived on the scene, the company was running at zero earnings. As he studied the events of the past year, he came to realize that several months prior to his arrival, they were actually tracking approximately 15 million in earnings. He asked members of the existing management team what had changed to cause such a dramatic drop in profitability.

He found out the board had become frustrated with the concept and in an attempt to beef up earnings, hired a new CEO. The new CEO ran a test in their main market to see if he could raise prices, but the method employed was deceptive. They used different colored plates and portion sizes to make it appear that the customer was getting a better value, even though the average price per plate had increased by one dollar. The test failed miserably, but in the CEO's ignorance, he instructed management to roll out the program nationwide by declaring, "The customer will adjust."

Unfortunately, for him and his board, their customers were pretty smart and did just that; they adjusted by leaving and eating elsewhere. By tilting the triangle, everyone lost: the company, customers, and employees.

For our third scenario, let's assume the employees decide to boost their earnings and start conspiring with customers by giving products away in exchange for cash payment under the table. Eventually the company will suffer a loss in profit and will not be able to sustain the business.

To share a personal experience, I was faced with this imbalance early in my career while managing an establishment. We employed around 75 of the most wonderful people you could ever hope to work with. One month upon reviewing our profit-and-loss statement, I noticed our cost of goods sold had increased dramatically. So I put a step-by-step plan in action to search out and uncover the reason for the increase. What we found was astonishing. Three of our smartest and brightest employees had come up with a devious scheme to pocket money and not ring-up sales.

If we had not uncovered this abuse in time, the establishment could have easily gone out of business. Of course, this would have jeopardized everyone's job, and our customers would have been forced to find another source of supply. These employees had tilted the triangle and put everyone at risk: the company, customers, and employees.

In a perfect world, the triangles of our lives would never be out of balance. Therefore, by placing the Trinity (God the Father, God the Son and God the Holy Spirit) over every area of your life, you are inviting Christ's covering, and coming into alignment with the Creator. You will naturally experience an eternal blessing: long-term peace and hope, which God promises for each of His creations.

> For I know the thoughts that I think toward you, says the LORD, thoughts of peace and not of evil, to give you a future and a hope. (Jeremiah 29:11)

Conclusion

Looking back on the material covered, we have peered into the spiritual realm. Showing that as beings created in God's image, we possess the three distinct characteristics of the Godhead: spirit, flesh, and soul. We explored the divine nature of creation and uncovered God's universe factory. We learned that our Father in heaven was not content to sit on His throne in the heavenly realm, but came down to earth in the flesh through Jesus Christ and empowered mankind through His Word, granting us revelation by the power of His Holy Spirit. We came to understand that our finite minds couldn't fully understand an infinite God. That our cosmos is growing at breakneck speed and all of God's creation in the spirit will live on for eternity.

We looked at Satan's intention to corrupt our world through the societies in which we live. We showed how he has done so by deceiving mankind from generation to generation, slowly eroding the moral and ethical fiber our country was founded upon. We came to the realization that most of us have been clueless and naively unaware of the effect the enemy's societal decay has had on our nation as a whole.

Next, we exposed Satan's Set-Up, the method employed in order to fulfill his evil intentions, knowing he was not omnipresent. We saw how he used original sin to his advantage by planting an evil seed in every heart born from the union between man and woman.

However, since God brings good out of every situation, we looked at how God used Satan's plan against him to create a culture of free will. By which every one of us has the opportunity to choose where they want to spend eternity. In essence, Satan became God's opportunity by providing a way for mankind to be saved from eternal destruction. We exposed the enemy's eternal agony; every time Satan attacks a born-again believer and they confess their sins, repent from those sins and turn back to God, Satan is destined to experience death and resurrection. Over and over again, that is his ultimate insanity.

We continued by showing that as a result of S.I.N., we have all become addicted in some way to the societies we live in and have ignorantly compromised the values established by our Founding Fathers. The addictive erosion becomes evident as we look back through history at the corruption birthed from previous generations.

However, we learned that inherent in each one of us there is good news; God is still in charge. When we are weak and don't have the strength to overcome those addictions, God is right there waiting to take our hand and guide our path.

Unfortunately, we came to realize that most of us are complacently content to just play life. We ignorantly follow other people in hopes they won't lead us off the cliff of life, leading to eternal separation from God. Oftentimes, we listen to individuals or church officials who relate scripture based on their own interpretation and risk embracing skewed theological thinking. We do so because we want to justify our self interest in hopes of fooling God into not judging our unrighteous behavior.

We saw how most of us continue to pull away from anyone or anything that gets close to our real life issues. When in reality we should be pressing in so we can break the hold they have on us. Of course, when the pain becomes unbearable, most of us do cry out in hopes that someone, somewhere is listening. Then we are finally open to embrace the freedom available through Christ by dealing with those issues, thus breaking the grip sin has on our life.

We exposed the three primary plays that the enemy has been running successfully for years: temptation, accusation, and deception. We learned that there are many options that stem from these three primary plays and gained insight on how not react to those plays.

We learned not to defend our actions or engage an enemy that doesn't care about the right or wrong of an issue, but whose only goal is to cause division. We learned that the only way to mount an adequate defense was to put on the invisible armor of God daily so He will be able to protect our spiritual beings.

We explored the concept of climactic deliverance, which is not a quick fix. That we are instantly delivered from sin when we made a true heartfelt decision to place our trust in Jesus Christ for our salvation. Thereby gaining immediate access into His eternal kingdom. Life then becomes a process where our spiritual skills are honed and the seed of S.I.N. is slowly removed from our hearts.

The Lord continues to bring about change in our lives as we share our faith with others, and as we read and study God's word. As we connect with a good Bible-based church filled with the Holy Spirit. As we determine to give Him the first fruits of our day and the final moments before drifting off to sleep.

Then we stepped on the Lord's perpetual stairway, one that never breaks down. We were relieved to learn that the Lord's stairway is one directional and regardless of whether we are walking up or down; we will always be traveling upward.

We learned to embrace the practice rounds of life—our life experiences—which are preparing us for our eternal destiny. The fact that our practice rounds become our object lessons by which we are able to communicate effectively to strengthen others, especially the younger generation.

We saw how we are all pieces of God's eternal puzzle. Even though our pictures might be missing a few pieces and appear incomplete, His puzzle will ultimately bear a perfect image. The image He preordained before creation. Like God, we too need to keep the end in mind.

Finally, we learned how important it is to place the Triune nature of God over every aspect of our lives in order to maintain proper balance. In doing so, we experience His blessings over our family, business, church, and societal families.

At the very beginning of the book, I challenged you with a question, and we have explicitly explored and defined the answer through these pages. It is my hope that you now have no doubt in your heart of the correct answer God desires to hear from all of His children. So once again, I ask on His behalf:

> If you were to die tonight, transported to heaven finding yourself standing at the pearly gates and the Almighty God of the Universe asked you, "Why should I let you in to Heaven?" What would your answer be?

Well, do you know the answer? If so, then brace yourself and get ready, because one day you too will be standing on the edge of eternity, ready to receive your crown of eternal life and declare your...

FREEDOM FROM S.I.N.

WE WOULD LIKE TO OFFER YOU A FREE GIFT

Each of us is an *Innately Unique Creation*. We have explored in FREEDOM FROM S.I.N. that each of us have been created with a body, mind, and spirit. We showed how God through the Trinity is Father, Son, and Holy Spirit; Jesus is the Way, the Truth, and the Life; and Satan is out to kill, steal, and destroy.

Therefore, we would challenge that each of us also have three unique qualities that we contribute to any endeavor or task we undertake.

For this reason we created a survey called the "iUC Questionnaire" to assist you in getting in touch with those qualities. Please visit our website to take advantage of this free gift. Our website can be found at http://www.mtoleadership.com

The purpose of MTO Leadership Development is to EXPOSE the enemy within each of us, IDENTIFY our unique qualities, and IGNITE christians with a call to action. We invite you to explore the website for more information and to obtain links to other books and materials to assist you on your spiritual journey through life.

To order additional copies of this book and to purchase the FREEDOM FROM S.I.N. STUDY GUIDE please visit www.freedomfromsin.com

The study guide, used in conjunction with the book, spans nine weeks and is a great tool for Sunday school classes, and small group study.

The Author is available to speak or to host half-day and full-day seminars. Please contact info@freedomfromsin.com to schedule.

Appendix

BIBLIOGRAPHY

1. *International Bible Society.* [Online]
2. www.greatsite.com. *World Bible Society.* [Online]
3. [book auth.] James VanderKam and Peter Flint. *The Meaning of the Dead Sea Scrolls: Their Significance for Understanding the Bible, Judaism, Jesus, and Christianity.* Copyright 2002, p. 22. A good site to visit for more information and to view images of the scrolls can be found at www.deadseascrolls.org.il
4. *Webster's Revised Unabridged Dictionary.* 1996, 1998 MICRA, Inc.
5. Strong's concordance / Blue Letter Bible. "Dictionary and Word Search for Logos/Phos (Strong's 3056/5457). *Blue Letter Bible.* [Online] 1996-2008. [Cited: August 4, 2008.] www.blueletterBible.com.
6. Strong, James. *Strong's Exhaustive Concordance of the Bible.* Madison NJ: Abingdon, 1890. # G1510
7. WordNet 1.6, 1997 Princeton Universtiy. *Dictionary.com.* [Online] www.dictionary.com.
8. *Webster's Revised Unabridged Dictionary.* MICRA, Inc. 2008.
9. *Hubble Site.* [Online] 1996. http://hubblesite.org/newscenter/newsdesk/archive/releases/1996/21/.
10. Strong, James. *Strong's Exhaustive Concordance of the Bible.* Madison NJ: Abingdon, 1890. # H1961.
11. Barry A. Kosmin and Ariela Keysar. [Online] Institute for the Study of Secularism in Society and Culture, Trininty College, Hartford, CT., 2001 data. http://b27.cc.trincoll.edu/weblogs/AmericanReligionSurveyARIS/reports/ARIS_Report_2008.pdf (pg.3)
12. *Nasa.gov.* [Online] http://rst.gsfc.nasa.gov/Sect20/A1.html.
13. *The American Heritage Dictionary of the English Language. Fourth Edition.* s.l.: Houghton Mifflin, 2004.
14. National Association of Gang Investigators Association.
15. Psychology.jrank.org/269/Gangs. *Psychology.jrank.org.* [Online] http://psychology.jrank.org/pages/269/Gangs.html.
16. National Infrastructure Protection Plan. 2006.
17. Special report of the National Gang Crime Research Center - Project GANGFACT. s.l.: The National Gang Crime Research Center, 1996.
18. Jr., Louis A. Perez. *On Becoming Cuban.* s.l: The Universtiy of North Carolina Press, 1999. Page 497.
19. Bureau of Western Hemisphere Affairs, U.S. Department of State, August 2008.
20. www.archives.gov/exhibits/charters/charters_of_freedom_6.html. *Archives.gov.* [Online]
21. *The American Heritage New Dictionary of Cultural Literacy, Third Edition.* s.l: Houghton Mifflin Company, 2005.
22. The Declaration of Independence. July 4, 1776.
23. *The American Heritage Science Dictionary.* s.l: Houghton Mifflin Company, 2002.
24. The Barna Group, Ltd. [Online] 2008. http://www.barna.org. Americans' On-the-Go Lifestyles and Entertainment Appetites Fuel Increasing Reliance Upon Technology; February 7, 2006
25. National Center for Health Statistics Health, United States; WithChartbook on Trends in the Health of Americans. Hyattsville, MD: s.n., 2006.

26. AAA Foundation for Traffic Safety. 2008.
27. Dictionary.com Unabridged (1.1) Random House, Inc. [Online] Dictionary.com
28. Copyright © 2012 EvanTell, Inc. All rights reserved. www.evantell.com
29. Oswald Chambers Publications Association, LTD.
30. Stairway to Heaven by Led Zeppelin. Recorded: 1971 Songwriter: Led Zeppelin Producers: Jimmy Page Copyright : 1971.
31. Strong, James. *Strong's Exhaustive Concordance of the Bible.* Madison NJ: Abingdon, 1890. #G862
32. Wilson, John A. *The Burden of Egypt,* 80. s.l: The University of Chicago Press.
33. Washington and Lee University
34. www.jewishvirtuallibrary.org/jsource/Judaism/613_mitzvot.html

The 613 Mitzvot

According to Sefer Hamitzvot of Rambam

248 Positive Mitzvot
P1: Believing in Gd
P2: Unity of Gd
P3: Loving Gd
P4: Fearing Gd
P5: Worshiping Gd
P6: Cleaving to Gd
P7: Taking an oath by Gd's Name
P8: Walking in Gd's ways
P9: Sanctifying Gd's Name
P10: Reading the Shema twice daily
P11: Studying and teaching Torah
P12: Wearing Tephillin of the head
P13: Wearing Tephillin of the hand
P14: To make Tzitzis
P15: To affix a Mezuzah
P16: Hakhel during Sukkos
P17: A king should write a Torah
P18: Everyone should write a Torah
P19: Grace after meals
P20: Building a Sanctuary for Gd
P21: Revering the Beis Hamikdosh
P22: Guarding the Mikdosh
P23: Levitical services in the Mikdosh
P24: Ablutions of the Kohanim
P25: Kindling the lamps by the Kohanim
P26: Kohanim blessing Israel
P27: The Showbread
P28: Burning the Incense
P29: The perpetual fire on the Altar
P30: Removing the ashes from the Altar
P31: Removing tameh persons from the camp
P32: Honoring the Kohanim
P33: The Priestly garments
P34: Kohanim bearing the Ark on their shoulders
P35: The oil of the Anointment
P36: Kohanim ministering in watches
P37: Kohanim defiling themselves for deceased relatives
P38: Kohein Gadol should only marry a virgin
P39: Daily Burnt Offerings
P40: Kohein Gadol's daily Meal Offering
P41: The Shabbos Additional Offering
P42: The New Moon Additional Offering
P43: The Pesach Additional Offering
P44: The Meal Offering of the Omer

FREEDOM FROM S.I.N

P45: The Shavuos Additional Offering
P46: Bring Two Loaves on Shavuos
P47: The Rosh Hashana Additional Offering
P48: The Yom Kippur Additional Offering
P49: The Service of Yom Kippur
P50: The Sukkos Offering
P41: The Shabbos Additional Offering
P42: The New Moon Additional Offering
P43: The Pesach Additional Offering
P44: The Meal Offering of the Omer
P45: The Shavuos Additional Offering
P46: Bring Two Loaves on Shavuos
P47: The Rosh Hashana Additional Offering
P48: The Yom Kippur Additional Offering
P49: The Service of Yom Kippur
P50: The Sukkos Offering
P51: The Shemini Atzeret Additional Offering
P52: The three annual pilgrimages
P53: Appearing before the Lrd during the Festivals
P54: Rejoicing on the Festivals
P55: Slaughtering the Pesach Offering
P56: Eating the Pesach Offering
P57: Slaughtering the Pesach Sheini Offering
P58: Eating the Pesach Sheini Offering
P59: Blowing the trumpets in the Sanctuary
P60: Minimum age of cattle to be offered
P61: Offering only unblemished sacrifices
P62: Bringing salt with every offering
P63: The BurntOffering
P64: The SinOffering
P65: The GuiltOffering
P66: The PeaceOffering
P67: The MealOffering
P68: Offerings of a Court that has erred
P69: The Fixed SinOffering
P70: The Suspensive GuiltOffering
P71: The Unconditional GuiltOffering
P72: The Offering of a Higher or Lower Value
P73: Making confession
P74: Offering brought by a zav (man with a discharge)
P75: Offering brought by a zavah (woman with a discharge)
P76: Offering of a woman after childbirth
P77: Offering brought by a leper
P78: Tithe of Cattle
P79: Sanctifying the Firstborn
P80: Redeeming the Firstborn
P81: Redeeming the firstling of a donkey
P82: Breaking the neck of the firstling of a donkey
P83: Bringing due offerings on the first festival

THE 613 MITZVOT

P84: All offerings to be brought to the Sanctuary
P85: Bring all offerings due from outside Eretz Yisrael to Sanctuary
P86: Redeeming blemished offerings
P87: Holiness of substituted offerings
P88: Kohanim eat the residue of the Meal Offerings
P89: Kohanim eat the meat of the Consecrated Offerings
P90: To burn Consecrated Offerings that have become tameh
P91: To burn the remnant of the Consecrated Offerings
P92: The Nazir letting his hair grow
P93: Nazirite obligations on completion of vow
P94: All oral submissions to be fulfilled
P95: Revocation of vows
P96: Defilement through carcasses of animals
P97: Defilement through carcasses of eight creeping creatures
P98: Defilement of food and drink
P99: Tumah of a menstruant
P100: Tumah of a woman after childbirth
P101: Tumah of a leper
P102: Garments contaminated by leprosy
P103: A leprous house
P104: Tumah of a zav (man with a discharge)
P105: Tumah of semen
P106: Tumah of a zavah (woman with a discharge)
P107: Tumah of a corpse
P108: The law of the water of sprinkling
P109: Immersing in a mikveh
P110: Cleansing from Leprosy
P111: A leper must shave his head
P112: The leper must be made distinguishable
P113: Ashes of the Red Heifer
P114: Valuation of a person
P115: Valuation of beasts
P116: Valuation of houses
P117: Valuation of fields
P118: Restitution for Sacrilege
P119: The fruits of the fourthyear planting
P120: To leave the corners (Peah) for the poor
P121: To leave gleanings for the poor
P122: To leave the forgotten sheaf for the poor
P123: To leave defective grape clusters for the poor
P124: To leave grape gleanings for the poor
P125: To bring Firstfruits to the Sanctuary
P126: To set aside the great Heaveoffering
P127: To set aside the first tithe
P128: To set aside the second tithe
P129: The Levites' tithe for the Kohanim
P130: To set aside the poorman's tithe in the third and sixth year
P131: The avowal of the tithe
P132: Recital on bringing the Firstfruits

P133: To set aside the Challah for the Kohein
P134: Renouncing as ownerless produce of the Sabbatical year
P135: Resting the land on the Sabbatical year
P136: Sanctifying the Jubilee year
P137: Blowing the Shofar in the Jubilee year
P138: Reversion of the land in the Jubilee year
P139: Redemption of property in a walled city
P140: Counting the years till the Jubilee year
P141: Canceling monetary claims in the Sabbatical year
P142: Exacting debts from idolaters
P143: The Kohein's due in the slaughter of every clean animal
P144: The first of the fleece to be given to the Kohein
P145: Devoted thing to Gd and the Kohein
P146: Slaughtering animals before eating them
P147: Covering the blood of slain birds and animals
P148: Releasing the mother before taking the nest
P149: Searching for the prescribed signs in cattle and animals
P150: Searching for the prescribed signs in birds
P151: Searching for the prescribed signs in grasshoppers
P152: Searching for the prescribed signs in fishes
P153: Determining the New Moon
P154: Resting on Shabbos
P155: Proclaiming the sanctity of Shabbos
P156: Removal of chometz on Pesach
P157: Recounting Exodus from Egypt on first night of Pesach
P158: Eating Matzah on the first night of Pesach
P159: Resting on the first day of Pesach
P160: Resting on the seventh day of Pesach
P161: Counting the Omer
P162: Resting on Shavuos
P163: Resting on Rosh Hashana
P164: Fasting on Yom Kippur
P165: Resting on Yom Kippur
P166: Resting on the first day of Sukkos
P167: Resting on Shemini Atzeret
P168: Dwelling in a Sukkah for seven days
P169: Taking a Lulav on Sukkos
P170: Hearing a Shofar on Rosh Hashana
P171: Giving half a shekel annually
P172: Heeding the Prophets
P173: Appointing a King
P174: Obeying the Great Court
P175: Abiding by a majority decision
P176: Appointing Judges and Officers of the Court
P177: Treating litigants equally before the law
P178: Testifying in Court
P179: Inquiring into the testimony of witnesses
P180: Condemning witnesses who testify falsely
P181: Eglah Arufah

P182: Establishing Six Cities of Refuge
P183: Assigning cities to the Levi'im
P184: Building fences on roof; and removing sources of danger from our dwellings
P185: Destroying all idolworship
P186: The law of the apostate city
P187: The law of the Seven Nations
P188: The extinction of the seed of Amalek
P189: Remembering the nefarious deeds of Amalek
P190: The law of the nonobligatory war
P191: Appoint a Kohein to speak to the people going to war and send back any man unfit for battle
P192: Preparing a place beyond the camp
P193: Including a digging tool among war implements
P194: A robber to restore the stolen article
P195: To give charity
P196: Lavishing gifts on a Hebrew bondman on his freedom
P197: Lending money to the poor
P198: Lending money to the heathen with interest
P199: Restoring a pledge to a needy owner
P200: Paying wages on time
P201: An employee is allowed to eat the produce he's working in
P202: Unloading a tired animal
P203: Assisting the owner in loading his burden
P204: Returning lost property to its owner
P205: Rebuking the sinner
P206: Loving our Fellow Jew
P207: Loving the convert
P208: The law of weights and measures
P209: Honoring scholars
P210: Honoring parents
P211: Fearing parents
P212: Be fruitful and multiply
P213: The law of marriage
P214: Bridegroom devotes himself to his wife for one year
P215: Circumcising one's son
P216: Law of the Levirite Marriage
P217: Law of Chalitzah
P218: A violator must marry the maiden he has violated
P219: The law of the defamer of his bride
P220: The law of the seducer
P221: The law of the captive woman
P222: The law of divorce
P223: The law of a suspected adulteress
P224: Whipping transgressors of certain commandments
P225: The law of unintentional manslaughter
P226: Beheading transgressors of certain commandments
P227: Strangling transgressors of certain commandments
P228: Burning transgressors of certain commandments

P229: Stoning transgressors of certain commandments
P230: Hanging after execution, transgressors of certain commandments
P231: Burial on the day of execution
P232: The law of the Hebrew bondman
P233: Hebrew bondmaid to be married by her master or his son
P234: Redemption of a Hebrew bondmaid
P235: The law of a Canaanite bondman
P236: Penalty of inflicting injury
P237: The law of injuries caused by an ox
P238: The law of injuries caused by an pit
P239: The law of theft
P240: The law of damage caused by a beast
P241: The law of damage caused by a fire
P242: The law of an unpaid bailee
P243: The law of a paid bailee
P244: The law of a borrower
P245: The law of buying and selling
P246: The law of litigants
P247: Saving the life of the pursued
P248: The law of inheritance

365 Negative Mitzvot

N1: Not believing in any other Gd
N2: Not to make images for the purpose of worship
N3: Not to make an idol (even for others) to worship
N4: Not to make figures of human beings
N5: Not to bow down to an idol
N6: Not to worship idols
N7: Not to hand over any children to Moloch
N8: Not to practice sorcery of the ov
N9: Not to practice sorcery of the yidde'oni
N10: Not to study idolatrous practices
N11: Not to erect a pillar which people will assemble to honor
N12: Not to make figured stones on which to prostrate ourselves
N13: Not to plant trees in the Sanctuary
N14: Not to swear by an idol
N15: Not to divert people to idolatry
N16: Not to try to persuade an Israelite to worship idols
N17: Not to love someone who seeks to mislead you to idols
N18: Not to relax one's aversion to the misleader
N19: Not to save the life of a misleader
N20: Not to plead for the misleader
N21: Not to oppress evidence unfavorable to the misleader
N22: No benefit from ornaments which have adorned an idol
N23: Not rebuilding an apostate city
N24: Not deriving benefit from property of an apostate city
N25: Not increasing wealth from anything connected with idolatry
N26: Not prophesying in the name of an idol
N27: Not prophesying falsely
N28: Not to listen to the prophesy made in the name of an idol

THE 613 MITZVOT

N29: Not fearing or refraining from killing a false prophet
N30: Not adopting the habits and customs of unbelievers
N31: Not practicing divination
N32: Not regulating one's conduct by the stars
N33: Not practicing the art of the soothsayer
N34: Not practicing sorcery
N35: Not practicing the art of the charmer
N36: Not consulting a necromancer who uses the ov
N37: Not consulting a sorcerer who uses the ydo'a
N38: Not to seek information from the dead
N39: Women not to wear men's clothes or adornments
N40: Men not wearing women's clothes or adornments
N41: Not imprinting any marks on our bodies
N42: Not wearing Shatnes (mixture of wool and linen)
N43: Not shaving the temples of the head
N44: Not shaving the beard
N45: Not making cuttings in our flesh
N46: Not settling in the land of Egypt
N47: Not to follow one's heart or eyes
N48: Not to make a covenant with the Seven Nations of Canaan
N49: Not to spare the life of the Seven Nations
N50: Not to show mercy to idolaters
N51: Not to allow idolaters to settle in our land
N52: Not to intermarry with a heretic
N53: Not to intermarry with a male from Ammon or Moav
N54: Not to exclude the descendants of Esav
N55: Not to exclude the descendants of Egyptians
N56: Not offering peace to Ammon and Moav
N57: Not destroying fruit trees in time of siege
N58: Not fearing heretics in time of war
N59: Not forgetting what Amalek did to us
N60: Not blaspheming the Great Name
N61: Not violating a shevuas bittui (oath of utterance)
N62: Not swearing a shevuas shav (vain oath)
N63: Not profaning the Name of Gd
N64: Not testing His promises and warnings
N65: Not to break down houses of worship or to destroy holy books
N66: Not leaving the body of an executed criminal hanging overnight
N67: Not to interrupt the watch over the Sanctuary
N68: Kohein Gadol may not enter Sanctuary at any but prescribed times
N69: Kohein with blemish not to enter Sanctuary from Altar inwards
N70: Kohein with a blemish not to minister in the Sanctuary
N71: Kohein with a temporary blemish not to minister in Sanctuary
N72: Levites and Kohanim not perform each other's allotted services
N73: Not to be intoxicated when entering Sanctuary; and not to be intoxicated when giving a decision on Torah law
N74: Zar (nonkohein) not to minister in Sanctuary
N75: Tameh Kohein not to minister in Sanctuary
N76: Kohein who is tevul yom, not to minister in Sanctuary

N77: Tameh person not to enter any part of Sanctuary
N78: Tameh person not to enter camp of Levites
N79: Not to build an Altar of stones which were touched by iron
N80: Not to ascend the Altar by steps
N81: Not to extinguish the Altar fire
N82: Not to offer any sacrifice whatever on the Golden Altar
N83: Not to make oil like the Oil of Anointment
N84: Not anoint anyone with special oil except Kohein Gadol and King
N85: Not to make incense like used in Sanctuary
N86: Not to remove the staves from their rings in the Ark
N87: Not to remove the Breastplate from the Ephod
N88: Not to tear the edge of the Kohein Gadol's robe
N89: Not to offer sacrifices outside the Sanctuary Court
N90: Not to slaughter holy offerings outside the Sanctuary Court
N91: Not to dedicate a blemished animal to be offered on the Altar
N92: Not to slaughter a blemished animal as a korban
N93: Not to dash the blood of a blemished beast on the Altar
N94: Not to burn the sacrificial portions of blemished beast on Altar
N95: Not to sacrifice a beast with a temporary blemish
N96: Not to offer a blemished sacrifice of a gentile
N97: Not to cause an offering to become blemished
N98: Not to offer leaven or honey upon the Altar
N99: Not to offer a sacrifice without salt
N100: Not to offer on Altar the "hire of a harlot" or "price of a dog"
N101: Not to slaughter the mother and her young on the same day
N102: Not to put olive oil on the mealoffering of a sinner
N103: Not to put frankincense the mealoffering of a sinner
N104: Not mingle olive oil with mealoffering of suspected adulteress
N105: Not put frankincense on mealoffering of suspected adulteress
N106: Not to change a beast that has been consecrated as an offering
N107: Not to change one's holy offering for another
N108: Not to redeem the firstling (of a clean beast)
N109: Not to sell the tithe of cattle
N110: Not to sell devoted property
N111: Not redeem devoted land without specific statement of purpose
N112: Not to sever the head of the bird of Sinoffering during melikah
N113: Not to do any work with a dedicated beast
N114: Not to shear a dedicated beast
N115: Not slaughter the Korban Pesach while chometz in our possession
N116: Not leave any sacrificial portions of Korban Pesach overnight
N117: Not allow meat of Korban Pesach to remain till morning
N118: Not allow meat of 14 Nissan Festival Offering remain till day 3:
N119: Not allow meat of Pesach Sheini offering to remain till morning
N120: Not allow meat of thanksgiving offering to remain till morning
N121: Not to break any bones of Pesach offering
N122: Not to break any bones of Pesach Sheini offering
N123: Not to remove Pesach offering from where it is eaten
N124: Not to bake the residue of a meal offering with leaven
N125: Not to eat the Pesach offering boiled or raw

N126: Not to allow a ger toshav to eat the Pesach offering
N127: An uncircumcised person may not eat the Pesach offering
N128: Not to allow an apostate Israelite to eat the Pesach offering
N129: Tameh person may not eat hallowed food
N130: Not to eat meat of consecrated offerings which have become tameh
N131: Not eating nosar (beyond allotted time)
N132: Not eating piggul (improper intentions)
N133: A zar may not eat terumah
N134: A Kohein's tenant or hired servant may not eat terumah
N135: An uncircumcised Kohein may not eat terumah
N136: Tameh Kohein may not eat terumah
N137: A chalalah may not eat holy food
N138: Not to eat the mealoffering of a Kohein
N139: Not eat Sinoffering meat whose blood was brought into Sanctuary
N140: Not to eat the invalidated consecrated offerings
N141: Not to eat unredeemed 2nd tithe of corn outside Yerushalayim
N142: Not consuming unredeemed 2nd tithe of wine outside Yerushalayim
N143: Not consuming unredeemed 2nd tithe of oil outside Yerushalayim
N144: Not eating an unblemished firstling outside Yerushalayim
N145: Not eat sinoffering and guiltoffering outside Sanctuary court
N146: Not to eat the meat of a burnt offering
N147: Not eat lesser holy offerings before blood dashed on Altar
N148: A zar not to eat the most holy offerings
N149: Kohein not to eat first fruits outside Yerushalayim
N150: Not eating an unredeemed tameh 2nd tithe, even in Yerushalayim
N151: Not eating the 2nd tithe in mourning
N152: Not spend 2nd tithe redemption money, except on food and drink
N153: Not eating tevel(produce heaveoffering and tithes not taken)
N154: Not altering the prescribed order of harvest tithing
N155: Not to delay payment of vows
N156: Not to appear in Sanctuary on festival without sacrifice
N157: Not to infringe on any oral obligation, even if without an oath
N158: Kohein may not marry a zonah
N159: Kohein may not marry a chalalah
N160: Kohein may not marry a divorcee
N161: Kohein Gadol may not marry a widow
N162: Kohein Gadol may not have relations with a widow
N163: Kohein with disheveled hair may not enter the Sanctuary
N164: Kohein wearing rent garments may not enter Sanctuary
N165: Ministering Kohanim may not leave the Sanctuary
N166: Common Kohein may not defile himself for dead (except some)
N167: Kohein Gadol may not be under one roof with dead body
N168: Kohein Gadol may not defile himself for any dead person
N169: Levites may not take a share of the land
N170: Levites may not share in the spoil on conquest of the Land
N171: Not to tear out hair for the dead
N172: Not to eat any unclean animal
N173: Not to eat any unclean fish
N174: Not to eat any unclean fowl

N175: Not to eat any swarming winged insect
N176: Not to eat anything which swarms on the earth
N177: Not to eat any creeping thing that breeds in decayed matter
N178: Not to eat living creatures that breed in seeds or fruit
N179: Not to eat any swarming thing
N180: Not to eat any animal which is a nevelah
N181: Not to eat an animal which is a treifah
N182: Not to eat a limb of a living animal
N183: Not to eat the gid hanasheh (sinew of the thighvein)
N184: Not to eat blood
N185: Not to eat the fat of a clean animal
N186: Not to cook meat in milk
N187: Not to eat meat cooked in milk
N188: Not to eat the flesh of a stoned ox
N189: Not to eat bread made from grain of new crop
N190: Not to eat roasted grain of the new crop
N191: Not to eat fresh ears of grain
N192: Not to eat orlah
N193: Not to eat kilai hakerem
N194: Not to drink yayin nesach (libation wine for idol worship)
N195: No eating or drinking to excess
N196: Not to eat on Yom Kippur
N197: Not to eat chometz on Pesach
N198: Not to eat an admixture of chometz on Pesach
N199: Not to eat chometz after noon of 14 Nissan
N200: No chametz may be seen in our homes during Pesach
N201: Not to possess chametz during Pesach
N202: A Nazir may not drink wine
N203: A Nazir may not eat fresh grapes
N204: A Nazir may not eat dried grapes
N205: A Nazir may not eat grape kernels
N206: A Nazir may not eat grape husks
N207: A Nazir may not rend himself tameh for the dead
N208: A Nazir may not rend himself tameh by entering house with corpse
N209: A Nazir may not shave
N210: Not to reap all harvest without leaving a corner for the poor
N211: Not to gather ears of corn that fell during harvesting
N212: Not to gather the whole produce of vineyard at vintage time
N213: Not to gather single fallen grapes during the vintage
N214: Not to return for a forgotten sheaf
N215: Not to sow kilayim (diverse kinds of seed in one field)
N216: Not to sow grain or vegetables in a vineyard
N217: Not to make animals of different species
N218: Not to work with two different kinds of animals together
N219: Not preventing a beast from eating the produce where working
N220: Not to cultivate the soil in the seventh year
N221: Not to prune the trees in the seventh year
N222: Not reap a selfgrown plant in the 7th year as in ordinary year
N223: Not gather selfgrown fruit in the 7th year as in ordinary year

THE 613 MITZVOT

N224: Not to cultivate the soil in the Jubilee year
N225: Not to reap the aftergrowths of Jubilee year as in ordinary year
N226: Not to gather fruit in Jubilee year as in ordinary year
N227: Not to sell out holdings in Eretz Israel in perpetuity
N228: No to sell the open lands of the Levites
N229: Not to forsake the Levites
N230: Not to demand payment of debts after Shmitah year
N231: Not to withhold a loan to be canceled by the Shmitah year
N232: Failing to give charity to our needy brethren
N233: Not sending a Hebrew bondman away emptyhanded
N234: Not demanding payment from a debtor known unable to pay
N235: Not lending at interest
N236: Not borrowing at interest
N237: Not participating in a loan at interest
N238: Not oppressing an employee by delaying payment of his wages
N239: Not taking a pledge from a debtor by force
N240: Not keeping a needed pledge from its owner
N241: Not taking a pledge from a widow
N242: Not taking food utensils in pledge
N243: Not abducting an Israelite
N244: Not stealing money
N245: Not committing robbery
N246: Not fraudulently altering land boundaries
N247: Not usurping our debts
N248: Not repudiating our debts
N249: Not to swear falsely in repudiating our debts
N250: Not wronging one another in business
N251: Not wronging one another by speech
N252: Not wronging a proselyte by speech
N253: Not wronging a proselyte in business
N254: Not handing over a fugitive bondman
N255: Not wronging a fugitive bondman
N256: Not dealing harshly with orphans and widows
N257: Not employing a Hebrew bondman in degrading tasks
N258: Not selling a Hebrew bondman by public auction
N259: Not having a Hebrew bondman do unnecessary work
N260: Not allowing a heathen to mistreat a Hebrew bondman
N261: Not selling a Hebrew bondmaid
N262: Not to afflict one's wife or espoused Hebrew bondmaid by diminishing food, raiment or conjugal rights
N263: Not selling a captive woman
N264: Not enslaving a captive woman
N265: Not planning to acquire someone else's property
N266: Not coveting another's belongings
N267: A hired laborer not eating growing crops
N268: A hired laborer not putting of the harvest in his own vessel
N269: Not ignoring lost property
N270: Not leaving a person who is trapped under his burden
N271: Not cheating in measurements and weights

N272: Not keeping false weights and measures
N273: Judge not to commit unrighteousness
N274: Judge not accept gifts from litigants
N275: Judge not to favor a litigant
N276: Judge not avoid just judgement through fear of a wicked person
N277: Judge not to decide in favor of poor man, out of pity
N278: Judge not to pervert justice against person of evil repute
N279: Judge not to pity one who has killed or caused loss of limb
N280: Judge not perverting justice due to proselytes or orphans
N281: Judge not to listen to one litigant in absence of the other
N282: A court may not convict by a majority of one in a capital case
N283: A judge may not rely on the opinion of a fellow judge, or may not argue for conviction after favoring acquittal
N284: Not appointing an unlearned judge
N285: Not bearing false witness
N286: Judge not to receive a wicked man's testimony
N287: Judge not to receive testimony from litigant's relatives
N288: Not convicting on the testimony of a single witness
N289: Not killing a human being
N290: No capital punishment based on circumstantial evidence
N291: A witness not acting as an advocate
N292: Not killing a murderer without trial
N293: Not sparing the life of a pursuer
N294: Not punishing a person for a sin committed under duress
N295: Not accepting ransom from an unwitting murderer
N296: Not accepting a ransom from a wilful murderer
N297: Not neglecting to save the life of an Israelite in danger
N298: Not leaving obstacles on public or private domain
N299: Not giving misleading advice
N300: Not inflicting excessive corporal punishment
N301: Not to bear tales
N302: Not to hate another Jew
N303: Not to put another to shame
N304: Not to take vengeance on another
N305: Not to bear a grudge
N306: Not to take the entire bird's nest (mother and young)
N307: Not to shave the scall
N308: Not to cut or cauterize signs of leprosy
N309: Not ploughing a valley where Eglah Arufah was done
N310: Not permitting a sorcerer to live
N311: Not taking bridegroom from home during first year
N312: Not to differ from traditional authorities
N313: Not to add to the Written or Oral Law
N314: Not to detract from the Written or Oral Law
N315: Not detracting from the Written or Oral law
N316: Not to curse a ruler
N317: Not to curse any Israelite
N318: Not cursing parents
N319: Not smiting parents

N320: Not to work on Shabbos
N321: Not to go beyond city limits on Shabbos
N322: Not to punish on Shabbos
N323: Not to work on the first day of Pesach
N324: Not to work on the seventh day of Pesach
N325: Not to work on Atzeret
N326: Not to work on Rosh Hashana
N327: Not to work on the first day of Sukkos
N328: Not to work on Shemini Atzeret
N329: Not to work on Yom Kippur
N330: Not have relations with one's mother
N331: Not have relations with one's father's wife
N332: Not have relations with one's sister
N333: Not have relations with daughter of father's wife if sister
N334: Not have relations with one's son's daughter
N335: Not have relations with one's daughter's daughter
N336: Not have relations with one's daughter
N337: Not have relations with a woman and her daughter
N338: Not have relations with a woman and her son's daughter
N339: Not have relations with a woman and her daughter's daughter
N340: Not have relations with one's father's sister
N341: Not have relations with one's mother's sister
N342: Not have relations with wife of father's brother
N343: Not have relations with one's son's wife
N344: Not have relations with brother's wife
N345: Not have relations with sister of wife (during her lifetime)
N346: Not to have relations with a menstruant
N347: Not to have relations with another man's wife
N348: Men may not lie with beasts
N349: Women may not lie with beasts
N350: A man may not lie carnally with another man
N351: A man may not lie carnally with his father
N352: A man may not lie carnally with his father's brother
N353: Not to be intimate with a kinswoman
N354: A mamzer may not have relations with a Jewess
N355: Not having relations with a woman without marriage
N356: Not remarrying one's divorced wife after she has remarried
N357: Not having relations with woman subject to Levirate marriage
N358: Not divorcing woman he has raped and been compelled to marry
N359: Not divorcing a woman after falsely bringing evil name on her
N360: Man incapable of procreation not to marry a Jewess
N361: Not to castrate a man or beast
N362: Not appointing a nonIsraelite born King
N363: A king not owning many horses
N364: A king not taking many wives
N365: A king not amassing great personal wealth
(34)

www.ingramcontent.com/pod-product-compliance
Lightning Source LLC
LaVergne TN
LVHW041331080426
835512LV00006B/403